D1328345

# The Politics of School Accountability

## Public Information about Public Schools

Edward Wynne

McCutchan Publishing Corporation
2526 Grove Street
Berkeley, California 94704

E0171
CARDINAL MEYER LIBRARY
MARIAN COLLEGE OF FOND DU LAC

Copyright 1972 by McCutchan Publishing Corporation
All Rights Reserved
ISBN 0-8211-2250-9
Library of Congress Catalogue Card No. 74-190055
Printed in the United States of America

To Helen, Bridget Janna, and Adam

Who were tolerant and helpful.

Thank you, and love.

# Contents

# Acknowledgments

This book was largely written while I was on a U.S. Office of Education fellowship at the University of California at Berkeley. When I began to consider how to utter my gratitude to those who helped me, I realized that, by giving first thanks to the university, I could be sure I had honored my principal benefactor. The university granted me the fellowship when I had interesting but uncertain qualifications. It made able colleagues available to me, and they provided me with counsel and helpful criticism. Its libraries fed my research. The fellowship requirements were loose enough for me to find the free time I wanted. Where I differed with those requirements, the university structure usually permitted the evolution of useful compromises. The grace and beauty of its grounds made me a little more willing to develop a long-range approach to large issues. Unquestionably, with the dispute arising about it, the university has major changes lying ahead. But as these changes transpire, I hope that their designers find means to retain the medley of qualities that has been so helpful to me and, I am sure, to many others.

While the counsel I received came largely from persons connected with the university, in all cases I could sense their acts also reflected their personal values; they, too, should receive my warm thanks. My counselors include Professors Geraldine J. Clifford, James W. Guthrie, and Melvin Webber. We have had our differences, but perhaps this is symptomatic of the difficulty of the task or the subtlety of their diverse visions. But through the whole effort, their time, counsel, and attention was available when I asked, and my effort is the better for it. Special thanks are due to Jim Guthrie, who was both my counselor and fellowship advisor.

Other faculty members and graduate students have been of considerable help. Peter Marris gave me time and thoughtful counsel at an important early stage. Martin Trow suggested methods of attack. Guy Benveniste, Gerald Hayward, Frederick Wirt, and Marvin Gentz have also assisted.

Help has also come from outside the university. Conversations with James S. Coleman and his writings have both contributed in important ways. Ellen Lurie, of the United Bronx Parents, gave me access to her experience, and prevailed on some of her very busy friends to make themselves available for interviews. Both Ellen and her friends may disagree somewhat with my conclusions, but they displayed great tolerance to an academic outsider.

Finally, I must acknowledge the assistance—both emotional and intellectual—of my children and my former wife, Helen. The book is about the public and the schools. Helen's common sense, lay-oriented questions, and support of my efforts provided me with invaluable intellectual and emotional help. My children, whose progress in school I was able to view as both parent and an experimentor (usually), tolerated my many questions about what was happening to them and what they thought about it. Their pithy answers kept me in touch with a potent reality.

It is certain that these many counselors do not all agree with everything I have done. However, despite their diversity of views, they all displayed a common desire to be helpful. Because of this diversity, I must emphasize that the views stated in this effort are mine and are not the responsibility of these parties.

# Introduction

At this time, accountability is an "in" word among educators, and school-oriented professionals. Like many educator catchwords, it is open to numerous interpretations: for example, that schools are responsible for making all students learn or that communities can hire and fire their own school administrators and teachers. Obviously, accountability has not yet developed a widely accepted precise definition. But vagueness is a common element of many rallying cries. Unfortunately, vagueness prevents clear analysis.

This book is an effort to wring out some of the vagueness and examine the phenomena of school accountability in an historic and interdisciplinary light. When we approach accountability in that manner, we will discover it has a long history as an educational issue and that its current prominence is related to many other trends in politics, the social sciences, and the personal value systems of Americans. Thus, a broad-gauged analysis will better equip us to handle the day-to-day issues that accountability will generate.

Before going further, I submit a definition: by accountability, I mean systems or arrangements that supply the general public, as well as schoolmen, with accurate information about school output performance—test scores and other data that show how well groups of children are learning in school. Accountability may be applied to an individual school, a school district, or to schools throughout a whole state or the nation. In each instance, parent and political groups are concerned with the operation of the particular school configurations rendering "accounts." This definition of accountability is congruent with the definition usually applied in business, the field in which accountability practices have reached the highest development. It suggests that simple, unglamorous, honest information about school performance can be a crucial element in school change.

Of course, there are divided opinions about the importance of accurate statistics to education improvement. For example, one academic who read the manuscript for this book proposed that greater interest in school reform would be promoted by recounting anecdotes about unwise principals or cruel teachers rather than by focusing on accountability issues. In a sense, his proposal is right. No one I know favors cruel teachers. So we are all united against cruelty to children and achieve a warm feeling of togetherness. However, once we try to get a precise definition of cruelty and develop operating rules, problems arise: for example, the obvious kinds of cruelty, like beating a child, are comparatively rare. Unfortunately, the changes we need in schools may require far more subtle tools than prohibitions against beatings.

The first tool, I suggest, is a set of systems to collect and disseminate far more accurate information about student learning than is available now. For example, almost no contemporary school system has an effective accountability system. As a result, school decision-makers cannot give serious attention to the issue of whether current policies help children learn better than proposed changes. It is impossible for them to consider such issues, since no routine well-planned measurements are taken to show the effect of school decisions and policies on learning. If this lack of measurement is remedied, schools will become more accountable. Other important changes will then take place in school policies and decision-making. The changes may well be for the better.

Any further progress towards accountability will involve a series of continuing interactions, or even conflicts, between:

1. The state of the art of education output research (or learning measurement);
2. Professionals engaged in education research;
3. Schoolmen;
4. The public and public spokesmen;
5. The media;
6. General public expectations about the relation of research and policy; and
7. Students.

This book is an analysis and forecast of these interactions. I hope it will help members of all these groups better understand where they are and where they are going. It shows that the accountability movement represents a resurgence of important continuing trends that have shaped American education and our whole society. As a result, the current interest in accountability may be the harbinger of vital longer-range educational change. If we understand the fuller picture, we will become better equipped to make our own day-to-day decisions about matters such as:

1. Laws governing school personnel and administrative practices;
2. The determination of school goals;
3. Teacher and administrator hiring practices;
4. School-community relations;
5. School salary patterns;
6. The dissemination of information about school performance;
7. Media reporting of school developments;
8. School district management policies;
9. The evaluation of programs; and
10. The management of education research.

To understand the operation of educational accountability, we must consider it from many perspectives. Different readers, with different backgrounds and interests, will naturally find these perspectives of varying interest or novelty. They may choose to focus on those chapters that are of greatest interest to them. The chapters cover the following materials:

1. Chapter 1 is a general discussion of the need for educational feedback and includes a model for school accountability (Figure 1, p. 8).
2. The past, current, and foreseeable future of the state of the art of output measurements will be described in chapter 2.
3. The history of various past and present efforts to develop accountability systems for education will be discussed in chapters 3 and 5, to show how this part of the model operated in the past.
4. The findings and implications of the past output measurement research are discussed in chapter 4 to indicate the kinds of issues accountability might bring to light.

5. The actual impact of the public on public school policy-making is not always clearly recognized. Well-informed persons assume that school policy decisions are made by school administrators with the legitimization of lay school boards. But in many important instances this has not been the case. To clarify this matter, several historically important instances of school policy-shaping are considered in chapter 6 to place the issue of public intervention in a historical perspective.

6. The media and the attitudes of mediamen toward school accountability will inevitably affect the course of events. These attitudes and patterns of reporting are discussed in chapter 7.

7. The forces attempting to generate school accountability systems are related to larger nationwide efforts to promote social accounting systems for other national concerns, such as hunger, health, etc. Inevitably, these patterns of social accounting will interact. Therefore, these complementary efforts are described in chapter 8 to give a fuller understanding of school accountability developments.

8. The public's attitude toward school accountability will inevitably be affected by public expectations about the role of schools. To what extent do some citizens see it as a device for generating a sense of community rather than an institution for transmitting cognitive knowledge? Of course, different citizens and groups emphasize different priorities, but the consideration in chapter 9 of these shifting priorities and social needs is an important part of any analytical effort.

9. The term *accountability* has its roots in business practices. Numerical accountability concepts have several thousand years of business history behind them. Chapter 10 will survey and analyze this history to see what implications it has for school accountability.

10. Chapter 11 includes a synthesis of all these threads, an attempted forecast, and some policy recommendations.

11. Chapter 12 is a checklist of measures that institutions and persons can take to promote school accountability.

12. The appendixes include three relevant articles that do not appropriately fit into the body of the book.

# 1

# The Issue

> They, the economists, seem to revolve in their eternal circle of landlords, capitalists, and laborers, until they seem to think of the distinction of society into those classes as if they were one of God's ordinances, not man's, and as little under human control as the division of day and night. Scarcely any of them seem to have proposed to himself as a subject of inquiry, what changes the relations of those classes to one another are likely to undergo in the progress of society; to what extent the distinction itself admits to being beneficially modified, and if it may not, in a certain sense, tend to disappear entirely.
>
> John Stuart Mill[1]

In 1955, Mrs. Rosa Parks refused to get up from a "Whites Only" seat in a Montgomery, Alabama, bus. Her defiance of Jim Crow helped ignite a train of events that may not be settled in this century. Nearly every American over twenty has sensed the revolutionary impact of these events. The attitudes of many whites towards blacks, and of blacks towards whites, have significantly changed. Indeed, blacks even look at each other differently. New institutions and new laws have arisen. Some contend the changes are far too little. Regardless of the justice of this charge, the changes represent important revisions in the past conduct of the persons and institutions involved.

Probably many who have lived through the whole progression

have sometimes been moved to wonder whether back in 1955 anyone could have thought such change was possible. We may even go on to wonder what other changes still face us. If we are concerned about public education in America—a comparatively static enterprise—we might finally reflect whether potent change forces exist even within that institution. This book focuses on that question.

In particular, it will consider whether the current emphasis on school accountability, as I defined that term in the Introduction, may trigger radical education change.

In other words, if parents are given information about school output, just as stockholders are given information about corporate effectiveness, what may happen?

The book proposes that if school accountability to the public becomes widespread, new conflicts will arise between schools and the public; as a result of these conflicts, public expectations about how schools should be run, and what they should achieve, will change. These changing expectations will generate new demands on schools, and promote radically new modes of school operations. The new modes may cover revised personnel practices, hours, types of buildings, administrative arrangements, and means of instruction. Concurrently, the quality, nature, and quantity of education research will increase, and the mass media will change their techniques for reporting educational activities. I shall term such large-scale, important changes *macrochange.*

All these potential changes will evolve from the interaction between schools and the public over output information, or "accounts" (a) created by education researchers, (b) who apply specific research techniques, and (c) have their findings disseminated to the public by the mass media. While the book focuses on educational change, it clearly has implications for other public institutions and concerns that are the subject of research, such as health or defense.

In the largest sense, this public interest in accountability can be viewed as part of our nationwide interest in consumerism; that is, as part of the effort to see that our continuously evolving institutions are still sensitive to the needs of their ultimate consumers—whether those users are auto drivers, food purchasers, medical patients, the parents of students, or the students themselves.

On the whole, these potential developments in education may be viewed as improvements or reforms. However, the aim is not so much to argue for accountability as to examine the proposition, describe the probable changes, and consider their implications. To achieve these goals we shall have to approach the question with a special degree of openness. We may better understand the complexity of this matter if we return for a moment to the refusal of Mrs. Parks. That act, too, was an important component in a pattern of macrochange.

Of course, her refusal was not the "cause" of the civil rights revolt. It was really one of an almost infinite succession of other causes that can be traced far back into time, and the continuing effects of those causes can be followed to the black activism today. But suppose we were asked to forecast race relations developments five or ten years before Mrs. Park's courageous act. Looking forward from such a point and anticipating important change might have seemed presumptuous. But my proposition about accountability involved making a major forecast about educational change. Is not such a forecast just as difficult to attempt as one for civil rights?

Of course, any such forecast must be speculative. Nevertheless social science should not reserve its concerns only for matters susceptible to clear-cut studies. Macrochange did occur in civil rights. The change was greater than many persons anticipated. The change was rooted in events that were apparent to many contemporary students of the problem, though most of them failed to evaluate properly their larger significance. Does accountability by means of output measures of school performance represent another force for macrochange?

Such measures are being applied and publicized more and more frequently. The Coleman Report on equality of education opportunity, which was issued in 1966, is a dramatic example.[2] The report supplied much of the evidence for the president's Message on Education Reform, issued in March 1970.[3] It has also been used as ammunition in debates about local control and to support proposals for education change such as contracting and voucher systems.

Again, consider the National Assessment. The assessment is an effort to produce a continuous series of measures of how well young Americans are learning in and out of school.[4] The assessment gave its first nationwide tests in the spring of 1970. A continuous succession of tests of various age groups will be conducted (indefinitely, I hope, like weather studies or the census). The assessment will be issuing data about learning performance over the next few years. The *Christian Science Monitor* observed that many states are planning their individual, statewide assessments.[5] Thus, the assessment is the first step in a wave of such efforts. As the *Monitor* said, "the floodgates are open." Things are also happening on the local level. In many school districts throughout the country—especially in urban areas—the question being asked is: "How well are children learning, and how can we find out?" For example, the New York City School Board has entered into a contract with the Educational Testing Service to design an accountability system.[6] The system will attempt to supply the board and the public with periodic reports about the learning performance of students on a school-by-school basis, in a format that will permit meaningful comparisons of interschool effectiveness.

In some areas, experiments are being attempted where contractors are paid to bring students up to a certain level of performance and are paid less if they fail. These arrangements naturally involve educators, school boards, and the public in controversies over the significance of the contractor's commitment and the "account" he must finally render.[7] Other experiments are proposed where parents will be given vouchers to "buy" education for their children from either public or private schools.[8] These experiments assume that the parent "purchasers" will be given meaningful and accurate information about the performance of the competing schools. These developments will surely raise the question: "Why can't ordinary public schools make similar information public?"

Also, schooling at all levels is absorbing more and more of our lives and using a growing proportion of our national wealth. It is inevitable that we will become more curious about how well the system is working. As a result, we will more and more often hear the word *evaluation* used with reference to education; while the word encompasses many different meanings, it frequently assumes some measurement of the amount of learning achieved by students.

All of these developments are facilitated by the growth of computer technology. This growth provides us with an increasing ability to amass and analyze output data. In sum, events relating to accountability via output measurements are arising with increasing frequency.

## Accountability and Feedback

This increasing interest in accountability is related to the larger issues of feedback to the public in our postindustrial society. Since the concept of feedback is crucial to this analysis, some further discussion is appropriate. The concept was well-defined in a metaphor offered by the mathematician Norbert Weiner.[9] He analyzed the task faced by anyone concerned with evaluating or carrying out a policy, including an administrator, a voter, or a politician. He said the task was comparable to that faced by the helmsman of a ship: to decide the ship's course, steer the ship in that direction, *determine the actual course the ship follows,* and redirect the ship when wind or other events require alteration of the planned course. The collection and analysis of information about the inevitable divergence between the planned and actual courses is the process of feeding back information to the helmsman. Presumably, the feedback will induce the correction of steering errors.

In most complicated enterprises, much necessary feedback is collected by special systems designed for the purpose. For instance, a modern nautical helmsman receives feedback via a sextant, compass, maps, radar, etc. Even in the prehistoric past, primitive helmsmen applied comparatively complex feedback systems. The more efficient the feedback system, the more ambitious the enterprise that can be attempted. (Consider the feedback mechanism needed by the astronauts and ground control!) Conversely, without effective feedback, complex enterprises face grave risks. In the 1960s Congress was appropriating funds for an ambitious national food distribution program, but had no means of discovering that in reality thousands of people who were suffering from severe malnutrition were not being reached by the program. No feedback apparatus had been designed to supplement the distribution effort.

Feedback is found in all successfully persisting operations, because the first direction or policy set almost inevitably needs revision over time; feedback is essential to wise revision. However, while institution builders always concern themselves with the initial policies of their institutions, they often fail to create feedback systems. Perhaps they assume they are creating policies or organizations that will never need correction. In addition, feedback structures are often costly and thus compete with inevitable economy pressures.

But there are more substantial resistances to feedback than indifference or economy. The simple truth is that feedback often tells us we are wrong. If we were always right, we would not need it. Humans naturally resist the establishment of feedback systems because they do not like to hear that they are mistaken and will have to change their conduct. This hostility exists even if the feedback is secret and available only to the subject. Despite this resistance, the world is filled with feedback. We watch where we are driving and thus receive feedback. When we participate in conversations, we observe the reactions of our companions, and vary the pace and substance of our conversation as a result of receiving feedback. Successful doctoral candidates in graduate school pay attention to the comments (or feedback) of their committee, and pass their requirements. However, in all these situations, the feedback recipient is highly motivated to "stay with it"; i.e., not to have an auto accident, to participate in the conversation, or to attain a degree. As a result he accepts the unpleasantness of discovering mistakes and correcting them. But if he could drive without observing the road, talk without watching his audience, or attain his degree without satisfying his committee, he might turn off much of his feedback.

It is evident that the development of feedback systems conflicts with the widespread human desire for quiescence and tranquility. One of my undergraduate students expressed the idea very nicely. I observed that many students neglected to pick up their corrected and graded term papers and were satisfied simply with receiving their grade in the mail. I said, "Their desire to avoid the discomfort of seeing the details of their mistakes and incorrect perceptions defeats feedback. If you were sailing from London to New York and followed this pattern, you would never get to New York." "That's true," he answered, "but you'd probably still reach some part of America!"

In the long run, some people might still conclude that a world without feedback would be empty and dull. Therefore, even if it were possible, they might refuse to drive without reacting to the road; talk without audience response, though the response might be indifference; or receive a doctorate without being "pressured." But different human beings evidently desire or seek feedback with varying intensity and are more or less adept at dealing with the criticism and tension that is part of the process. Similarly, some humans are better at transmitting criticism or feedback to others. But despite these natural variations, it is clear that the search for, and the acceptance of, feedback cannot be taken for granted. Still, there are some pressures that drive administrators toward feedback.

Sometimes, an administrator courts obvious, immediate danger by rejecting feedback. In such instances, he either seeks and accepts feedback and keeps on his toes, or he is "eliminated." In this situation there is usually no public problem. But in other instances, ignoring certain feedback or failing to set up feedback collection systems may not produce immediate harm. The bad effects may be delayed for months or years, or the administrator may believe, or claim, that such effects are the fault of some other part of the system. In these cases, the absence of a feedback system may act as a shield from guilt or blame or postpone indefinitely the discovery that things aren't working.

The issue of feedback becomes even more involved in a postindustrial society, where the effects of large, complex institutions and processes are not easy to perceive. In the case of such complex institutions, which include schools, we can characterize the feedback as either *intuitive* or *nonintuitive.* I believe these distinctions were first suggested by Daniel P. Moynihan. The distinctions are not precise. However, they suggest the difference between (a) impressions gathered from students, friends, simple news articles, report cards, and firsthand observations and (b) information deliberately collected and analyzed by independent professional researchers and by specially designed collection systems. Inevitably, nonintuitive feedback about pollution, health, traffic problems, crime, etc., will grow in importance in forming policy for many of our larger institutions. To a large degree this book is about nonintuitive feedback from schools.

## The Plan of Analysis

This book's method of analysis is suggested by the model in Figure 1. The model is adapted from one first proposed by the political scientist David Easton.[10]

Public *schools* receive their *resources* from the *public*: parents, legislators, school board members, etc. At the same time, the *demands* of the *public*—expressed as laws, votes, civil service regulations, etc.—determine the essential character of *schools.* The *de-*

*mands* thus finally determine the nature of *school output*, i.e., students.

The *public* receives *feedback* about school operations. The great

Figure 1

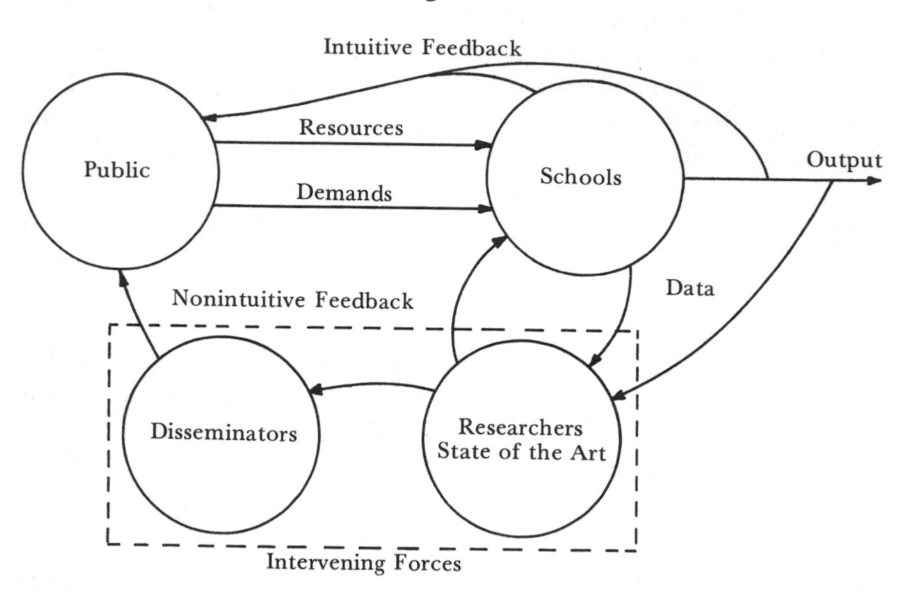


proportion of this feedback is *intuitive.* The *intuitive feedback* comes from their observations of students, schools, and graduates and through the media.

*Education researchers* are improving the *state of the art* of educational measurement and statistical analysis. This permits better forms of *nonintuitive feedback* on school operations. The measurements can be applied to either students or graduates. Presumably, the *researchers* will pass their *nonintuitive feedback* on to school and school administrators. If the *researchers* also want to inform the *public* of their findings and thus facilitate accountability, it will usually be necessary for them to use an intermediate medium, i.e., the *disseminators.* Essentially, *disseminators* are the media, i.e., television and the press, but they can include conferences, speeches, and popular books. Clearly the *public's nonintuitive feedback* system is very complicated. It requires *researchers* committed to accountability, a particular level of *state of the art,* and sympathetic and informed *disseminators.*

Presumably, if the public finds its thinking reshaped by new nonintuitive feedback, it will change its demands on schools, schools will change, and the result will be a change in the learning of their students.

The relationships sketched here are complicated; a change in any one part of the model can affect the whole entity. If reporters became extremely interested in nonintuitive feedback, the level of media coverage and thus the amount of accountability might increase considerably even though the state of the art and the interest of researchers stayed the same. If researchers developed simple and reliable accountability systems equivalent to weather reports, the cost-of-living index or the census, accountability might also increase, even though the researchers and the press were still comparatively disinterested. (It is true these other statistical systems are also imperfect. Despite their shortcomings, they are far more accurate than their educational equivalents. Indeed, there are no existing educational output equivalents. We know with some precision what the weather has been in the past; the census is far superior to any raw population estimate made by someone traveling about the country; and the cost-of-living index accurately portrays the general price trends, though it may err in some particulars.)

## Footnotes

1. In H. A. Innis, *Empire and Communications* (Oxford: The Clarendon Press, 1950), p. 2.

2. James S. Coleman et al., *Equality of Educational Opportunity* (Washington, D.C.: Government Printing Office, 1966).

3. Richard M. Nixon, "Education Reform," *Weekly Compilation of Presidential Documents* 6, no. 10 (March 3, 1970): 304-314.

4. *Christian Science Monitor,* 15 August 1970, p. 1

5. Ralph W. Tyler, "National Assessment: History and Sociology," in *New Models for American Education,* ed. James W. Guthrie & Edward Wynne (Englewood Cliffs, N.J.: Prentice-Hall, 1971), pp. 17-34.

6. *New York Times,* 9 February 1971, p. 1.

7. Leon Lessinger, "Engineering Accountability for Results," *Phi Delta Kappan*, 52, no. 4 (December 1970): 217-225.

8. Ester M. Swanker & Bernard E. Donovan, "Voucher Demon-

stration Projects," *Phi Delta Kappan* 52, no. 4 (December 1970): 244.

9. Norbert Weiner, *The Human Use of Human Beings* (Boston: Houghton Mifflin, 1950).

10. David Easton, "An Approach to the Analysis of Political Systems," *World Politics* 9 (April 1957): 383-400; idem, *A Framework for Political Analysis* (Englewood Cliffs, N.J.: Prentice-Hall, 1965).

# 2
# School Output Measures: Basic Concepts

To attain awareness always requires a measure of valor.

Alvin W. Gouldner[1]

An output is the essential product of any entity or system. Determination of the essence is an extraordinarily difficult conceptual task. What is the essential product of General Motors: profits, automobiles, or transportation? Is the essential product of a police operation arrests and convictions or public tranquility? Is the product of education graduates or knowledge? If the product is knowledge, what is that? Is it humor? Reading? Persistence?

What we sense from discussions about essential products is that complex systems rarely have one simple essential product. Suppose General Motors made large profits for several years, but produced absolutely nothing or only grossly unsafe automobiles. If this happened, it is likely that embarrassing questions would be asked in Congress or the media. If its automobiles worked but it made no profit, other problems would arise. On the other hand, a great diversity of allegedly essential products makes it impossible for administrators to make focused choices on priorities; reasonable arguments can be made for such a great range of alternatives that the organization tends to lose its sense of direction. In such situations, to satisfy the operating necessity of routinized choice, the organization may accept a visible, plausible, but peripheral product as its practical essence. However, when pressed the organization will still contend that it is striving for its historic prolix goals. But this generality masks the trivia that have replaced these overambitious goals. So careful discussions about essential products can stimulate organizations to reconsider and redefine their goals. Typically, such discussions—when they are constructive—also reveal that more than one essential product (but fewer than ten!) must be recognized and concurrently pursued.

When we have decided what outputs are appropriate for a system, we can then try to see how well the system is working. But to do this, the outputs must be so defined that we can measure the amounts produced. This, too, is tricky. "Measurement of a previously unmeasured concept is seldom accomplished in one fell swoop. Measures of concepts, like their meanings, evolve slowly."[2] So, in the case of education, we become concerned with deciding what is better or worse reading, how to identify greater persistence, or what is a good sense of humor. However, the often repeated contention of measurement experts has been that if a quality can be defined it presumably exists in varying quantities: there can be more or less of it; if the quality can be recognized, the differences in quantity can be measured.

Obviously, the development of output measures rests on a complex, lengthy, implicit dialectic process. Almost no output or measurement will perpetually serve as a major test of an institution's performance. New concepts of appropriate outputs arise over time; new measurements are created for old definitions; different disciplines, different interest groups, and different technologies and philosophies may all affect this process. How have these broad principles been applied in the American education system?

## Essential Learning Outputs

Schools are only one of the sources of human learning. Mass media, family, interpersonal relationships, and jobs all contribute to the refinement and enlargement of individual knowledge. Learning continues throughout adult, or postschool, life. This theme of lifetime learning from many processes is appropriate in a nation founded on the precepts of the Enlightenment and premised on an educational process resulting from the free flow of ideas. Surely effective output measures should measure knowledge acquired both in and out of school.[3] We may even be able to identify the effects of different out-of-school knowledge systems. This might permit us to assess the relative contribution of many knowledge-diffusing institutions: press, families, television and radio, libraries, legislatures, jobs, sports, military service, and so on. Although I accept these propositions, this chapter will largely focus on output measures for elementary and secondary school systems.

One of the most common of school output measures involves calculation of the numbers of students "processed," the number of years of schooling received, the number of graduates, and so forth. These data suggest one definition of what is an essential school product. The goal is to keep a certain number of youths subject to school processes for a certain amount of time. Such data naturally excite concern about the rate and number of dropouts. Though these data may not tell us about quality of knowledge acquired, they are often part of the statistics already maintained by schools. Rough-and-ready data, such as years of schooling, have been important tools for economists, who have studied the relationship between the output of education (defined in this manner) and the economic growth of nations.[4]

Despite its usefulness for some purposes, "graduate output" has obvious shortcomings as a measurement tool. We must assume differences in school efficiency and variations in the amount of knowledge received by degree holders. Not all schools can be equally effective: not all educators are equally skillful. Without this assumption, the most economical education procedure would be to reduce all education costs to the minimum and provide all graduates with cut-rate degrees. Once we reject this course, and agree there are differences in the quality of school output, we become concerned with *effects* of education as an output. How much knowledge do graduates acquire? Then another question arises: How can we produce the best effect for a given cost level, and how can we ensure that certain minimum effects (beyond the receipt of a diploma) are being produced? In order to answer this question, we need more refined output definitions and measurement tools.

In considering the knowledge output of elementary and secondary schools, the question of international comparisons will arise. For instance, *Toward a Social Report,* issued by the U.S. Department of Health, Education and Welfare, included data suggesting that American students at certain age levels were learning less mathematics than their contemporaries in foreign countries.[5] While such studies highlight significant issues, the entire formal and informal educational system of a society produces a total product. Failure in producing any one effect on a child may be the by-product of success in producing another effect. Americans may learn more history or creativity than the Japanese at the expense of learning math. This is not to propose inadequate mathematics teaching per se, but to emphasize the problems of international comparisons, especially those focused on one subject. I suggest that the most productive comparisons, for the moment, can be made between schools within our country, where there is some agreement on what we hope to attain.

## The Methodology of School Output Evaluation

The first goal of school output evaluation is to determine what kinds of knowledge and how much knowledge a student has acquired. That is a task in measurement.

At this moment, it is evident that most citizens (and many educators) identify such measures almost entirely with reading and mathematics scores on objective (or short answer) tests plus exams such as the college boards. Undoubtedly, these are the most widely used output measures. However, the "knowledge" measured can be more than facts learned and traditional cognitive skills such as algebra or map reading. It can also cover more subtle values; it depends on the objectives and quality of the test instrument. For instance, President Nixon's 1970 Message on Education Reform urged that a National Institute of Education develop "new measures of educational output. In doing so, it should pay as much heed to what are called the *immeasurables* of schooling (largely because no one has yet learned to measure them) such as responsibility, wit and humanity as it does to verbal and mathematical achievement."[6]

Actually, some psychometricians might contend we have such subtle instruments available today, although they would agree that at their present state of development such instruments may be ill-suited for use in large-scale studies.[7]

As an example of more subtle measurement, consider this recently developed measure of potential artistic creativity: the subjects, who have had some experience in painting, are presented with a table containing a number of jars and other objects, asked to select several, place them on another table, and paint a still life within a specified time limit. While this is being done, a trained examiner keeps notes of (a) the manner in which the subjects examine the objects before selecting any, (b) the particular objects examined, and (c) the way in which the paintings develop. The examiner's observations are kept on a carefully designed form. The data on the form is analyzed to see (a) the number of ways in which the subjects have studied the facets of the objects before selecting them—looked at them from all sides, held them, felt their texture, etc.—(b) the extent to which the subjects have considered objects that were not usually considered by other subjects, and (c) the point during the painting process when the shape and pattern of the painting became apparent. Previous research had demonstrated that more persistently creative artists had usually examined objects in more different ways, had examined the less noticed objects, and had developed the final form of the painting at later stages than other artists. Thus, the "test" has proved to be a useful predictor of later creative painting talent.[8]

Obviously, the development and application of such subtle measurements is neither simple nor cheap. However, it suggests that we can find out far more than we do now—if we are patient and feel that the information is important.

Fortunately there is an aspect of modern output measurement that creates important options for test designers: output measurements are aimed at overall school efficiency rather than individual student learning. This means that statistical sampling techniques can be used to measure the learning of an appropriate sample of the students. For instance, suppose we are using four different tests to measure four outputs of a school. Each test can be administered to a separate quarter of the students. An appropriately designed sample, which included even smaller proportions of students, might be ample for evaluative purposes, even in a small school. The National Assessment (which we will discuss more fully later) is using a less than 1 percent sample of 130,000 student subjects to assess the performance of all American schools.[9] Again, the well-known national pre-election polls are usually based on samples of fewer than 10,000; that is, less than .2 percent of our voters. Sampling systems, such as election polls, are not precisely accurate. They do not pretend to be. Their purpose is to approximate what opinion is. Similarly, a school output measure based on a small sample might say that, based on our 2 percent sample, 77 percent of the students in the whole school—give or take about 3 percent—know their home phone numbers. For most purposes, such an approximation is all we need. Of course, such data does not tell us what any specific child knows, and the individual parent or teacher also wants information about particular children. However, this precise kind of information need not be produced by the general output measurement sampling process. If needed, it can be developed in each class by the teacher.

There is another advantage to sampling: it permits the use of varied and more elaborate types of tests and measurements. For instance, objective or short answer tests are not appropriate for many measurement purposes; some measurements are better derived from more discursive written answers, interviews, and other exercises. All of these approaches are feasible via sampling, if the techniques have been properly validated, since the tests can be carefully administered by trained examiners to a fraction of the student population.

## The National Assessment

Efforts are underway to design and apply varied instruments. The National Assessment has been a leading force in this development. Samples of some of the questions used by the assessment follow:

On this calendar, draw a ring around the date which is two weeks after December 8. (Mathematics, age 9)

Show on this picture a clock face where the hands will be at 9:30. (Mathematics, age 9)

The noonday temperatures in a town in New Jersey were recorded for one week. The temperature the first day was 30 degrees Fahrenheit, the second day it was 25, the third day it was 30, the fourth day it was 31, the fifth day it was 29. What season of the year was this most likely to have been? (Science, age 9)

We are going to have a PTA meeting in our school on Monday evening at seven p.m. Will you write a little note inviting your parents to attend? (Writing, age 9)

The examiner says, "I am going to play a little tune. When it is finished, will you hum the tune for me?" (Music, age 9)

The examiner says, "I am going to play a song you have often heard." (After the song has been played, the examiner asks, "Can you tell me the name of the song?" (Music, age 9)

The examiner says, "Can you sing, or play a musical instrument? Sing or play something for me." (Music, age 9)

Here are four pictures. Do some of them seem alike to you? Which ones? (Art, age 9)

Here is an article which tells you how to make a paper hat. Here is the material. See if you can make a hat. (Reading, age 13)

Check the word below that means the same as *being.* (Writing, age 17)

While babysitting for your 2-year-old brother, one afternoon you hear a scream from the basement. When you get there, you see an open bottle of acid. Your brother can't talk so you don't know whether he drank any of the acid. Check which of the actions listed below you should do first. (Science, age 17)

The Constitution of the United States says that members of the Supreme Court are to be appointed for lifetime. Write below one reason for this law. (Citizenship, age 17)

Describe an experiment that you might do to show that plants give off oxygen. (Science, age 17)[10]

As we can sense, the assessment has tried to develop questions that permit prose answers and invite student reflection but are susceptible to structured grading.[11] In other words, by experimenting, we can devise a grading scale that permits a trained examiner to grade all the possible correct answers to the Constitution question with comparative consistency. The examiner needs training, and the development of the question requires experiments and time, but it can be done.

The assessment questions expose other differences between traditional achievement testing and more recent developments in measurement. Traditional tests are graded almost solely in terms of percentiles or number scores; the scores tell us the number or proportion of correct answers given by the subject and where he stands in relation to other students tested. Students are characterized as reading at six months behind national levels in reading, for example, or two years ahead. Such tests are described as *norm referenced,* i.e., above or below the norm. Tests of this sort do not give us an idea of what absolute skills the student possesses; only a highly trained specialist knows what is meant by *reading at the fifth grade level, at the 27th percentile for tenth grade math,* and so on. However, these scoring characteristics reflect the current uses of the tests and the concepts of their designers rather than the essentials of output tests.

The scoring systems and tests are aimed at identifying "deviant" students, i.e., those in the top or bottom 10 or 20 percent. This information permits school counselors or college admission personnel to draw simple conclusions; some colleges want applicants from the top 10 percent, students in the bottom 20 percent go into remedial reading, etc. For such purposes, an abstract, comparative score is satisfactory.

The traditional norm referenced tests had poor powers of discrimination at the highest or lowest levels, i.e., the top or bottom 5 percent. Though one could identify the best and worst learners, there were not enough very hard or very easy questions to enable one to make distinctions within the deviant groups. An Einstein might have nearly the same score as just a very smart child.

On the other hand, instruments such as those applied by the assessment permit testers to give feedback to nontechnicians, as well as experts, about the actual skills or knowledge students possess. Such tests are described as *criterion referenced.* Their scores can be translated to recognizable information. Also, they do not rely on gross, offensive interstudent comparisons as much as the norm referenced tests. On any norm referenced test, 50 percent of the students, by definition, are *subnormal;* criterion references focus more on what students know or need to know, than on how they compare to others. This is not to say that comparisons are an irrelevant measure; it is useful to know when someone is exceptionally adept or inadept, and that requires comparison. However, comparisons are only one standard of performance, and they can be overemphasized. In addition, one can sense that the assessment measures many levels of knowledge for each group; i.e., there are both very hard and very easy questions asked in all areas. These factors increase the amount of information the testing system can transmit and the number of people who can use the feedback, thus enlarging the usefulness of the system.

To illustrate the character of assessment results and conclusions, here is a report of the results of four (of the eleven) writing exercises given to nine-year-olds:

101. When asked to write a thank-you note to their grandmother for the birthday gift of a puppy, 88% of the 9s wrote a legible letter expressing their thanks for the gift, while 11% of the 9s did not write a letter which met all three requirements.

102. Of the 9s, 35% wrote a letter of invitation to a play which included

the necessary information of date, time, and place. While 83% wrote a letter and mentioned the play, slightly more than 60% included the date and time, and 48% included the place. Thus while 9s did give some of the required information, only about a third completed all the requirements for this task. A large proportion of the 9s provided information which would ordinarily be included in an invitation but which was not required for this task—75% included a greeting, 52% included the name of the sender (writer), and 33% included a closing.

103. Nines listened to a recording of a telephone conversation between Mary and Billy, and were asked to write a note including certain bits of information which Mary gave to Billy. Parts of the information were included by 68% or more of the 9s, but only 31% of them included all the required bits of information.

104. Nines were asked to address an envelope, given all the information which should be placed on a properly addressed envelope. Six bits of information were required for the task to be scored acceptable; 28% of the 9s did the task successfully. As with the first three exercises reported above, many 9s included some of the required information, but not all of it.[12]

Incidentally, it's obvious that reporting of this sort has implications for the traditional report card. There are many variations in local school practices of reporting to parents, and the policies, like most other types of feedback, serve numerous divergent needs. They inform the parents how well their child and the teacher are performing. They may enable the teacher to induce the parents to pass important or enlightening information back to the school. They may motivate the parents to offer more help to their child or increase or diminish their demands. They enable the students to appreciate their strengths and weaknesses. They can stimulate students to greater efforts by offering implicit rewards or reprimands. They can help all concerned perceive the competence of the student in comparison with other students. For example, if the student plans to be a professional musician or writer, he should be far more proficient than most other students in music or literature; merely being good is not enough.

This variety of reporting needs stimulates diverse local policies. The cards may have letter grades, number grades, test scores, or narrative analysis. They may come with a mandatory parent-teacher (and sometimes child) conference or be tied to criterion measures such as used by the assessment. But in any case, as assessment data becomes more widespread, it's likely that written reporting to parents will move in the direction of criterion assessment. An example of a report card reflecting criterion approaches is shown in Figure 2.

Figure 2. Report card for the language arts areas used from kindergarten through fourth grade

LANGUAGE ARTS PROGRESS REPORT

PUPIL______________________ SCHOOL______________________

| LANGUAGE ARTS AREAS | LEVEL A | LEVEL B | LEVEL C |
|---|---|---|---|
| AUDITORY DISCRIMINATION | Recognizes: Sounds, Rhyming words | Hears: Consonants in various positions in words, consonant combinations. Matches sounds to symbols. | Hears consonant combinations. Identifies sounds in words. Distinguishes vowel sounds. |
| VISUAL DISCRIMINATION | Matches, Recognizes likenesses and differences. Moves eyes from left to right. Identifies objects. | Identifies and matches: Upper and lower case letters, color words. | Discriminates between similar symbols. Recognizes common components, plural endings. |
| LISTENING | Knows sounds. Reacts to games and stories. Follows simple directions. | Gives reasons for reactions to stories, recordings. Follows 2-step directions | Replies and reacts to questions. Follows 3-step directions. Forms visual images. |
| ORAL EXPRESSIONS | Avoids immature speech, organizes ideas. Enjoys and participates in speaking activities. | Retells, in sequence, short stories heard. | Retells, in sequence, stories heard and read |
| MOTOR SKILLS AND HANDWRITING | Traces, copies and draws basic shapes. Handles materials properly. Recognizes writing as a form. Copies name correctly. | Writes names, letters, ITA characters, words. | Writes: short words, simple sentences, stories. Copies: Simple sentences, short stories. |
| WORD ANALYSIS | | Uses picture and letter clues to identify words. | Matches pictures and beginning sounds. Uses consonant clues to identify words. Blends symbols to form new words. |
| WORD STUDY | Develops vocabulary through listening and speaking | Displays curiosity about words. | Uses picture dictionary. Identifies similar words quickly. Recognizes words rapidly. Understands meanings of |

TEACHER ____________________ CONFERENCE DATES ____________

| LEVEL D | LEVEL E | LEVEL F | LEVEL G |
|---|---|---|---|
| Hears: Differences between single consonants and blends, parts in compound words | Hears: Vowel digraphs, phonograms, "r" influenced words, contractions, triple blends | Hears: Vowel digraphs, Schwa sound, syllables | Hears: Multi-syllables in words, accent |
| Recognizes: Vowels, compound words, prefixes, blends, common components. Makes transition to T.O. | Recognizes: Vowel digraphs, "r" influenced words, word parts, contractions, triple blends, prefixes and suffixes | Recognizes: Parts of words, syllable patterns | Recognizes: Common components of words, syllables |
| Comments to others. Gets meaning from context or voice. Reacts to speaker. Retells main ideas | Follows 4-step directions. Respects ideas of others. Answers questions. Retells story in sequence | Follows 5-step directions. Shows adequate concentration. Evaluates critically. Listens with responsibility for facts, ideas, etc. | Adapts skill to purpose. Recognizes: Sound pattern, important ideas |
| Shares and interprets information. Role plays in small groups. Applies acceptable speaking standards | Uses acceptable speaking standards. Recounts in order. Shows vocabulary growth. Participates in oral activities | Selects topics and plans talks. Gives book reports from simple notes. Develops ideas and keeps to subject. Respects opinions of others | Keeps interest of audience. Speaks in complete, concise sentences. Keeps talks within a time limit. Chooses variety of sentence beginnings. Includes necessary and correct facts in proper sequence. Gives report which develops one main incident |
| Attempts to write legibly | Writes neatly and legibly. Slants and spaces letters properly and uniformly | Makes clear distinction between capital and lower case letters | Applies standards for good writing to daily classroom and homework assignments |
| Uses phonics to attack words. Sounds compound words | Uses: Vowel digraphs "r" influenced vowels. Sounds word parts. Attacks words independently | Uses schwa sound. Divides words into syllables. Accents words | Unlocks multi-syllable words. Applies rules of accenting. Changes meaning through use of prefixes and suffixes |
| Identifies and uses comparison words. Understands some antonyms | Makes personal dictionary. Selects words precisely. Understands | Uses exact descriptive words. Understands homonyms. Gets meaning from contextual clues. Builds words | Understands syllabication. Builds words from less regular components. Substitutes descriptive words for |

Obviously, designing such a report card is a substantial effort; at the same time, it simplifies the eventual tasks of grading and of focusing student, parent, and teacher attention on the student's learning strengths and weaknesses. However, a criterion-oriented card does not diminish the usefulness of parent-teacher meetings and, perhaps, additional comparative data.

Of course, the assessment is not without its critics. Some of them seem to be motivated, at least in part, by a desire to escape being accountable. Other critics have contended that the scope of the assessment is too narrow, and its methods still inadequate. One suggested that these latter shortcomings justify the total abandonment of the assessment.[13] Unquestionably, the assessment's methods can be refined. When it is looked at carefully, its limited character is evident. Its annual operating budget is about $3 million. This is slightly more than .01 percent of the annual operating costs of American elementary and secondary education. Its total research costs—perhaps $10 million—are a miniscular proportion of the costs of the enterprise it is trying to discover how to assess. Of course, such a comparatively minute effort, with almost no operating experience, will have many inadequacies. However, it is not clear that the solution is abandonment of the effort.

## Measuring Other Outputs

Sampling and careful measurement have other implications for education policy beyond measuring traditional teaching outcomes. Modern child rearing has placed growing responsibilities on the school and at the same time has increasingly cut it off from public life and public observation. For example, urban society children spend most of their time in the company of their peers, family, or teachers. This represents an extraordinary narrowing of the range of experiences historically offered the young. Even in the immediate past—say twenty-five to thirty-five years back—children spent far greater proportions of time at jobs, neighborhood stores, or in contact with more remote relatives or other adults who were not child-oriented professionals.

These earlier patterns changed with the diminishment of child labor, the lessening of farming as an occupation, the growth of age-homogeneous suburbs, and the lengthening and intensification of formal education (not only has the number of school years grown, but the number of school days per year has also significantly grown). The matter is further complicated by the patterns of teacher recruitment, certification, and retention. These forces all tend to limit the type of person who comes into teaching (i.e., takes a college level education program), is hired, and chooses to stay. All this means that child rearing has been diverted from the mainstream of adult life or left to narrow classes of adults running a restricted institution. This isolation may not be for the best for either children or the schools. It argues that we must give careful attention to what is happening to the children we are raising (historically speaking) in this radically new mode. Thus, it may become appropriate to wonder how much children are enjoying school, whether they are prepared for the jobs they seek after graduation, whether they are technically and emotionally mature enough for college work, etc.

As an instance, suppose we are concerned about student drug use. A sampling technique that guaranteed confidentiality to student-respondents might be an excellent means of studying student knowledge, attitudes, and practices in regard to drugs. Two groups of my undergraduate students have conducted such surveys in local high schools. In both cases, the surveys faced strong opposition from the administrators. Each survey turned up a far higher rate of student use of hard and soft drugs than the administrators forecast. The survey also suggested a high degree of student tension and fear about drugs—even among many users. The students wanted more counseling about drugs.

Incidentally, all surveys of group knowledge and conduct patterns become extrainformative if they have been continuously applied over some time. Then, we can see changes in attitudes and get a better sense of what is happening. For example, suppose 30 percent of the students in a survey say they do not like school in 1972. That is interesting, but the 30 percent figure means much more if the dislike figure in the same survey in 1970 was 50 percent or 15 percent. Two successive index numbers permit comparisons and are more than twice as valuable as one.

## Teaching for the Test

Another matter that arises is concern about "teaching for the test." This refers to a belief that teachers are able to increase student test scores significantly by narrowly focusing instruction on the expected subject matter of the test. Essentially, the term *teaching for the test* is pejorative; it implies that knowledge acquired for such purposes will be ephemeral, and that the measurements have trivial value. Let me offer a vivid example of this belief:

A parent activist in the experimental Ocean Hill-Brownsville school district in New York City told me of an inservice training course for teachers he had audited during 1969. The course was conducted by middle-echelon school administrators. These instructors and the teachers attending the course agreed it was important to improve the reading scores of the lower income students attending their schools, especially in the light of increasing community pressures for better school performance. As a solution, the instructors suggested drilling students on the types of words typically found on the standard reading tests. For instance, one instructor suggested, "If *bonnet* is a word common on such tests, and the students don't get the idea, go out and buy the record 'Put on Your Easter Bonnet.' Play it to the students. When the scores improve as a result of such efforts, the parents will love you." The activist was horrified at this approach to teaching.

The activist is, I believe, largely correct. However, the story involved an extensive series of misunderstandings, though they were, perhaps, more the fault of the educators than the parents. First, no one defends the actual advanced leaking of specific planned test questions (unless the questions cover large general topics). If that were done, the test would not be a test. Of course, such leakage sometimes happens; but the answer is to apply better administrative controls, not to abolish tests.

But what about teaching that focuses on the types of material that one can predictably expect on the test? Numerous experiments have shown that scores can be *somewhat* improved by crude, "forcing" techniques such as the one suggested in the story.[14] However, the effects are probably the result of two different forces:

1. The simple increase in mechanical test-taking skills: filling out a form, sizing up a test, and so on. Students with little experience in such matters can improve their scores slightly with instruction in how to take a test. And, in a world where we fill out tax forms, maintain checking accounts, and submit employment applica-

tions, these are important skills. If students have not learned them, the schools may well be at fault.

2. The effect of rote instruction and drill in the expected substance of the test: e.g., spelling, vocabulary, or math. Such instruction, too, is sometimes slightly helpful. But if the teacher does not know the precise items on the test in advance, cramming is not a useful tool for significantly improving scores if the student is unlearned in the first place.

For instance, experimenters attempted to improve the reading scores of young Mexican-American students, who typically performed poorly. Efforts to drill them in test-type words consistently failed to produce any success. Finally, the experimenters discovered that the children's major problem was failure to understand certain key concept words: front, back, soon, later, etc. Lacking this understanding, they could not begin to comprehend the material being taught. The need was not to give them more time in reading, but to understand why they were having trouble learning, remedy that problem, and then teach them how to read. The experimenters set out to develop a new system to teach the concept words. The new system was substantially different from those regularly used by the students and relied heavily on students teaching each other. The developing system was monitored by frequent tests of the concept words to see whether the system was doing the job or needed improvement. From time to time, as the developers received feedback from the tests, they revised and improved the system. When the system was finally complete, the students had learned the concept words, and their reading scores improved substantially. The new system was then made available to other schools.[15]

In other contexts, it is evident that a major problem in teaching reading to poor learners is motivation. If the teacher can motivate the children, the skill may follow; if not, drill may simply drive the children to further withdrawal.

Thus, the concern over teaching for the test can mask many issues. Do we mean teaching particular leaked test items? That is wrong. If we want to, we can stop it by better administration. Do we mean increasing children's skills in doing certain kinds of paper work? Perhaps this is not a bad idea in our paper-oriented society. Do we mean using excessive rote and drill? This is usually poor teaching and actually does not significantly help test scores, although many educators do not know this. Finally, do we mean teaching students the concepts and skills that high scores on well-constructed tests try to measure, just as the better reading scores of the Mexican-American students evolved from learning concept words? Of course, in the short run, ill-advised teachers and administrators may use inappropriate methods of teaching for the test; the answer to this is better-trained teachers, and better-developed ways to teach. In the long run, with better leadership, tests stimulate the development of such improvements, just as the new system for the concept words evolved from concern about reading scores.

## Footnotes

1. Alvin W. Gouldner, *Enter Plato* (New York: Basic Books, 1965).
2. Russell L. Ackoff, "Towards Quantitative Evaluation of Urban Services," in *Public Expenditures in the Urban Community,* ed. Howard G. Schaller (Washington, D.C.: Resources for the Future, 1964), p. 94.
3. Wilbur J. Cohen, "Education and Learning," *Annals* 373 (September 1967): 79-101.
4. W. L. Hansen, ed., "Symposium on Rates of Return on Investment in Education," *Journal Of Human Resources* 2 (Summer 1967): 291-374.
5. HEW, *Toward a Social Report* (Washington, D.C.: U.S. Government Printing Office, 1969), p. 68; see also Torsten Husen, "International Impact of Evaluation," in *Educational Evaluation: New Roles, New Means: The Sixty-eighth Yearbook of the National Society for the Study of Education, Part 2,* ed. Ralph W. Tyler (Chicago: University of Chicago Press, 1969), pp. 335-360. Tyler is an authority in this field, and the collection is comprehensive.
6. Richard M. Nixon, "Education Reform," *Weekly Compilation of Presidential Documents* 6, no. 10 (March 3, 1970): 306.
7. Donald J. Dowd & Sarah C. West, "An Inventory of Measures of Affective Behavior" (*affective* means relating to emotions, values or human relations), in *Improving Educational Assessment and an Inventory of Measures of Affective Behavior* (Washington, D.C.: Association for Supervision and Curriculum Development, National Education Association, 1969), pp. 90-158; Lewis B. Mayhew, "Mea-

sures of Non-Cognitive Objectives in the Social Studies," in *Evaluation in Social Studies: Thirty-fifth Yearbook of the National Council for Social Studies,* ed. Harry D. Berg (Washington, D.C.: The Council, 1965); Jack C. Merwin & Frank B. Womer, "Evaluation in Assessing the Progress of Education to provide Bases of Public Understanding and Public Policy," in *Educational Evaluation,* pp. 305-334.

8. M. Csikszentmihalyi & J. W. Getzels, "Discovery Oriented Behavior and the Originality of Creative Products: A Study With Artists," *Journal of Personality and Social Psychology* 19, no. 1 (1971): 47-52.

9. See, e.g., *Educational Evaluation;* Tyler, "National Assessment: History and Sociology," in *New Models for American Education,* ed. James W. Guthrie & Edward Wynne (Englewood Cliffs, N.J.: Prentice-Hall, 1971); Harry L. Miller & Roger R. Woock, *Social Foundations of Urban Education* (Hinsdale, Ill.: Dryden Press, 1970), pp. 211-220 (a useful, semipopularized survey of current research); Edward Wynne, "School Output Measures As Tools for Change," in *Education and Urban Society,* 2, no. 1 (November 1969): 3-21.

10. Department of Elementary School Principals, National Education Association, *National Assessment of Educational Progress: Some Questions and Answers* (Washington, D.C.: Department of Elementary School Principals, NEA, 1967), p. 12; Committee on Assessing the Progress of Education, *Demonstration Package, Form for Age 17* (Ann Arbor, Mich.: Committee on Assessing the Progress of Education, 1968).

11. Merwin & Womer, op. cit.

12. National Assessment of Educational Progress, *Writing, National Results, 1970, Report 3* (Washington, D.C.: U.S. Government Printing Office, 1970), pp. 12-13.

13. Martin T. Katzman & Ronald S. Rosen, "The Science and Politics of National Assessment, *The Record* 71, no. 4 (May 1970): 571-587.

14. Frank B. Womer & N. Ksihor Wahi, "Test Use," in *Encyclopedia of Education Research,* 4th ed. (New York: Macmillan Co., 1969), p. 1463.

15. Ralph J. Melaragno & Gerald Newmark, *Final Report, A Pilot Study to Apply Evaluation-Revision Procedures in First-Grade Mexican American Classrooms,* TM-3930/00/00 (Santa Monica, Calif.: System Development Corp., May 17, 1968).

# 3

# Accountability: A Hundred-Plus Years of Trying

Even in slight things, the experience of the new is rarely without some stirrings of foreboding.

Back in 1936, I spent a good part of the year picking peas. I started out early in January in the Imperial Valley and drifted northward, picking peas as they ripened, until I picked the last peas of the season in June, around Tracy. Then I shifted all the way to Lake County, where for the first time I was going to pick string beans. And I still remember how hesitant I was that first morning. I was about to address myself to the string beans. Would I be able to pick string beans? Even the change from peas to string beans has in it elements of fear.

In the case of drastic change, the uneasiness is of course deeper and more lasting.

Eric Hoffer[1]

In considering the history of output measures, we must be sensitive to the distinction between accountability efforts sponsored by schools, and those thrust on schoolmen, essentially by external groups. The distinction is important because of the mechanics of collecting data. With some types of institutions, the public or researchers can garner nonintuitive feedback without institutional cooperation: we can measure air pollution without the help of automobile companies; we do not need to ask cigarette companies who smokes. This is not ordinarily the case in school accountability. Because achievement data should include large numbers of school age children and often cover diverse topics, the instruments probably should be administered in schools. We also want information about school inputs (teacher qualifications, expenses per child, and the like). Thus school cooperation is essential in school evaluation. Tensions have persistently arisen over this matter.

## School Accountability, An Historic Concept

The concept of output accountability for educators arises naturally for laymen. Two millenia ago, Plutarch advised:

> Fathers, themselves, ought every few days to test their children, and not rest their hopes on the disposition of a hired teacher; for even those persons will devote more attention to the children if they know they must from time to time render an account.[2]

Some simple, intuitive, output measures as Plutarch proposed have probably been the major basis of school accountability over most of educational history. However, events are making this intuitive feedback more and more inadequate. In general, children are now acquiring more and different formal knowledge than their parents. Inevitably, parents are less able to evaluate the instruction their children receive. The information explosion, the growth of the school curriculum, and the tendency for children to attend school longer than their parents, have diminished the effectiveness of first-hand observation as an assessment tool.

In addition, larger, more bureaucratic school structures discourage parents from attempting to evaluate the learning of their children. If you feel your child is not being taught math well in high school, to whom do you complain? The principal? The guidance counselor? Your child's math teacher for this term? His math teacher last term? The chairman of the high school math department? The school district math curriculum committee that decided on the textbook to buy? The textbook publisher? The writer of the textbook? A school board member? If your complaint is justified, how much can any one of these individuals do about it? In other words, it is one thing to hold accountable a tutor you personally hire; it is another to attempt to check on a large school system. Inevitably, other less intuitive accountability techniques have begun to emerge.

## The Office of Education: The Original Vision

Some early American attempts to measure output have considerable contemporary significance. In the early nineteenth century, educational reformers and school administrators strove to create a federal commitment to improving elementary and secondary education.[3] Henry Barnard was one of the most persistent of these reformers. Barnard was firmly convinced of the need for better data. He felt such data might be a key tool for fostering educational improvement; they would disclose the most successful practices, which could then be applied in other school systems. In 1838 and 1839 Barnard, then a Connecticut school official, was personally responsible for having questions about the national level of literacy inserted for the first time in the 1840 census. He accomplished this by making a series of personal visits to President Van Buren.

From about 1840 forward, educational groups sporadically attempted to have Congress establish a national agency for promoting federal education concerns. During the same period, the farmers lobby was trying to create a new federal agency for assisting agriculture. The developments arising from these two efforts present an interesting contrast. The farmers got their agency, the Department of Agriculture, in 1862. The educators won the creation of the Department of Education (the predecessor to the present Office of Education) in 1867.

The congressional arguments for the education agency directly relied on the agricultural precedent. The legislation, for example, provided that the Department of Education, like Agriculture, should "collect such statistics and acts as shall show the condition and progress of education in the several States and Territories." Congressman Samuel W. Moulton, in arguing for the bill in 1866, made the agriculture parallel quite clear:

> The Department of Agriculture at the seat of Government here does not invade any rights of property in the States. What does it do? What we propose for the Department of Education in this bill. It gives the result of experiments, it collects facts from California, from Maine, from all of the States, and all parts of the world, prepares those facts in popular form and presents them to the people. Here are two hundred and fifty Representatives of the people. What has been the greatest demand made on you? Has not the greatest demand from your constituents been for the Agricultural Report? The demand has been for agricultural information, seeds and plants, the results of experiments, etc.

The Department of Agriculture applies only to one class of men. The bureau we propose here applies to every man, woman, and child in the country . . .

We do not propose to go into Ohio or any other State, but we propose to correct whatever is wrong or mischievous in any of these State systems by pointing out and showing to them that their systems are wrong and what the better plan would be; just the same as the Bureau of Agriculture, by disseminating information all over the land, giving the results of experience, corrects errors in the method of the cultivation of lands, and promotes the interests of agriculture in the different States.[4]

The bill was passed, and Barnard, wholly committed to an information collection perspective, became the first commissioner. Barnard and his successors failed dismally at their task. The office was badly underfunded by Congress, and entirely without resources to collect the data Barnard wanted to obtain. We can be sure from his prior interest in census data on literacy that part of the data he hoped to acquire was school output information. A historian of the office's early years concluded that one reason for the gross underfunding was the comparative coolness of professional educators to the concept of an active Department of Education (that they had been only mildly interested in promoting).

The later comparative history of the education and agriculture agencies is extremely significant. Over the years, Agriculture maintained its focus on information collection, research, and dissemination. It has had continuously enlarging budgets and staff, and much of its energies have been directed at being a resource for farmers, who welcome its information. Farm agencies have vigorously lobbied for expansion and enlargement of its services. Today, the department has an annual budget of about $7 billion and over 105 thousand employees. Between 1850 and 1965, agricultural productivity performance has increased from 4.1 persons fed by one farmer to 37 persons.

Education, on the other hand, started as an agency of minimal size, and stayed there. It never found out a great deal about schools, and it never obtained significant support from great numbers of educators. After World War II, the federal budget for the Office of Education began to grow, and today it is at about $5 billion. However, the office has only a staff of about 2000 employees (compared to Agriculture's 105 thousand) employees. So most of the money is simply turned over to local schools. At the same time, the office—as opposed to Agriculture—has neither the staff, the tradition, nor the base of research to provide really useful information about how the money should be spent. But the problem is probably the fault not of the office but of its constituency; farmers aggressively want to grow more corn or cattle; it is not so clear that improved learning is as important a school goal. So the educators' agency never had the pressure from its constituency to do the job that Congressman Moulton had in mind. And while we know a lot about the production of corn, cotton, and hogs, no one has any idea whether, or how much, education productivity per teacher has increased between 1867 and 1970. We have never collected such data.

At the present time, the Office of Education is helping to support National Assessment, which is aimed at some of the same types of data that concerned Barnard. I shall discuss some of the assessment's problems later, and we shall see that school indifference and hostility to data collection still faces the office today.

## Other Early Output Measurement Efforts

Some of Barnard's reforming contemporaries also saw the value of accountability. Horace Mann, another early nineteenth-century school reformer, became engaged in a controversy with Boston schoolmasters over the quality of education in the schools. He persuaded the local school committees to administer uniform written exams to a sample of students. The results corroborated his criticisms. Perhaps for this reason, his new evaluation technique was not adopted.

In 1895-97, Joseph Mayer Rice persuaded schools to administer to sixteen thousand students a spelling test he had devised. The results showed no correlation between the amount of time that schools spent in spelling lessons and the achievement of their pupils. However, Leonard Ayres reports:

> The presentation of the results brought the investigation under almost unlimited attack. The educators . . . united in denouncing as foolish, reprehensible, and from every point of view indefensible, the effort to discover anything about the value of teaching by finding out whether or not the children could spell. They claimed that the object of such work was not to teach the children how to spell, but to develop their minds.[5]

Rice, a pediatrician with training in psychological measurement, continued his interest in measurement and evaluation. In 1902 he wrote an article in *The Forum,* a journal of social criticism, in which he proposed further organized efforts toward school accountability:

> It may be said, without exaggeration, that up to the present time the science of pedagogy has been in its entirety a structure based on no stronger foundation than one of opinions. Now that it has been demonstrated that we have a ready means of learning with what success each teacher is meeting, and therefore a basis for studying why certain schools are successful, and therefore others not, there ought to be no delay in taking advantage of it.[6]

Rice understood the problems in financing the proposed efforts. The next year he wrote:

> A most important problem remains to be solved. The inductive method applied to pedagogy necessitates the examination of pupils in many different schools and localities, the marking of thousands upon thousands of papers from many different points of view, the construction of elaborate statistical tables, etc., etc.; and a source of revenue must be provided to pay for the travel and the clerical hire.[7]

Rice therefore established a department of educational research under the auspices of *The Forum* to implement his research plans, but lack of funds and the great hostility of educators forced him to discontinue the enterprise. He attributed the hostility of the school administrators to "some of the things (such as the spelling study) I said of our country in my series of articles on the Public School System of the United States, published in *The Forum* some nine years ago."[8]

The administrators might frustrate the proposals made by Rice, but in the early twentieth century the application of efficiency and rationalization was being urged on all public institutions, due in part to the popularity of the management approaches being developed by Fredrick Taylor. The educators could not ignore these public trends. They had to take some steps, and they did. In the early 1900s, the adoption of "businesslike" statistical methods appeared as an important theme in school administration.[9] This development had no relation to sensitive evaluation, however; the business themes applied by schools evolved into a ritualistic mimicry of Taylor's scientific management movement. The innovations caricatured Taylorism, demonstrating its weaknesses and none of its strengths. Thus, when school administrators attempted to increase student learning "scientifically," they treated the rate of student promotion through grades or the amount of time spent in various classes as indices of school efficiency, without considering whether either promotion or time in class was related to learning.

In modern terminology, they focused on input—what they exposed students to—and rejected Rice's proposals to focus on output—actual student learning. Such conduct demonstrated the shallow knowledge of the administrators concerned. The efficiency cult deprived the schools of benefits that might have been produced by a sensitive application of Taylorism. In addition, it generated great hostility to rationalization among school reformers. The scars of this hostility persist today.

## The Testing Movement

Standardized testing began to appear in schools not too long after the rejection of Rice's proposals. However, it was adopted to measure *pupil performance* rather than *school performance.* In other words, it was acceptable to measure how well students learned but not how well schools taught. A major development in the pattern occurred during World War I. Behavioral psychologists were employed to advise the Army on how to classify and identify the talents of millions of draftees. Their recommendations involved large-scale adoption of objective, uniform tests. It became dramatically evident that the tests were a useful means of analyzing performance of different subjects in widely scattered locations. The schools followed suit and have made continuous use of similar tests for the same reasons: to identify students' talents, thereby facilitating rational assignment, and to discover the student's shortcomings for diagnostic purposes.[10] In 1964, all of the seventy-five public high schools queried in one study used the standardized test in one way or another, while 75% of the elementary schools used similar measures.[11]

There have been many criticisms of tests and charges of excessive reliance on test-taking rather than on more substantive skills. For example, the charge has been made that the tests are being used to stigmatize ghetto children, by compelling them to learn skills and vocabularies irrelevant to their life. However, the charges may miss the point that the Greek root of the word *educate* means to bring out from. Presumably, we hope that ghetto children will not be compelled to spend their lives entirely in the ghetto. Thus, the tests are means of measuring the success of the school in helping to bring these youths out of their present environment into another one. It is true that the school does not always succeed in attaining such goals, but measurement and tests are one means of seeing how well it is succeeding.

One study on this topic observed that:

> the elixir of the "culture-fair" or "culture-free" test has been pursued through attempts to minimize the educational loading to test content, or to reduce the premium on speed of response. However, these efforts have usually resulted in tests that have low validity for academic prediction purposes and little power to uncover hidden potentialities of children who do poorly in the common run of academic aptitude and achievement tests . . . . Many bright, nonconforming pupils, with backgrounds different from those of their teachers, make favorable showings on achievement tests, in contrast with their low classroom marks.[12]

The research has consistently demonstrated that the tests are useful predictors of later school performance. For example:

> A student at the highest level of academic aptitude (based on eleven separate score levels of performance on standard college entry exams) has more than four times as much chance of obtaining a B average or better in college as did a student at the lowest level of academic ability: 74 chances in 100 versus only 16 chances in 100.[13]

There is another basic question of relevance: How important is success in the subjects on which school grades are based for later success in life? Are better students better businessmen, lawyers, or doctors? The answer to this question will require much more study.[14] However, no serious analyst has proposed that illiteracy advances a person's prospects. Also, both the test and school curriculum have been undergoing continuous refinement.

The test movement was further accelerated by increasing college enrollment after World War II. Colleges considering applicants from many geographic areas found tests a convenient way to compare applicant performance. Inevitably, schools tended to evaluate students by standards that meshed with those used by colleges to which they might apply, and test scores became a national communication tool for certain groups.

College admission practices also produced another evaluative use of test scores. Admission counselors at colleges needed to know how to weight the grading systems of schools and school systems; what did a B average, or being in the top quarter in a particular school mean in national comparisons? Some schools and school districts have prepared descriptions of their high schools, which analyze the achievement test score patterns of their student bodies (and their letter-grading systems) in a detailed and coherent form. The outlines are prepared for college counselors to enable them to estimate the significance of school grading systems and, incidentally, the general academic caliber of the students. Figure 3 is an extract from such an outline distributed by the high school in Berkeley, California.

It is evident that this format gives college counselors a useful picture of some of the characteristics of the school. There are very few school publications about test scores (for public release) that match its clarity. I suspect that colleges receive well-organized and comparatively clear data because they wield power. If the data are obscurely presented, the school's graduates are less likely to be admitted.

The proposal has been made that such test results should be used to assess the performance of school administrators, as well as the performance of students.[15] However, this approach has not received systematic attention from school administrators or from many education researchers other than Rice. One recent study of techniques for evaluating administrators made no reference to whether the students under that administrator were learning.[16]

It is also true that "raw" achievement test scores have important limitations as accountability measures. Educators see large variations in average scores between schools within the same district, and they suspect that the variations reflect more than differences in school administration. Therefore, it might be unjust to evaluate performance by simply comparing median scores between schools. In addition, researchers—applying rather simple analytic techniques—have demonstrated a consistent, strong correlation between per pupil expenditures by different school districts and the average level of per district pupil performance on tests. In other words, the greater the

## FIGURE 3

STANDARDIZE TESTS – Class of 1969

| Test | Year Administered | Students | Mean |
|---|---|---|---|
| PSAT | 1967 | 429 | |
| Verbal | | | 47 |
| Math | | | 50 |
| LORGE-THORNDIKE | 1966 | 1045 | |

| | Mean | | | Upper Quartile | Median | Lower Quartile |
|---|---|---|---|---|---|---|
| Verbal | 102.7 | 52%ile | (S.D. – 19.176) | 117 | 102 | 87 |
| Non-Verbal | 104.5 | 51.5%ile | (S.D. – 17.696) | 117 | 104 | 91 |
| Total | 103.7 | 51%ile | (S.D. – 19.176) | 117 | 104 | 90 |

GRADE DISTRIBUTION – Class of 1969

Percentages of final grades for 1059 juniors at the end of the 1967-68 school year.

A – 18%
B – 31%
C – 27%
D – 13%
F – 11%

Average grade index for all students in this class for junior year was 2.40 on a 4 point scale.

per pupil expenditures, the higher the pupils' scores. This was construed to mean that more dollars would provide better quality education. Despite school indifference to output accountability, however, external pressures have developed for the application of such measures.

## The Tradition of State Responsibility

In almost all states, school districts exercise their power under state delegation. Thus, a state school agency has final responsibility for the quality of education offered. States also pay a substantial portion of local costs. The nature of state control varies widely, but this legal framework interjects a significant element into the question of by whom and how schools shall be evaluated.

In New York State, the State Board of Education (the Regents) has traditionally exercised a strong role in overseeing education offered throughout the state. It has consciously applied output evaluations. For over 100 years, at certain grade levels, students have been required to take state-designed, uniform Regents' exams covering a prescribed minimum curriculum. They include both subjective and objective questions. The tradition of these exams is a logical precedent for other types of output evaluations, since their basic purpose has been to test schools as well as students. Not too surprisingly, some educators look on such exams with disfavor. One complained that they demonstrate that "fully certified administrators and teachers are not *trusted* to provide adequate learning experiences without the pressure of statewide final examination."[17] There is little information about the precise comparative effect of these exams on the actual quality of schools.

In addition to the New York Regents' exam, many other states have assisted in the administration of objective tests to high school students throughout their local districts. However, the data from these programs was used for college selection or placement purposes or sometimes made available to local administrators for their own use. The data was not intended as an accountability tool.

## Accountability: 1950

Project Talent, funded by the Office of Education in 1959, was the first large-scale effort in modern school output evaluation in the

United States.[18] (John C. Flanagan, a principal developer of Project Talent, had served in the Air Force in World War II, and had assisted in the planning of personnel assignment systems.) Unlike Rice's proposals, the project was purely a research effort and had no apparent accountability goals.

Project Talent was feasible only with the development of computers. It compared the performance—on uniform, objective, and traditional tests—of a large number of pupils in many schools (whose identity was kept secret) against the level of expenditures, size of classes, qualifications of teachers, and socioeconomic background of the students in those schools. The objective was to discover the combinations of resources that worked best with certain combinations of students. Project Talent did not develop definitive answers, but it helped refine a method.

The data collected by the project is still being analyzed by researchers, and follow-up studies on former students are also being conducted to measure the long-range effect of school variables, e.g., how much effect did certain student performance levels or teacher characteristics have on later earnings, college performance, or perhaps even "fulfillment" in later life?[19]

Concurrently other forces for school change were at work. In 1954 the Supreme Court, in *Brown* v. *Board of Education,* held deliberate school segregation by race to be unconstitutional. One premise for the decision was that segregated schools had the *effect* of handicapping black students, even if their facilities and per pupil expenditures were equal to those of white schools. As the sociologist James S. Coleman pointed out, for the first time education policy shaping concerned itself not with the *inputs* in schools (dollars, teachers, real estate, etc.) but with the outputs or effects.[20] It began to appear that equality of opportunity might mean not equal inputs but equal learning. This emphasis gives a special thrust to accountability.

School desegregation in the District of Columbia was one illustration of the impact of the *Brown* decision on accountability. During desegregation, the system conducted a districtwide testing program to measure the achievement level of the pooled students. Shortly afterward, the congressional committee that oversees district affairs (composed primarily of southerners) commenced a series of hearings on the desegregated schools.[21] The test scores and their implications became a major issue. The scores communicated the fact that black pupils performed well below the academic level of white students in all their classes. The school officials were reluctant to reveal the data, and it appears local civil rights organizations also tried to keep them out of the record. Several committee members attempted to use the data to criticize desegregation. The hearings evolved into debates over the implications of the data. Did they suggest the latent inferiority of the black pupils? Did they reflect the previous segregation? Did they show that desegregation (in effect for only a short time and in an incomplete fashion) was ineffectual? Did it mean heterogeneous classes were impractical?

Of course the questions were not answered in any useful form at the hearing. Still, the debate prefigures the complex and shifting alliances that might evolve from output-oriented debates in the future. One side is sorry the data exists and tries to hide it. When it is revealed, disputes arise over its accuracy and interpretation. In a later dispute, both sides may change positions; for example, in succeeding debates, some civil rights spokesmen have become pro-test. Typically, none of the extreme militants on either side are interested in conducting an experiment to see what the usually ambiguous data really means.

The data from Project Talent became politically significant when Francis Keppel, the United States Commissioner of Education, testified on behalf of Title I of the Elementary and Secondary Education Act of 1965. Title I of the bill (which passed) proposed to appropriate about $1 billion a year for schools having concentrations of children from low-income families. Keppel emphasized that Project Talent and related research demonstrated that such children had low levels of school performance. Consequently, special funding for remedial programs was needed. The bill was passed, but the discussions about school output had another effect on Title I.

Previous federal school grant programs had only minimal evaluation requirements. An assessment of the effects of the National Defense Education Act of 1958 observed that the evaluation reports required by the act communicated only that the money had been spent; the evaluators could not find out what it had been spent for and could only guess at the effect of the expenditures.[22] The draft of Title I proffered by the administration provided that grantees should submit evaluations only at the end of the act's authorization of three years. During the hearings on the act, Senator Robert Kennedy observed that reporting and evaluation were

> not completely developed in the bill and that is why I wanted to have some discussion of it here. I think it is very important when we talk about the educational system in various communities. I think it is very difficult for a person who lives in a community to know whether, in fact, his educational system is what it should be, whether if you compare his community to a neighboring community they are doing everything they should do, whether the people that are operating the educational system in a state or in a local community are as good as they should be. I think it is very difficult for a citizen to know that. So you come in and say, "We have a certain percentage district. We are going to put $2 million in there."
>
> Now, that $2 million, because of the kind of board that you have, might just be completely wasted while $2 million in some other community might be used to help a child tremendously. If I lived in the community where the $2 million was being wasted, I would like to know something about that. I would like—I wonder if we couldn't just have some kind of system of reporting either through some testing system which could be established which the people at the local community would know periodically as to what progress had been made under this program. I think it would be very helpful to Congress and I think it would be very helpful to the people living in the local communities.[23]

At the urging of a small group of legislators, including Senator Kennedy and Congressman Scheuer, Title I was amended to require *annual* evaluations.

When Congress passed the Civil Rights Act of 1965, it directed the Office of Education to conduct a survey of equality of educational opportunity to assess the segregation existing in American schools. This "politically generated" survey (often called the Coleman Report after James S. Coleman, its principal designer) was the most elaborate piece of education research in American history. Not too surprisingly, important differences of opinion arose among the persons concerned with organizing the survey.[24] One group strove to collect data to emphasize the extent of segregation; others felt that attention should also be given to its effects, i.e., to the outputs of schools rather than just the scope of segregation. To a significant degree, the output orientation was adopted. Still, at the moment the survey was released, substantial efforts were made by federal officials to obscure some of its important implications (which are more fully discussed later). Nevertheless, the data bank developed by the survey has become a vital resource for analysis.

Even after the release of the Coleman Report, charges of burial continued to be uttered. Daniel P. Moynihan pointed out that the Office of Education had let the report go out of print a year after its issuance, and he contended that educators and many researchers were trying to ignore it out of sight. Moynihan sponsored a seminar and special issue of the *Harvard Education Review* to give prominence to the Coleman results and their implications.[25]

## School Administrators React Nationally

There had been continuing school-based resistance to these efforts. For instance, between 1968 and 1970, I interviewed thirty-five to fifty present or former school administrators throughout the country about the school release of output data to the public. These administrators generally agreed that schools almost invariably disclose output data only after internal disputes and usually only in response to vigorous public demands. As Michael Crozier has observed:

> It is clear that in any kind of organization there is a constant pressure to escape from reality. This tendency corresponds to what popular sentiment calls "bureaucratic tendencies." Centralization is one way to achieve it; completely impersonal rules are another. Both permit escape from an otherwise necessary adjustment. We shall describe as a "bureaucratic system of organization" any system or organization where the feedback process error-information-correction does not function.[26]

Thus we might conclude that school response to output evaluation efforts is an attempt to avoid the creation of a feedback process.

This avoidance of feedback is intensified by the comparative freedom from scrutiny that schools have obtained for themselves in the recent past.[27] As districts and all school operations become complex, school superintendents begin to dominate and manipulate school boards because of their superior information resources. Boards are not sufficiently informed to differ effectively with their superintendents.[28] For instance, one former school board member in Montgomery County, Maryland (an affluent suburb of Washington, D.C.) told me that in the early 1960s the superintendent gave the board members only the average scores for each school and did not give the names of schools with the scores. I inquired whether anyone had asked for the identities of the schools, that is, exactly who was doing better or worse? He told me the members "understood" that such a question would be seen by the superintendent as an intrusion into school administration and a threat to the principals of the schools. This personal observation about school board impotence is supported by broader surveys. A 1966 Gallup poll of school board members' opinions concluded that:

> In most communities, school board members say they are overwhelmed by problems of immediate concern—finding enough money in the budget to meet school needs, trying to keep up with population growth with new buildings and classrooms, meeting the problems of teacher shortages, seeking experienced teachers within budget limitations. These tasks occupy most of the time of the nation's school boards . . . . In many communities the local school board does not devote much time to the discussion of the curriculum or to innovative practices.[29]

But the issues between the superintendent and the board are not just withholding data and concealing issues with smoke screens of day-to-day trivia; the fact is that usually the key data is nonexistent. Nonexistence can be more prejudicial to the board's power than concealment. If data is concealed, it may be discovered or leaked. But if it has not been collected, it may take one or more years to develop an accountability system and put it in operation. Even when the data is collected at some future time, it becomes most useful after we have several years' collection as a comparison base.

Perhaps it is these forces for uninformed management that caused one researcher to conclude that "the New York City Board of Education's administration of business affairs is not an administration but a masonic order, with concentric circles of deeper and deeper mysteries."[30]

But behind these instances of administrative obscurity rests an important general principle: schools are far more innately reluctant to open their workings to public examination than most American institutions that have such intensive relations with the public. To see this reluctance in a comparative light, consider the signs typically seen outside Protestant churches. The signs usually name the pastor and the denomination; give the church phone number, the hours of services, and the subjects of services; and include an invitation to visit. In general, if a visitor or potential churchmember visits the pastor, he will be courteously received, and the workings of the church and its various activities will be explained to him. Contrast this with a public school. There is almost never an outside sign. The principal's name is not apparent, nor is the school phone number, the visiting procedure, or the name or contact point for any parent organization that exists. There rarely is any invitation for visitors to enter. Yet many schools will inform you that they have an open door policy—if you can find out about it.

Why does this contrast exist? Essentially, because if the minister turns away his church members, he will have no church, so he strives to engage them in church activities and make the church theirs, too. Conversely, the school does not clearly need the parents, only their children, and the law requires their attendance. The presence of the public is not welcome. After the public has been kept out for a while, the school begins to operate on the assumption that the public will not see the school's internal workings. When the school begins operating on that assumption, the entrance of the public will surely be disruptive, since the operation has not been designed to allow for their presence. All of this helps explain why, when I was a parents' committee member in a public school, a suggestion that the school put up an outside bulletin board met with endless objections. I have never heard so many reasons for not doing such a simple thing. Of course, to the school it was not a simple step; it was a very radical one.

Perhaps these patterns of school secretiveness explain why most parents react to school policy only with apathy. As one study disclosed, "many voters have little sense of any efficacy in their relationship to the schools. They despair of their own ability to do anything, of the possibility that school officials might care about what they think, and they find educational policy too complicated for them."[31] Let us see how schools applied these general principles to dealing with requests for accountability data.

Despite important public issues underlying the Coleman Report, complete sets of survey instruments were received from only 59 percent (689 out of 1170) of the high schools that participated. A disproportionately large number of big city school systems declined to participate in any way.[32]

The National Assessment, which is essentially trying to conduct a periodic nationwide sampling of student achievement, met with similar opposition. However, the assessment's promoters had time and influence. They knew of the previous patterns of resistance and moved deliberately, but with determination. Some quotes from a 1967 letter from the Executive Secretary of the American Association of School Administrators to the ASA membership demonstrate the spirit of that opposition:

> The project is a national testing program and as such will inevitably lead to the pressures of regional, state and local comparisons, and it will have national overtones for the dispensing of Federal Aid. The Carnegie Committee (which helped develop the project) has said that the program . . . might contribute a more accurate guide than we currently possess for allocating public and private funds, where they are needed, what they achieve and decisions affecting education . . . . Every school in an area which ranks below the national average would find itself branded by the low performance. It is a matter of the coercion and pressures of comparisons. . . . The National Assessment project would yield very little, if any, information on the performance of students in public and private schools which is not already known. The Executive Committee of AASA . . . recommends to its members and the educational institutions which they serve that they refuse to participate in the tryouts of these tests and the eventual testing program.[33]

This letter did not explain why the assessment was thought unacceptable, if the data it sought were already known. Nor was the letter too clear about how the members of the AASA, who were supposedly administrators following the bidding of their school boards, could simply "refuse to participate."

The assessment's promoters launched a vigorous campaign against the attack. Faculty groups at numerous colleges sent protest telegrams to the AASA. Newspapers such as the *Wall Street Journal* and the *Houston Post* carried critical editorials. The National Congress of Parents and Teachers and the National School Boards Association issued statements on behalf of the assessment. Concurrently, behind the scenes approaches were made. After much bargaining, the AASA agreed to cooperate on the condition that the planning board of the assessment be reconstituted to make it more "representative." A former president of the AASA became president of the reconstituted board. The board has since arranged for the administration of the assessment to be taken over by the Education Commission of the States, although the bulk of the assessment's funding is from the U.S. Office of Education. The commission, founded in 1966, serves as a clearinghouse for state educational policy-makers and is maintained by the state governments.

As another possible effect of the bargaining, the data from the assessment will be published on a regionally aggregated basis only, thus permitting comparison only among the quadrants of the country. Of course, no organization or individual is administratively responsible for a quadrant of America. It is likely that the limited size of the assessment's sample would not justify identifying city-by-city scores for comparison purposes; the proportion of the sample in each city might be too small to permit meaningful accountability. However, some interstate comparisons might be warranted. The fact is that the assessment promoters understood that one condition for gaining access to schools was to diminish the identifiability of the data they collected.

In an earlier chapter, I noted that the assessment was an enterprise of comparatively small scope with a relatively modest research base (considering the size of the enterprise being examined). Now that we see the pattern of resistance faced by the assessment, we can begin to understand the factors that shape our investments in research to collect data on education.

## Administrators React Locally

Citizens within individual school districts have frequently faced similar obstacles when seeking data. For example, in New York City in 1963:

> Parents were responsible for the reintroduction of and reemphasis on the basic academic criteria progress in reading and arithmetic, after researchers had willingly abandoned these to the interests of the vague, diffused and difficult-to-measure criteria involving social and personal functioning—these criteria had been abandoned and reinstated more for sociopolitical reasons than educational ones.[34]

One activist told me of her struggles to obtain meaningful output information from school administrators in her city, so she could publish interschool comparisons. "But you got the data," I said. "I've seen your tabulations."

"Yes! I stole it."

"How?"

"Simple. The board offices are a public building. At 4:45 p.m., I entered and went into the ladies' room. At 5:05 the building was empty. I walked into the offices, opened the files, and took what I wanted!"

I remember another episode that appears representative of the desire of school administrators to keep output data from public hands: I attended a meeting between our school superintendent and a number of parents who, like myself, had their children in a special school program. This was a suburban city with a population of about 125 thousand. At the meeting, I asked the superintendent whether it would be a good idea for some of the parents and teachers to meet together, formulate goals for the program, and arrange for a testing and evaluation system to see whether the goals were met. The superintendent replied that it was a good idea but impracticable: teachers would feel too threatened by the process. No other parent spoke up, and the matter was dropped. About a year later, another parent became interested in having the schools administer a particular IQ test to students. He thought that the district parents could then compare the school achievement scores of their children with students in different districts who had the same IQ, but different achievement scores. The comparative effectiveness of our district could then be evaluated. He met with the superintendent to ask that the test be administered and reported their conversation to me. His request was refused: on the grounds that (1) there was not time to arrange for the administration of the particular test, and (2) the district was trying to maximize other goals than those measured by traditional achievement tests. He asked the superintendent how progress toward these other goals might be evaluated. The superintendent said, "Only by observing the conduct of teachers in the classroom." The superintendent also said that he had observed classroom practices in many cities throughout the country, and while there were still shortcomings in our district, we were doing better than other schools. (Note the themes: there is no data; we shouldn't collect it; rely on my expert judgment.) The parent dropped the matter.

The superintendent's efforts to bury the data were probably motivated by a number of objectives. These may have included a desire to (a) avoid conflicts with his teachers and administrators, (b) escape accountability, (c) prevent "sterile" dissension, and (d) assist the school system in pursuing other goals than those measured by the tests. Regardless of his motives, however, the superintendent saw the inaccessibility of data as the key to control of school policy. This inaccessibility diminished the feedback and arguments available to other forces. However, since the system employed over 500 teachers, the lack of nonintuitive feedback also meant that the superintendent's control of his operation must rely largely on exhortation, since he would lack the necessary information to direct school policy in any other way. Thus, power based on the nonexistence of data may leave even the "powerful" with only the appearance of power.

This analysis suggests two types of power: relative power and absolute power. At present, the superintendent can be said to have relative power, i.e., more power than is held by school faculties or members of the community. If more output data was collected and disseminated, his relative power might diminish because members of the community or faculties would be better-equipped to dispute and reverse his judgments. Despite this diminishment, his absolute power to improve student learning might grow, because he could really analyze and affect the education process. He might receive a smaller proportion of a larger "power pie," but altogether, he'd have more pie.

It is likely that some administrators are more interested in the symbols and appearance of authority, i.e., relative power, than in real authority, i.e., absolute power. Indeed, such administrators may appear most frequently in education; they may represent the high proportion of "marginal men" some researchers have found among school administrators.

Tensions surrounding data disclosure have other implications for schools. Not only are output measures being applied for evaluation purposes, but also it is often proposed that such measures be integrated into more systematic forms of school administration, such as program planning budgeting systems (PPBS).[35] These new forms relate output measurements to program-budgeted school expenditures: a marked change from the traditional line item budget. Thus, a school district PPBS budget might have program items, such as foreign language learning, and list under each item a statement of the previous annual expenditure for this objective and a measurement of pupil attainment of goals. This compares to the present situation, where neither the administrator nor the board member is able to tell the annual expenditure for specific goals, since all teachers salaries are usually lumped together, and there is no output evaluation. It is hoped that PPBS, which is adapted from federal government practices, will focus discussion on what it costs to achieve certain specified performance goals and whether the goals are being attained.

Many proponents of PPBS are sympathetic to overall reform. However, they essentially view it as a management question. The organization chart looks cleaner when decisions all fit within the formal hierarchy. Therefore, they focus designs on getting output feedback to "school decision-makers," whom they identify as superintendents or other administrators. While they do not support secret data, they are somewhat uncomfortable with the disorderly process of public debate and policy-making. Therefore, such technocrats often release to the public only data of low priority.[36] I imagine the decision-makers are pleased with such a perspective.

I recall a discussion with a school administrator that sharply highlighted the issue of public release of data. The administrator argued that his staff should be careful about what data they made public, since he did not want any Daniel Ellsbergs on his staff (referring to the former defense consultant who leaked the lengthy study about Vietnam to the *New York Times* in the summer of 1971). Of course, whether Ellsberg acted rightly or wrongly is a subtle ethical issue, but it is clear that, to the administrator, Ellsberg's conduct was an act of betrayal. In other words, leakage of internal school information might be seen as equivalent to endangering national security! One way to prevent such dangerous leakages is not to collect information: then no temptations will arise. Thus, we may even wonder whether effective internal accountability programs will be developed to go with the new fiscal accounting unless they are supported by public demands. Perhaps we are seeing a modern revival of Taylorism in the schools, and, just as in the past, it is not a bad idea, but the form rather than the spirit may be followed, resulting in pseudo-rationalism and reaction against true rationalism.

There is also the issue of the reliability of data. In 1969 I interviewed a parent who worked on school issues in a community action program in a poor neighborhood of New York City, with many non-English-speaking parents. She told me that when reading tests were administered the teachers had children who were poor in

English "sit out" the tests. Thus, when schoolwide scores were reported, and parents made interschool comparisons, the "sit out" schools looked good, since their average did not include their "worst" pupils. She also showed me a report card that had a line for the student's reading test score. Beside the words *Reading score* was an asterisk. At the bottom of the card was the footnote *or teacher's estimate.* This meant that the reading score, which presumably would permit the parent to find out how well the school was teaching his child, might be the test score, or it might be a number the teacher found convenient to insert. The parent could not tell from the card whether the number inserted was a test score or a personal estimate.

A substitute teacher in New York City told me of overseeing the administration of a reading test to a class in an elementary school in the fall of 1969. The students remarked that they already knew something about the test, since the assistant principal had taken them out of class in small groups during the preceding few days to drill them on specific questions from the test administered.

In the summer of 1969, I interviewed seven persons active in movements to increase community control of schools in low-income neighborhoods of New York City. I particularly asked their opinions of the significance of output data as tools for accountability. None of them had any faith in the data made available by the schools they were criticizing. One or two of them conceded that honest testing systems might be devised to produce reliable data, but they were pessimistic. In connection with this, it is important to note that the National Assessment tests are to be administered not by school employees but by outsiders.

In 1971 the *New York Times* reported that there was widespread test leakage to students in the New York City schools who were about to take standard tests.[37] The leaks were assisted by some principals and teachers, who contended that they were acting in the interests of the students, who otherwise would do poorly on the tests. They did not explain how the children would be harmed by their poor performance, since the test results were not publicly linked with the children's names. The New York City School Board ordered an investigation.

In spite of the considerable opposition of school administrators illustrated in the preceding pages, the operation of output measurement and accountability systems has generated a considerable amount of data about school operations. This data has stimulated many developments in education research, which have important implications for the conduct of our schools and the future course of accountability.

## Footnotes

1. In Daniel P. Moynihan, "Sources of Resistance to the Coleman Report," *Harvard Educational Review* 38, no. 1 (Winter 1968): 23-36, p. 24.

2. Robert Ulich, *Three Thousand Years of Educational Wisdom* (Cambridge, Mass.: Harvard University Press, 1948), p. 96.

3. The following discussion derived from Donald R. Warren, "To Enforce Education: A History of the United States Office of Education" (Ph.D. diss., University of Chicago, 1968).

4. U.S., Congress, House, *Congressional Globe,* 39th Cong., 1st sess., 1866, 36, pt. 4: 3045.

5. See Ralph Tyler, "National Assessment: History and Sociology" in *New Models for American Education,* ed. James W. Guthrie & Edward Wynne (Englewood Cliffs, N.J.: Prentice-Hall, 1971), pp. 20-21. See also Jack C. Merwin, "Historical Review of Changing Concepts of Evaluation," in *Educational Evaluation: New Roles, New Means: The Sixty-Eighth Yearbook of the National Society for the Study of Education,* ed. Ralph Tyler (Chicago: University of Chicago Press, 1969), pp. 6-25.

6. Joseph M. Rice, "Educational Research," *The Forum* 34 (July 1902): 124.

7. Joseph M. Rice, "The Society of Educational Research," *The Forum* 35 (July 1903): 119.

8. Rice, "Educational Research," op. cit., p. 127.

9. Raymond E. Callahan, *Education and the Cult of Efficiency* (Chicago: University of Chicago Press, 1962).

10. Warren G. Findley, "Purposes of School Testing Programs," in *The Impact and Improvement of School Testing Programs,* ed. Warren G. Findley (Chicago: University of Chicago Press, 1963), pp. 1-27.

11. O. G. Brim, Jr. et al., *Use of Standardized Ability Tests in American Secondary Schools* (New York: Russell Sage Foundation, 1965); D. A. Goslin et al., *Use of Standardized Tests in Elementary Schools* (New York: Russell Sage Foundation, 1965).

12. "Guidelines for Testing Minority Group Children," *Journal of Social Issues* 20, no. 2 (April 1963): 138.

13. Alexander W. Astin, "Racial Considerations in Admission," in *The Campus and the Racial Crisis,* ed. David C. Nichols & Olive Mills (Washington, D.C.: American Council on Education, 1970), p. 116. See also Astin, *Predicting Success in College* (New York: Free Press, forthcoming).

14. See, e.g., Otis D. Duncan, *Socioeconomic Background and Occupational Achievement* (Ann Arbor: University of Michigan Press, 1968); Janet Combs & W. W. Cooley, "Dropouts: In High School and After School," *American Educational Research Journal* 5, no. 3 (May 1968): 342-362.

15. R. L. Ebel, "The Relation of Testing Programs to Educational Goals," in Warren Findley & Edward Wynne, "How to Measure a School's Performance," *American School Board Journal,* August 1968, pp. 5-9.

16. Educational Research Service, *Evaluating Administrative Performance* (Washington, D.C.: National Education Association, 1968).

17. H. M. Littlefield, "Who's Afraid of Regents Exams," *Teachers College Record* 68 (March 1967): 480.

18. John C. Flanagan et al., *Design for a Study of American Youth* (Boston: Houghton-Mifflin, 1962); Flanagan, "Evaluation in Program Development," in *Educational Evaluation,* pp. 228-234; Flanagan et al., *The American High School Student,* Final Report, Cooperative Research Project No. 635, U.S. Office of Education (Pittsburgh: Project Talent Office, University of Pittsburgh, 1964).

19. For example, see Coombs & Cooley, op. cit.; Flanagan, "Evaluation," op. cit.

20. James S. Coleman, "The Concept of Equality of Educational Opportunity," *Harvard Educational Review* 38 (Winter 1968): 7-22.

21. U.S., Congress, House, Committee on the District of Columbia, *Investigation of Public School Conditions, Hearings before the Subcommittee to Investigate Public School Standards and Conditions and Juvenile Delinquency in the District of Columbia,* 84th Cong, 2d sess., 1965.

22. P. E. Marsh & R. A. Gortner, *Federal Aid to Science Education* (Syracuse, N.Y.: Syracuse University Press, 1963), pp. 40, 60, 92.

23. U.S. Congress, Senate, Committee on Labor and Public Welfare, *Elementary and Secondary Education Act, Hearings, before a Subcommittee on Education,* 89th Cong, 1st sess., 1965, pt. 1: 514.

24. Catherine Caldwell, "Social Science as Ammunition," *Psychology Today* 4, no. 4 (September 1970): 38-44.

25. Moynihan, op. cit.; *Equality of Educational Opportunity,* special issue, *Harvard Educational Review* 38, no. 1 (Winter 1968).

26. Michael Crozier, *The Bureaucratic Phenomenon* (Chicago: University of Chicago Press, 1965), p. 186.

27. Burton R. Clark, "Sociology of Education," in *Handbook of Modern Sociology,* ed. R. O. Farris (Chicago: Rand-McNally, 1964), p. 760.

28. Willard Waller, *The Sociology of Teaching* (New York: Russell & Russell, 1932), p. 93, an older book with still valid perceptions. See also, David Rogers, *110 Livingston Street* (New York: Random House, 1968); Marilyn Gittell & T. Edward Hollander, *Six Urban School Districts: A Comparative Study of Institutional Response* (New York: Fredrick Praeger, 1968).

29. Gallup International, Inc., *School Board Members Reactions to Educational Innovations* (Princeton, N.J.: 1966).

30. John Thackery, "School Business, I," *The Center Forum* 3, no. 6 (1969): 12-13.

31. James D. Koerner, *Who Controls American Education?* (Boston: Beacon Press, 1968), p. 147.

32. Samuel Bowles & Henry M. Levin, "The Determinants of Scholastic Achievement," *Journal of Human Resources* 3, no. 11 (Winter 1968): 6. The details on the precise number and character of the non-participating districts could not be made public.

33. See Tyler, "National Assessment," op. cit., p. 29.

34. D. G. Fox, "Issues in Evaluating Programs for Disadvantaged Children," *Urban Review* 2 (December 1967): 5-9.

35. See, e.g., Harry J. Hartley, *Educational Planning-Programming-Budgeting: A Systems Approach* (Englewood Cliffs, N.J.: Prentice-Hall, 1968).

36. Henry S. Dyer, "Statewide Evaluation—What are the Priorities?" *Phi Delta Kappan* 51, no. 10 (June 1970): 558-559. For example, "Informing the public" was the *last* of six priorities cited by Dyer. See also Frank W. Banghart, *Educational Systems Analysis* (New York: Macmillan Co., 1969): Daniel L. Stufflebeam, *Evalua-*

*tion as Enlightenment for Decisionmaking* (Columbus: Evaluation Center, Ohio State University, 1968).

37. *New York Times*, 3 April, 1971, p. 1; New York, 7 April, 1971, p. 18.

# 4

# School Output Measures as a Research Resource: Fights over Ideas

The new control technology has tremendous scope and power. There is enormous need for new and better controls, and especially for controls that are quantitative and therefore not just matters of "opinion." But the new controls have this power and satisfy this need, precisely because they are not "neutral," precisely because they change both the events they record and observe and the men to whom they report and who they inform. What is needed therefore for those who are the designers of these controls is an attitude very different from that of the physical scientist or of the instrument maker. Theirs is a much greater power—but also a much greater limitation. They have to know that they can do much less—and have to know what they cannot do. But they also have to know that what they can do means more, much more—and have to impose on themselves the responsibility appropriate to this power.

Peter F. Drucker[1]

## The New Scene

Daniel Moynihan described a 1966 seminar on educational survey research conducted at Harvard University in the following terms:

Word got around that no one knows about education; that it was not easy to understand, but hard. The whole subject of schooling had been moribund because it had been thought to be easy; and guys who run a fast track are not interested in something easy. But by the end of the academic year, our seminar had grown to about 75 professors—became a conference, really. We had the whole top floor of the Harvard Faculty Club.[2]

Before development of this sort, the bulk of learning research (during the past forty to fifty years) was conducted by behavioral psychologists. There was a common pattern to their studies. They typically took two moderate size groups of subjects or students, subjected one group to a novel or experimental instructional technique, such as programmed learning or television, and offered "traditional instruction" to the other group. The psychologists then compared the difference in learning efficiency of the two groups by testing them with a common instrument. Almost invariably such experiments found that the difference between the two groups tested was statistically significant, but it usually was not large enough to justify changing classroom procedures. This approach was not an effective means of isolating the many factors beyond instructional methods that might influence learning: such as administrative practices, teachers' salary practices, students' home backgrounds, and differences in teacher training or competence. Indeed, this behavioral approach might even have its conclusions affected by unconsidered variations among these factors. One analyst offered observations of earlier education research that may still be pertinent:

The profusion of published studies and doctoral theses in education, and the frequency with which the term educational research is invoked, testifies to the vigor, if not the authenticity, of the scientific movement in education from 1920 to 1940. There is already contrary testimony, however, that the bulk of the research structure—research courses, dissertations, school research bureaus, journals, action research—has made little contact with what schools do, and that to maintain otherwise constitutes acute self-deception, if not fraud . . . . Research after 1920 has had its primary importance as an activity expected of an expert group, and not for its substantive contribution to either theory or practice.[3]

One reason the traditional approach could not effectively deal with a great diversity of variables was the lack of computers. Without computers, it was impracticable to develop methods to analyze the innumerable relationships in a real school that might invite study or affect experiments. Another problem was that the study of the numerous variables that presumably affect school performance would require a large data bank. Such a bank should be based on a broad sample of students. This means obtaining the cooperation of many schools or school systems and the amassing of considerable financial resources. In effect, large scale research required political backing to win school acceptance and funds. On the other hand, the analysis of the effect of a limited number of specified variables on a small group of students permitted experiments to be conducted on a modest scale. In general, the traditional research methods accepted school structure as given or as irrelevant. What was studied was the instructional "package" offered the student by the teacher, perhaps just because it was something research could focus on. The researchers involved did not need to have too much to do with schools or with politicians. It was a modest, but clean, business.

Over this period, the field of education research stayed at essentially a marginal level of operation. One survey concluded that educational research units (usually associated with universities) have shown, from 1910 until the early 1960s "a high mortality rate, and a severe organizational lag."[4]

Nevertheless, as Moynihan's remarks implied, two new forces are interacting. First, the disciplines and perspectives of education researchers are changing. Moynihan himself, for instance, is an atypical education researcher—outspoken, controversial, colorful, concerned with politics and politicians, and with a flair for catching the public eye, but still a technically competent academic. Another education researcher, James S. Coleman (whose work we mentioned earlier), did an important study in the late 1950s and then left education to do statistical research on the diffusion of innovations in medicine. His earlier study had important, concrete, and disturbing implications for high school operations but attracted little attention among educators. In the sixties, however, he returned to education research at the invitation of a prominent statistician temporarily working for the U.S. Office of Education. Economists have also begun to apply their statistical talents in the field.

As Moynihan suggests, these new researchers are attracted partly by the previous underresearching of the field; they believe that there are important things to be discovered. At the same time, their energy and prestige, sometimes acquired elsewhere, has given them leverage to urge and carry out projects requiring political support and substantial funding. For example, Coleman was personally consulted by President Nixon about education policy proposals, and Moynihan has helped promote a federally funded National Institute for Education to accelerate education research.[4] Incidentally, the planning for that institute is being conducted partly by staff from Rand, the research corporation originally founded to do military research—more newcomers.[5]

## The New Technologies

The new men are partly the product of new technologies, such as survey research. Survey research studies social processes by collecting and analyzing data from groups of sample subjects. For example, it is the basic technique used in political polling. In education, survey data is based on tests and other measurement instruments developed by psychologists. The subjects need not be in experimental situations. The data covers the performance or achievement of the subject, plus other information about the environment or events surrounding him. This might include his parents' amount of education; the number of students in his class; his race, sex, and teacher's qualifications and salary; and so on. By means of computers, comparisons are made—often using the statistical technique called regression analysis—between students' scores and the factors that seem most often associated with superior student performance.[6] The new researchers are experienced in these skills, which were first developed in the fields of statistics, economics, and sociology.

Regression analysis recognizes that there will inevitably be random genetic differences between students, so that we can tell very little by observing that one student in one school is doing better than another student in a different school. However, when we have data on a large number of pupils, individual differences average out; with a sample of fifty pupils from one school and a similar sample from another school, one can assume that they will each have about the same proportions of innately bright or dull students. If this is true, differences in average group performance become significant. This technique requires either carefully designed samples or large numbers of subjects. The students can be from a single district or a combination of districts. While some inputs, such as teacher qualifications or pupils' sex, may have only a small effect, we would still wish to measure its effect, since an influence based on a small effect might be important; even one affecting scores as little as 1 percent.

In other words, we might discover via regression that students with dictionaries in their homes tend to have scores 1 percent better than students from similar backgrounds without dictionaries. One percent is not a big difference, but dictionaries are pretty cheap—so the information might be useful. If fewer class periods of longer duration seem to help learning slightly, we might be encouraged to change scheduling systems radically in the hope of greatly improving learning scores. It is important to remember, however, that with a less carefully organized data pool, far larger variations in scores might still be statistically insignificant.

Perhaps the most common type of regression analysis is a comparison of the performance of students with common socioeconomic characteristics who have been in schools or classes with different characteristics. For instance, all students in the data bank with a common age and parents having less than a high school education (a significant socioeconomic indicator) might be identified by the computer. The computer could identify students in this group who achieved significantly better scores than others, i.e., the overachievers. Then, the computer would identify those school characteristics commonly found with the overachieving students and not found in the schools or classes of the underachievers. Do the "overs" and "unders" each have (a) the same proportion of certified teachers, or (b) the same pupil-teacher ratios? Where a connection appears between overachieving or underachieving and some school characteristic, computations are made to determine the correlation between the characteristic and the score.

The correlation is a statistical statement of the relationship between the two factors. A perfect correlation, such as the correlation between being a human and possessing a heart, is 1. An absolutely random event, like the chances for heads or tails when tossing a coin, has a correlation of 0. Of course, high correlations do not prove that one correlated thing causes or is caused by the other; if most murderers eat ice cream cones, there is a high correlation but no evidence that eating ice cream cones causes murders or that murder creates a craving for ice cream. But a high correlation often justifies further discussions and experiments. For example, if there is a correlation of .35 between high reading scores and having dictionaries in the home, we might design an experiment; find a group of students from similar types of homes and schools, who do not have dictionaries, test their reading scores; give dictionaries to some of them; then test both groups again later and see if the dictionary-owning students' scores have improved more than the scores of students without dictionaries. Naturally, a low correlation can also be important; it proves that there is little or no relationship between two factors.

The analytic powers of computers have been applied in education for only fifteen years. Within the next ten years, these devices will immensely increase their power to correlate more data at lower costs and to follow more complex analytic programs. Inevitably, the application of survey techniques will be intensified.

Survey research will not extinguish the need for focused experiments. However, it will seek to discover what affects students in real schools before turning to narrower studies. In sum, the new mode may focus on many factors that were ignored in the past.

All researchers using survey research admit there are shortcomings. For instance, a report of the U.S. Commission on Civil Rights states:

> It is difficult to compare a given characteristic of schools or students apart from other factors. The best teachers are most often found in schools whose students come from fairly affluent homes. These schools also tend to have the most advanced educational programs and the best educational facilities. Their students almost always are white. This make it very difficult to measure the effects of very high levels of school quality upon student bodies of either social or racial backgrounds. Similarly, the fact that most Negroes attend school almost exclusively with other Negroes makes it difficult to assess the relationship between racial composition of schools and student performance.
>
> Second, the process of education is very complex, and simple causal connections cannot be drawn. It may seem reasonable, for example, to say that a student's motivation to learn directly affects his academic performance. Thus, when it is found that students with strong motivation performed better, we can assume greater motivation improves performance. However, there undoubtedly is a complicating causal relationship in which levels of motivation and academic performance interact, each reinforcing the other.[7]

Survey research is undergoing continuous improvement. In early 1970 one knowledgeable researcher told me that the Coleman Report, authorized in 1964 and completed in 1966, was a good job, "considering how long ago it was done."

## What the Measurements Have Shown

### Educator Resistance

It is evident that educational administrators have evinced persistent hostility toward the efficient public application of such measures. The means of opposition have varied: disinterest in funding educational research, refusal to disclose data, criticisms about the legitimacy of the researchers, and shifting interpretations of the goals of school operations to make research findings less relevant are only a few examples.

Often the resistance has been comparatively effective, particularly since public interest in these debates has been relatively slight. Lacking public support, researchers have rarely had the muscle to go ahead on their own. It is possible that the effectiveness of professional resistance is diminishing. At least the frequency of output accountability efforts is increasing; perhaps some administrators are even becoming willing sincerely to assist accountability in their districts.

### What Students Learn

Americans of school age are acquiring more cognitive information than in the past, largely due to an increasing proportion of such youths attending school for increasingly long periods of time. It is possible that the *average* amount of information acquired per pupil per year is slightly less, but this may be the product of the higher percentage of children attending school, i.e., the overall ability of the attending pupils may be less, and the current pupil pool may be less capable of learning than the more selective former one. But more people are learning more, and probably both good and poor students learn more than such students did in the past.[8]

### The Attitudes of Students

We have no way to estimate changes in the pupils' noninformational skills, such as adaptability or persistence. Instruments to do this are being developed, but there are no baselines for comparisons. Thus, we have no clear way of knowing whether contemporary youths feel or act differently from youths in the past. This is a major lack, since the recent national youth unrest at the college and high school level raises important issues about how our current maturation structure affects the young.

### The Powerful Effect of Families on Students

There are wide variations among the median achievement levels of different socioeconomic groups of students, regardless of the quality of their schools. At the twelfth-grade level, black students (who usually come from poorer and less educated families), on the average, are reading three years behind national norms. Conversely, the students from college-educated families are, on the average, about two years ahead. Substantial variations among median achievement levels are also found for other socioeconomic groups.[9]

### How Much Difference Do Different Schools Make?

We know very little about how or whether different school inputs affect pupil learning. The analyses have tried to isolate the school factors—cost per pupil, teacher sex or age, class size, quality of teacher's college, whether the teacher is certified—associated with superior pupil performance. They have consistently found that the best performance predictor is not the quality of the school factors (such as cost per pupil, pupil/teacher ratio, quality of building, teacher certification, and the like, or any combination of these) but socioeconomic data, such as the amount of education the pupil's parents had or their income level. In other words, pupils from higher socioeconomic backgrounds tend to do well even in "poor" schools; pupils from low socioeconomic backgrounds tend to do poorly even in "good" schools.

The studies have also shown, however, that pupils from better-off homes usually go to good schools in the suburbs, or in the wealthier neighborhoods of cities. This means that these students, by their performance, give the school a good record of results. However, in the past it was concluded that the schools' traditionally good quality characteristics—small class size, higher teacher salaries, etc.—were the cause of the excellent results. But regression analyses show that the same kind of students in poor schools were performing about as well without the advantages of the good schools.

In other words, the formal school environment has much less influence on children's learning than their home situations. Apparently, the most important characteristics of better students are their skills and attitudes about school learning, and these skills are most often developed or better taught at home through interaction between parents and children.

The matter of causes of achievement has been further confounded by correlations disclosed in analyzing the socioeconomic composition of the student population in a classroom or school. The regression technique was used to identify students who were in classes composed largely of students from different backgrounds from their own, poor children in classes composed mainly of students from better-off families, etc. The theory was that the student mix in the class might have as much or more to do with student performance than the school variables. The data support the theory. Generally, students from lower-status families have better performance levels when they are in classes composed mostly of students from a higher socioeconomic status. The data about the effect of such mixing on the higher status students is not yet so clear, but there is a suggestion that their performance level is more resistant to depression than the lower status students' is to elevation, at least if there is a reasonable mix of higher socioeconomic status students.[10]

From such data, one might infer that to improve learning we should change the student environment rather than the school program. Such inferences have been used to support various arguments in behalf of school desegregation and bussing. In Norfolk, Virginia, a school desegregation plan that attempted to maintain a certain minimum percentage of middle-income whites in classrooms with low-income blacks (by means of leaving some blacks in all-black or segregated schools) was defended by some researchers as an appropriate step to promoting increased black achievement.[11]

The regressions have shown that questions about the student's college plans, and how he thinks he can control his life prospects, are important predictors. As part of the Coleman Report, students were asked not only if they hoped to go to college, but also whether they had taken concrete steps to get there; i.e., were they in college prep courses, had they read catalogues, were they planning to take entrance exams? They were also asked to check whether they believed success in life was largely dependent on (a) luck, (b) connections, or (c) personal effort.

The analysts called these questions the *fate questions.* The theory was that if you believe you can control your life and are taking realistic steps to do so, you will be more likely to apply yourself effectively in school. They found a high correlation between aggressive, optimistic answers to these questions and student scores.[12] Low status pupils who believed in fate control did significantly better than their peers who did not. (Incidentally, many low status children said they did want to go to college: their abstract aspirations were high enough, but they had not taken the appropriate steps; their aspirations were just fantasies, and presumably, they themselves understood them to be fantasies.) Data of this sort has been used by black power and decentralization proponents to argue that if blacks and parents were more active in running schools, their children would have more belief in the potency of their social group and, therefore, would learn better.

As already suggested, analysts have had great difficulty identifying school inputs that have important effects on the rate at which children learn. For instance, a critical analysis of the Coleman Report contended that it underestimated the effect of school inputs.[13] Yet the most effective school input identified in this "optimistic" analysis of the report—teacher quality, as measured by the teacher's verbal facility on an objective test—would move black students' performance at the twelfth-grade level up only 25 percent of the three-year achievement gap, if black students obtained 200,000 teachers with the verbal facility of the best teachers in America. The critics admit this suggestion is based on "incomplete" data.

The debate over the implications of the data has burst forth at many points. The Commission on Civil Rights said that there was no evidence that compensatory programs, which tried to help students catch up by giving them extra (traditional) resources, had significantly improved achievement.[14] Even allowing for the inadequacies in evaluations, Title I programs under the Elementary and Secondary Education Act have fallen short of expectations despite increased expenses ranging from 10 to 30 percent per child. In California, only 14 percent of the students in the 1968-69 Title I program had a progress rate that would indicate they might achieve median scores.[15] The data permitted a commentator to say "for all their variety the programs have generally suffered from one fundamental difficulty: they are based on sentiment rather than facts."[16]

In 1964 New York City, partly at the urging of the American Federation of Teachers, began the "More Effective Schools' program. In the program, a few schools with concentrations of disadvantaged pupils received large (up to 100 percent) increases in inputs for very small classes, teacher aids, and the like. An output evaluation, released to the press without comment on a Friday afternoon (and thus kept out of the weekday papers) admitted that the program, after two years, had failed significantly to improve performance.[17]

## The Implications of the Research

While the program-focused evaluations were directed at the achievements of children from low-income homes, their implications, as well as the findings of studies such as the Coleman Report, extend to all schools. They suggest that our knowledge about the effects of schools on the learning of middle-class children is equally limited, i.e., we do not know very well if, how, or how much current school inputs help any children learn.

Other commentators have contended that the data reflect the homogeneous nature of American public school practices: while there is a considerable nationwide range in school dollar input (average per pupil expenses in different districts run from $250 to $1,700 per child), the ways the money is spent are remarkably similar; more dollars simply buy better teachers and administrators with more college credits or degrees, more equipment, or lower pupil-teacher ratios.

Thus it is evident that, in a profound sense, American education is extremely centralized. That is, uniform college entrance requirements, high school credentialling policies, teacher-training institutions, and salary structures have all combined to make our schools follow almost all the same patterns of operations, for perhaps 20 million students—quite an impressive example of quiet centralization. So when we talk about local control of education, we forget that most of the real decisions have already been surrendered to these nationwide forces. These patterns have certain advantages: high school students with good college board scores in Oregon can comfortably apply to Florida colleges, knowing that their high school records will be accepted; families can move and expect their children to fit easily into the program of their next school; and well-qualified teachers can seek jobs in the national market. However, we may be paying too high a price for this valuable uniformity: our schools may be frozen in a bad stage, but we will never know it without some divergence. Using economic terminology, Coleman observed, "given the present organization of education in the United States, the marginal utility of expenditures for education as measured by increments of achievement is far less than it might be under other modes of organization.[18] A report on school innovation in New York State found: "Few innovations took place in the kind of people employed, in the way they were organized to work together, in the types of instructional materials they used, or in the times and places at which they taught. In short, schools as structured institutions remained the same."[19]

The point is well illustrated by the personal experience of the dean of the Graduate School of Education at Ohio State. He and some of his colleagues agreed to act as principals in difficult urban schools for a week. The dean admitted that his service was a prolonged state of siege.[20] He outlined the school improvements his experience suggested to him: abolition of compulsory attendance laws and autonomy for the principal in (a) selecting faculty without regard to teacher certification, (b) allocating his budget, and (c) establishing his own curriculum. Probably no public school principal has these simple elements of authority, which are possessed by any gas station manager or supermarket operator. It may be true that few principals ask for such change, but by the time they attain the principalship, they have had ten to fifteen years under the current system; it has become their home.

The innovation issue can be illustrated by the following metaphor: If you want to travel from Chicago to New York City, you have innumerable transportation choices: airplane, bus, private car, trains, horse, bicycle, etc. You can also choose within different modes—one busline or airline or another etc.—but you realize, advertising to the contrary, that the important choice is between the general modes because it depends on basic considerations such as time, finances, and taste. In education, if you want your child to learn reading, writing, math, or other cognitive skills, about all you can do in the United States is to send him to a public or private school. There are some differences between these schools, but most of the differences are apparently like those within the transportation modes. The choices are inconsequential. Therefore it is not too surprising that the regressions have suggested that usually one school or another really does not make much difference.

Incidentally, if we wanted to improve New York-Chicago travel, we would not be solely committed to seeking suggestions from the bus companies or airlines. If we asked their advice, they would tell us about enlarging their engines, improving the quality of meals, widening the seats, showing better movies, changing reservation arrangements, etc. We can be sure they would not suggest developing high-speed trains, intercity rockets, or long-range bicycle routes. Of course, these unusual alternatives will not spring up overnight, but the existing transporters are not likely ever to propose them. The unusual ideas will most likely come from outsiders who have no commitment to current arrangements.

In sum, despite the methodological issues dividing some analysts and divergent interpretations, the output data represent a powerful critique of established school doctrine. At best, the data says that we are not sure what is right. Considering our enormous investment in education—in doctrine, personnel, and dollars—this is a provocative confession of uncertainty.

President Nixon's 1970 Message on Education Reform (drafted with Daniel Moynihan's assistance) put it this way: "it is simply not possible to make any confident deduction from school characteristics as to what will be happening to the children in any particular school." The president also said: "when educators, school boards and government officials alike admit that we have a great deal to learn about the way we teach, we will begin to climb up the staircase toward genuine reform."

There is an ironic note to the "discovery" that school may make less difference in children's performance than we have thought. The discovery only reiterates a long-established principle. In 1916 John Dewey observed that, "schools are, indeed, one important method of transmission which forms the dispositions of the immature; but it is only one means, and compared with other agencies, a relatively superficial onc."[21] Despite their theoretical acceptance of Dewey's pronouncement, in practice American educators and the public have assumed that schools were the principal means of learning. This assumption encouraged schools to accept (and have thrust upon them) responsibilities that go far beyond their traditional role. For instance, in teaching disadvantaged children, schools today are perhaps given greater responsibilities for motivating their students than they ever had in the past. Indeed, if one were about to design a new school system, one might well question the current implicit American division of responsibility among home, society, and school for generating learning motivation.

## Footnotes

1. Peter F. Drucker, "Controls, Control and Management," in *Management Controls: New Directions in Basic Research,* ed. Charles P. Bonini (New York: McGraw-Hill, 1964), p. 295.

2. *New York Times,* 6 March 1970, p. 26.

3. Geraldine Jonich, *The Sane Positivist: A Biography of Edward L. Thorndike* (Middletown, Conn.: Wesleyan University Press, 1968), pp. 558-559. See also Lee J. Cronbach & Patrick Suppes, eds., *Research for Tomorrow's Schools* (New York: Macmillan Co., 1969).

4. Sam D. Sieber & Paul F. Lazarsfeld, *The Organization of Educational Research* (New York: Bureau of Applied Social Research, 1966), p. 102.

5. Roger E. Levien, Study Director, *National Institute for Education: Preliminary Plan for the Proposed Institute,* R-657-HEW, A Report prepared for Department of Health, Education and Welfare (Santa Monica, Calif.: Rand, 1971).

6. As examples, see James W. Guthrie et al., *Schools and Inequality* (Cambridge: MIT Press, 1971); Hendrick D. Gideonse, "The Relative Impact of Instructional Variables," *Teachers College Record,* 69, no. 7 (April 1968): 625-640; Thomas F. Pettigrew, "Return to the Common School," in James W. Guthrie & Edward Wynne, *New Models for American Education* (Englewood Cliffs, N.J.; Prentice-Hall, 1971); and Malcolm Provus, "Evaluation of Ongoing Programs in the Public School," in *Educational Evaluation: New Roles, New Means, Sixty-Eighth Yearbook of the National Society for the Study of Education, Part II,* ed. Ralph Tyler (Chicago: University of Chicago Press, 1969).

7. U.S. Commission on Civil Rights, *Racial Isolation in the Public Schools* (Washington, D.C.: Government Printing Office, 1967), p. 76.

8. U.S. Department of Health, Education and Welfare, *Towards A Social Report* (Washington, D.C.: Government Printing Office, 1969).

9. Pettigrew, op. cit.

10. Allan B. Wilson, "Educational Consequences of Segregation in a California Community," in U.S. Commission on Civil Rights, op. cit., vol. 2, pp. 165-206.

11. *New York Times,* 1 April 1970, p. 34.

12. Guthrie & Wynne, op. cit., p. 162.

13. Samuel Bowles & Henry M. Levin, "The Determinants of Scholastic Achievement, *Journal of Human Resources* 3, no. 1 (Winter 1968); James J. Coleman, "Reply," *Journal of Human Resources* 3 (Spring 1968): 235-246. See also Marion E. Shaycroft, *The High School Years: Growth of Cognitive Skills* (Pittsburgh: American Institutes for Research and School of Education, University of Pittsburgh, 1967); Guthrie et al., op. cit.

14. U.S. Commission on Civil Rights, op. cit., p. 138.

15. California State Department of Education, *Evaluation of Elementary and Secondary Education Act, Title I: Projects of California Schools* (Sacramento: California State Department of Education, 1967-1968).

16. Edward Gordon, "Is Compensatory Education Failing?" *College Board Review* 62 (Winter 1967): 7-11.

17. *New York Times,* 20 August 1967, p. 39; Harry L. Miller & Roger R. Woock, *Social Foundations of Urban Education* (Hinsdale, Ill.: Dryden Press, 1970), pp. 238-248.

18. Coleman, op. cit., p. 245.

19. Henry M. Bricknell, *Organizing New York State for Educational Change* (Albany: New York State Department of Education, 1962), p. 19.

20. Charles E. Silberman, *Crisis in the Classroom* (New York: Random House, Vintage Books, 1970), p. 451.

21. John Dewey, *Democracy and Education* (Toronto: Collier-Macmillan, 1944), p. 4.

# 5
# Current Accountability Efforts: Conflicts and Progress

> The most deliberate procedure for selecting ameliorative actions where strain exists or is to be avoided is reasoning. It is reverted to when involuntary modes of adaptation fail. Reasoning requires sustained attention, time, and deferring the time of relief from strain—all of them sacrifices which the human organism prefers to avoid. But they are sacrifices deemed to be necessary for the relief of a greater strain, the irritation of doubt.
>
> Raymond J. Chambers[1]

It is evident that accountability is a fluid and fast-moving field. But it is worthwhile to survcy some of the more recent developments to see the tendencies they reveal, with the realization that they will be overtaken by later events.

## National Developments

The federal requirements for Title I evaluations have forced all urban school districts to manifest some concern for accountability. These evaluations have centered on the question: have the disadvantaged students involved in the program learned better than before? Each evaluation has become part of a state evaluation report, and two distilled nationwide Title I Evaluation Reports have been produced by the U.S. Office of Education.[2] These reports have been the subject of controversy. Some persons have emphasized that the reports (as discussed earlier) have shown the programs to be ineffectual. Other evaluators have contended that the evaluations are deficient in their methodology and that school staff has been uninterested in frank evaluation. One reviewer characterized the second national Title I report as "urban eyewash."[3]

As one by-product of Title I and other federal legislation aimed at assisting educational planning and evaluation, many states have been working toward developing comprehensive evaluation systems. The federal catalyst has further stimulated them to attempt to mesh their efforts into an interstate reporting format.[4] Another by-product of these federal accountability concerns is the Office of Education's statistically-oriented booklet *Do Teachers Make a Difference?*[5] The contributors concluded that we had no firm idea whether different types of teachers made a difference, or how much, or why: profoundly provocative conclusions, in view of the fact that the federal government spends about $10 billion a year to assist education.

The National Assessment (largely supported by the Office of Education) has been administering tests since 1969 and has issued several reports.[6] The reports have excited only modest public interest, perhaps because of the lack of longitudinal data and more informative geographic labeling of test results. In other words, being told that so many children or citizens can meet certain performance criteria is not dramatically significant until we see (a) whether performance levels are related to higher or lower personal achievement such as employability, or (b) how one state compares with another. But such comparisons will take time to evolve.[7] Incidentally, it is ironic that, for all the criticisms we hear of the competitive use of tests, it is still true that the currently noncompetitive elements of the assessment—e.g., no comparisons between states or longitudinal comparisons— are a major reason for its limited visibility. But we can assume that as time passes, more comparisons will be made.

The operation of the assessment has stimulated research on test-related topics, such as the administration of tests at home rather than in school, oral rather than written tests, group rather than individual tests, nonobjective rather than objective tests, and the reliability of tests administered by the students' regular teachers.

The contractors who did the development work for the assessment tests are now using their competence to create equivalent testing systems for individual states, school districts, and other units.

While such tests will contain different materials from the assessment, the design costs would be diminished because of the exploratory efforts for the assessment.

## State Developments

A number of states are now planning or undertaking structured output evaluation efforts. A nationwide survey of all such programs emphasized the dynamic situation when it concluded that:

> state assessment plans and programs are currently in a highly fluid state, with new developments occurring daily. Accordingly, the facts and surmises presented in this report may well be out-of-date within a matter of months. It is for this reason that the entire survey should be viewed only as a snapshot of the situation existing early in the year 1971. It is for this reason also that we hope this survey will be the first in a series by which, eventually, it will be possible to chart some trends.[8]

There is a considerable variety to the state efforts, and we will only discuss a few of the more noteworthy programs. As one such instance, the system being developed in Pennsylvania offers insights into the statewide accountability process. The Pennsylvania effort began in 1963, when the Pennsylvania legislature passed an act which provided, with artful simplicity, that the state board of education:

> Shall develop an evaluation procedure designed to measure objectively the adequacy and efficiency of the educational programs offered by the public schools of the Commonwealth. The evaluation procedure shall be so constructed and developed as to provide each school district with relevant comparative data to enable directors and administrators to more readily appraise the educational performance and to effectuate without delay the strengthening of the district's educational program. Tests developed under the authority of this section to be administered to pupils shall be used for the purpose of providing a uniform evaluation of each school district and the other purposes set forth in this subdivision. The State Board of Education shall devise standards for performance upon the completion of the evaluation procedure required by this section.

Public conferences and committee meetings were held to define the goals to be measured. The participants included a number of members of the public. Ten educational goals were articulated. They included cognitive and affective values, e.g., "the habits and attitudes associated with responsible citizenship," "mastery of the basic skills

50171
CARDINAL MEYER LIBRARY
MARIAN COLLEGE OF FOND DU LAC

in the use of words and numbers," and "help every child prepare for a world of rapid change." The Educational Testing Service was retained to help develop criteria, tests, and procedures to measure the goals. The procedures included the collection of data about student socioeconomic status and various school inputs.[9]

The first Pennsylvania tests were administered six years later, in the spring of 1969, partly because of the complexity of the design process and partly because of inadequate funds for administration and planning. The first report of results noted that school cooperation was obtained on the condition that no individual school would be identified and no school names would be attached to the data. Actually, from the data in the first report, it is impossible to tell anything about the performance of any particular school or school district in Pennsylvania. The report makes no reference to enlarged disclosure plans for the future test results.[10]

Since 1966 New York State has required schools to administer uniform objective achievement exams (as well as the traditional Regents' exams) to all pupils in grades three, six, and nine. The tabulated results are published annually in a format that permits median score comparisons between: (1) metropolitan areas (Standard Metropolitan Statistical Areas), (2) major cities, (3) smaller communities, and (4) individual schools within communities. The tables do not include information on the socioeconomic status of students, and the state admits that its reporting system has other significant omissions. However, there is a commitment to developing refined tests and data collection instruments to use for comparative and analytic purposes.[11]

In California, legislation was passed in 1968 to establish the framework for a statewide pupil-testing program.[12] The act requires that the state board of education annually report to the legislature—on a district-by-district basis—on a number of factors, including the median scholastic ability and achievement of pupils. The evaluation plan was developed by a committee (appointed by the state department of education) composed largely of professional educators. A limited number of copies of the first evaluation have been released, in a format that handicaps effective analysis.

In Michigan, the state department of education began a statewide assessment program in 1969-70. The program was focused largely on cognitive goals and was partly supported by funds and legislation authorized by the legislature with the encouragement of the governor. To win the cooperation of school districts, the department promised that they would not release data on individual districts to anyone but local school administrators. The statewide data—without individual district labeling—was released by the department in the fall of 1970. In a short while, the department was deluged by requests for labeled data by districts:

The Chairman of the Senate Appropriations Committee wanted the data, the House Appropriations Committee wanted the data, the House Education Committee wanted the data, the House Special Committee on the Quality of Elementary and Secondary Schools wanted the data, the Legislative Fiscal Agency wanted the data, and several individual legislators wanted the data for their districts. In addition, there was considerable sentiment among individual members of the State Board of Education which supervised the Department that public disclosure of the data should be made. The Department was caught squarely between the interest of competing groups—on the one hand, legislators and other state officials who demanded the data, and on the other hand local school personnel who felt they had been assured that no such disclosure would be made.[13]

Like rational men, the department staff attempted to duck the issue, and asked data seekers to seek the data from individual school districts. The requesters usually refused to accept such referrals. The Michigan legislature had also passed a law that provided that test results should be one of the criteria to be used to identify needy districts entitled to special state aid. Some degree of district identification would be needed to carry out this requirement.

Eventually, the combination of the pressures from the legislature and governor, plus the requirements of the state aid legislation, forced the department to release the labeled data. Naturally, this reversal of policy provoked angry responses from the school administrators. One administrator contended that "The Michigan Educational Assessment Program is really politics masquerading as research. Promise after promise has been broken. Plans have been dictated and changed by the legislature . . . ."[14] Despite these tensions and recriminations, the Michigan program will continue, with minor modifications.

## Issues Raised by State Efforts

The state efforts have raised other issues beyond the predictable questions of labeling of results and the implications of the data. Two of these issues have been what goals should be measured in the testing programs, and who should define the goals? In several instances, the goals have simply been determined by the adoption of existing standard tests. The advantages and disadvantages of this process are apparent. On one hand, the existing tests are relatively adequate measures of certain cognitive skills and have undergone considerable development. On the other hand, these measures focus on only a fraction of the cognitive and affective skills children must acquire. Another alternative used by some states is to have a committee of educators determine the goals to be measured. This offers expedition but leaves the decision-makers open to charges of excessive manipulation. The final alternative has been to have laymen, or committees of laymen and educators, conduct the goal-articulation process. Such a procedure is not always expeditious, but it does create a substantial base of citizen interest in the ultimate testing program and tends to legitimize the effort. Perhaps the most ambitious example of such citizen-based efforts is found in California. There,

> the California School Boards Association gathered statements of educational philosophy and goals from virtually every school district in the state. An analysis of the material from some 400 districts resulted in 18 definitions of basic goals. Although these 18 goal statements were given no official sanction by the state education authorities, the activity in and of itself has reportedly influenced state legislation, which now calls for the development of a common state curriculum, modified by local options, and which specifies further that the common curriculum shall be based upon some common set of goals and objectives agreed to in advance.
>
> Concurrently with the work of the California School Boards Association, another group of citizens and educators was also concerning itself with the formulation of educational goals for California. That was the Advisory Committee on Achievement and Evaluation set up by the Education Committee of the California Assembly. After well over a year of hearings, the Advisory Committee recommended to the legislature that a state commission on educational goals and evaluation be established, and during the 1969 regular session a Joint Committee on Educational Goals and Evaluations was given a mandate to tackle the problem.
>
> The Joint Committee, whose members are drawn from the Senate, the

Assembly, and the State Board of Education, has appointed still another group of educators and citizens to form an Advisory Committee for Guidelines on Goals. Meantime, working with a staff of consultants, the Joint Committee has decided to require each school district to develop its own goals and objectives based upon the forthcoming Guidelines. Ultimately these local goals are to be added to goals developed by the State Department of Education, by educational specialists, and by citizen advisors. Combined and edited, these goals and objectives will be submitted to the State Board of Education in 1973 together with an evaluation system designed to measure their attainment.[15]

One outcome of these multistate developments was a suggestion that state education department staff members concerned with goal articulation receive training in the application of Delphi techniques. The Delphi technique is a means of using circulated and recirculated questionnaires and discussions to stimulate group members to move toward a well-thought-out consensus.

It is clear that these goal-definition steps will inevitably excite more interest and productive debate as the abstract goals become means of defining measurements and the measurements become tools for directing policy. Thus, no controversy may arise if we establish a goal such as "helping students to become adequate parents." But if we agree on some instrument to measure whether students are learning to be "adequate parents," and over time the measures show that student adequacy at these skills and attitudes is diminishing, the discussion will grow sharper. Someone will propose a tax increase to improve the effectiveness of the adequate parent program; others will want to take funds away from some other school program to finance the needed improvement.

At that moment, the necessity of the "adequate parent" goals will become a live issue. The scope of citizen and administrator interest will widen. Questions will be asked: Just how important is this goal? Who recommended its priority? Is the instrument applied really meaningful? And so on. As a result of such controversies, we will find out exactly how important the goal under fire really is to the citizens of a state or locality. Incidentally, at that moment, careful work by the earlier goal selection committee and the measurement experts can begin to pay off. If the committee members are effective and influential citizens, they can speak out to explain and justify their priorities, and the measurement experts can show their instruments make sense, if they do.

But goal-setting is only one of the issues prompted by state-fostered accountability. Another question has arisen about sampling versus broader testing of more (or all) students. The sampling approach permits more diversified data collection with less cost in dollars or time. However, data collected through sampling does not permit local schools to identify the skill or performance level of their individual students. All the district knows is whether it is generally achieving or not achieving a goal. Therefore, if the district wishes to correct a low level of performance, the state sampling data does not let it know which particular students need special help. Such information would require administering all tests to all students. To overcome this problem, some states practice universal testing. They administer the entire test battery to all students and make the results available to districts for diagnostic purposes.

The interest in universal testing is understandable. However, I suggest that it will tend to diminish the flexibility of state and district accountability programs. The truth is that the matter of appropriate goals—at both the state and local levels—is still largely unsettled. For the time being it is probably sensible for us to "hang loose." Sampling facilitates such an approach. It encourages the creation of diverse instruments and the striving for diverse goals, and it diminishes the costs and pressures generated by the testing process. Furthermore, it is likely that there will be interdistrict differences in goal priorities. An upper-middle-income district might perceive that most of its students are several years ahead of national reading norms and that brief, simple reading tests will suffice to spot individual deviant students. The same district might be troubled about student drug abuse or student readiness to work in traditional job settings. Statewide sampling might develop instruments to pick up these local issues; if the state-published results excited district concern, the district could apply its own individual testing program to focus on these issues, while generally avoiding the reading issue. A district with a large proportion of blue-collar families might justifiably decide to adopt a reading-focused emphasis. In other words, sampling provides all districts with a diversity of information, and stimulates them to decide local measurement priorities. Universal testing provides more detailed and specific information of more limited scope. It may unduly narrow our testing horizons at an early stage.

In some states, the test scores have been applied in state aid formulas: low scores on traditional cognitive tests have become one of the criteria for identifying districts (or schools) that need additional fiscal aid. The theory is simple: if the students do poorly, the school system needs more financial help. However, as one survey observed, in such states,

> some school principals who are serious about their responsibilities are beginning to talk of deliberately over-speeding test administrations, so that school performance measured by the tests will not come up to the mark. Their reasoning apparently is that if failure is to be rewarded, then it is folly to be successful.[16]

Another issue arising from enlarging state involvement is implicit in the foregoing discussion: there are a great number of persons and institutions interested in these matters, and coordination and communication will be difficult. For example, there are state departments of education, state legislatures, local school districts, the National Assessment program, the evaluations required for federal programs such as Title I of the Elementary and Secondary Education Act, and objective tests administered for college entrance and school placement. Many of these entities and systems look to different constituencies with different values and training. While one could contend that the general principles of accountability are relatively simple, many of the details of implementation do become complex. Even with the best of good will, misunderstandings and conflicts will arise. The matter will be compounded by the profound potential for conflict that the collection and release of accountability data generates.

## School District Developments

There have been a number of efforts within school districts to collect and use output evaluation for intradistrict accountability. One group in New York City, the United Bronx Parents, prepared training materials for parents on school evaluation, including the use of comparisons between interschool reading averages.[17] The materials had titles such as "Would you like to know how *your* school compares with the rest of the schools in the Bronx?" and "How to make a school visit." The former described the reading scores and other pertinent data for 110 elementary schools and included a simple, accurate description of the captions for each column in the report.

The United Bronx Parents work principally with low-income families. They are financed by funds from both the Office of Economic Opportunity and the Urban Coalition. I visited their office, and my impression was that their three or four full-time staff members were dedicated people with impressive talents. While they were clearly engaged with the neighborhood problems, their research director, who organized the data and taught the training sessions, was a Phi Betta Kappa and summa cum laude university graduate. In other words, starting a new strategy takes unusual talents. One of the group's aspirations was to make reading scores a focal issue. However, as a community-based organization, they had to react to local priorities. For example, many parents in the district felt that school lunch programs were important. So that had to be fought for, even though the staff may have felt that other issues were more important. Another staff aspiration was to move toward becoming more self-supporting by using dues received from parents. This would free the organization from obligation to funding agencies. But their constituency lives on the edge of survival. (Dante could have obtained ideas for the Inferno by walking through the east Bronx.) Clearly, the parents' organization has a desperate time keeping a long-range perspective in an environment with cruel day-to-day tensions.

In 1968 the Poor People's Campaign asked the Office of Education to "increase the accountability of local schools receiving Federal assistance by requiring that per pupil expenditures dropout and survival rates and reading levels be made available to the public on a regular and periodic basis." The office replied that Title I evaluations were public documents.[18] However, it appeared that the campaign lacked the resources to raise this issue at a local level, since I was unable to find any signs of local follow-up action.

The Office of Education has required school districts to establish parents' advisory committees to affect the policies of local Title I programs. Theoretically, such committees could use their status to increase the degree of program accountability by demanding better and more objective evaluation. Undoubtedly, this has occurred in some cases, but not too frequently.

Some local school systems have shown an interest in developing effective open accountability systems. In February 1971 the New York City School Board announced the signing of a contract between the board and the Educational Testing Service to design an accountability system for the school district. Later, Kenneth B. Clark, a black psychologist and educator, criticized one of the key assumptions underlying the proposed design: that schools with students from different backgrounds might be expected to have different levels of performance.[19] Clark contended that it would be irresponsible for an accountability system to accept performance variations due to such socioeconomic factors. Since the Educational Testing Service's design plan assumes the participation of citizen committees in the design process, it is likely that this issue will arise at later stages.

The Columbus, Ohio, school district has developed perhaps the best accountability communication system now in operation. Some of the details of the system are described in Appendix A. The most prominent product of the system is an annual, school-by-school output report, which is easily available to all citizens. One page of the 175-page report is reproduced on the following pages. The Report includes an informative twenty-five-page introduction.[20]

## Performance Contracting

One outgrowth of the growing emphasis on school accountability and the apparent failure of many of the compensatory education programs designed on traditional lines is the proposal that private contractors be paid to teach students with payment partly conditioned on the production of measurable, prespecified results. Inevitably, such arrangements will require a written statement of the goals to be attained and reliable measurement systems to see if they have been achieved. This procedure is clearly equivalent to traditional business accounting practices.

The first such modern arrangement between a contractor and a public school occurred in 1969. Therefore, the educational contracting process is still in its infancy. If it continues and grows, it will be subject to change and development. However, a sketch of its brief history and discussion of its implications is still pertinent.

The performance contracting programs currently in operation involve private contractors who have taken over a school responsibility, usually for the instruction of children from low-income families where the school has not had significant success. Frequently, the programs involve reading or math. Of course, these are also subjects

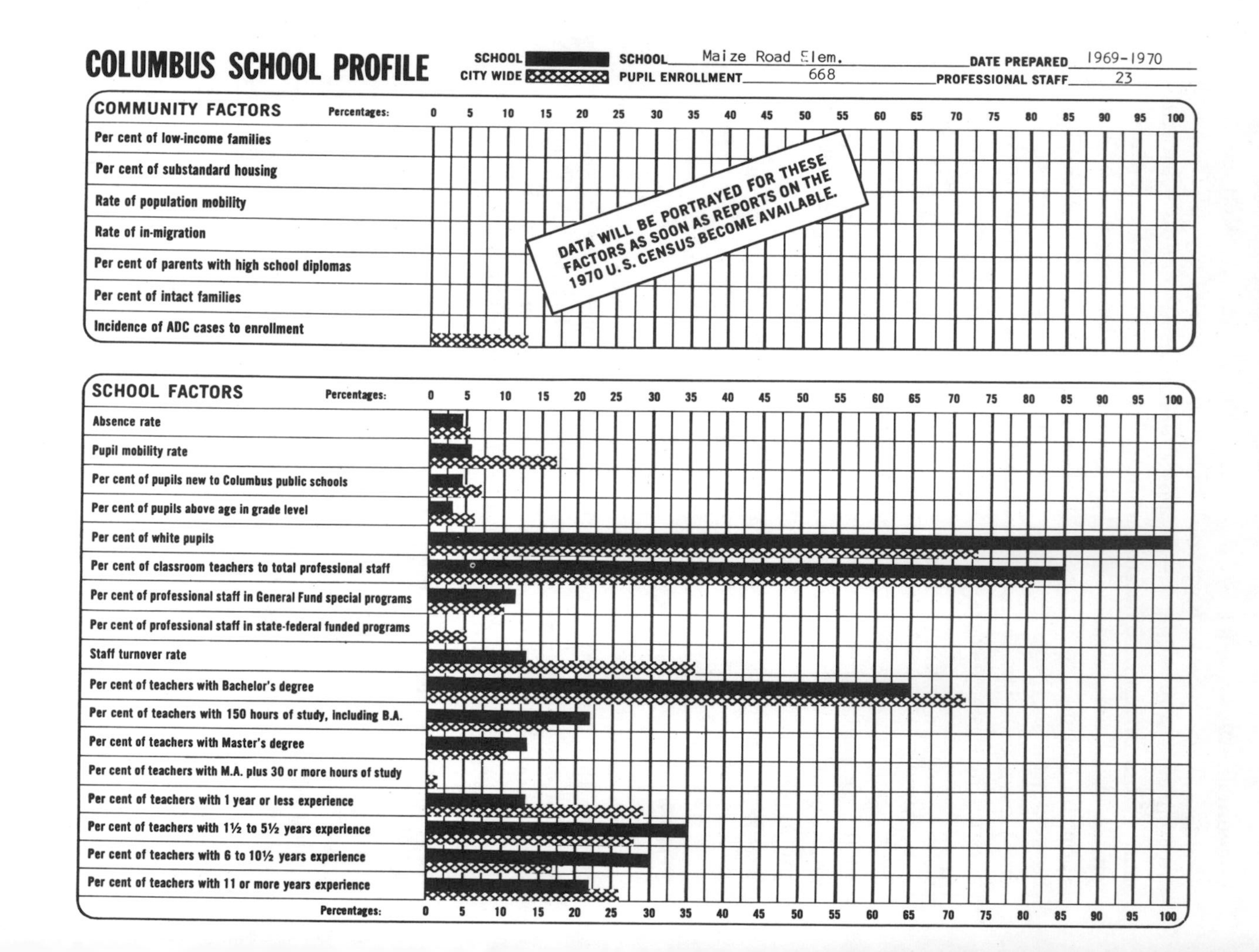
COLUMBUS SCHOOL PROFILE
SCHOOL
CITY WIDE
SCHOOL Maize Road Elem.
PUPIL ENROLLMENT 668
DATE PREPARED 1969-1970
PROFESSIONAL STAFF 23
COMMUNITY FACTORS
Percentages:
0 5 10 15 20 25 30 35 40 45 50 55 60 65 70 75 80 85 90 95 100
Per cent of low-income families
Per cent of substandard housing
Rate of population mobility
Rate of in-migration
Per cent of parents with high school diplomas
Per cent of intact families
Incidence of ADC cases to enrollment
DATA WILL BE PORTRAYED FOR THESE FACTORS AS SOON AS REPORTS ON THE 1970 U.S. CENSUS BECOME AVAILABLE.
SCHOOL FACTORS
Percentages:
0 5 10 15 20 25 30 35 40 45 50 55 60 65 70 75 80 85 90 95 100
Absence rate
Pupil mobility rate
Per cent of pupils new to Columbus public schools
Per cent of pupils above age in grade level
Per cent of white pupils
Per cent of classroom teachers to total professional staff
Per cent of professional staff in General Fund special programs
Per cent of professional staff in state-federal funded programs
Staff turnover rate
Per cent of teachers with Bachelor's degree
Per cent of teachers with 150 hours of study, including B.A.
Per cent of teachers with Master's degree
Per cent of teachers with M.A. plus 30 or more hours of study
Per cent of teachers with 1 year or less experience
Per cent of teachers with 1½ to 5½ years experience
Per cent of teachers with 6 to 10½ years experience
Per cent of teachers with 11 or more years experience
Percentages:
0 5 10 15 20 25 30 35 40 45 50 55 60 65 70 75 80 85 90 95 100

## STANDARD SCORES

BELOW AVERAGE — AVERAGE — ABOVE AVERAGE

| ACADEMIC APTITUDE | Level | Year | 20 | 30 | 40 | 50 | 60 | 70 | 80 |
|---|---|---|---|---|---|---|---|---|---|
| Verbal | School | 1969 | | | | | | | |
| | City | 1969 | | | | | | | |
| Non-verbal | School | 1969 | | | | | | | |
| | City | 1969 | | | | | | | |

## NATIONAL NORM GRADE PLACEMENT

| ACHIEVEMENT | Number Tested | Level | Year | Median Score | % Above Norm |
|---|---|---|---|---|---|
| Reading (Vocabulary) | 95 | School | 1968 | 6.8 | 67 |
| | 108 | School | 1969 | 7.1 | 79 |
| Grade Tested: 6 | 8277 | City | 1969 | 6.0 | 50 |
| Reading (Comprehension) | 95 | School | 1968 | 7.3 | 72 |
| | 108 | School | 1969 | 7.3 | 76 |
| Grade Tested: 6 | 8279 | City | 1969 | 6.0 | 51 |
| Language (Mechanics) | 95 | School | 1968 | 6.5 | 64 |
| | 108 | School | 1969 | 7.0 | 70 |
| Grade Tested: 6 | 8254 | City | 1969 | 5.7 | 45 |
| Language (Expression) | 95 | School | 1968 | 6.6 | 64 |
| | 108 | School | 1969 | 7.0 | 71 |
| Grade Tested: 6 | 8253 | City | 1969 | 5.3 | 42 |
| Language (Spelling) | 95 | School | 1968 | 6.5 | 63 |
| | 108 | School | 1969 | 7.0 | 66 |
| Grade Tested: 6 | 8251 | City | 1969 | 6.0 | 50 |
| Arithmetic (Computation) | 97 | School | 1968 | 6.1 | 67 |
| | 108 | School | 1969 | 6.6 | 68 |
| Grade Tested: 6 | 8291 | City | 1969 | 5.9 | 50 |
| Arithmetic (Concepts) | 97 | School | 1968 | 6.7 | 70 |
| | 108 | School | 1969 | 7.1 | 85 |
| Grade Tested: 6 | 8285 | City | 1969 | 5.9 | 56 |
| Arithmetic (Application) | 97 | School | 1968 | 6.5 | 68 |
| | 108 | School | 1969 | 9.4 | 80 |
| Grade Tested: 6 | 8279 | City | 1969 | 6.0 | 53 |

Grade scale: GRADE 1, GRADE 2, GRADE 3, GRADE 4, GRADE 5, GRADE 6, GRADE 7, GRADE 8, GRADE 9, GRADE 10, GRADE 11, GRADE 12

○ National Norm median for grade tested   □ National Norm upper and lower quartiles for grade tested where we have developed the most refined measurement instruments. The contractors have sometimes accepted responsibility for the whole school operation, though they have more typically taken over only one component, while the students otherwise continued regular school attendance. The contractors have been profit and nonprofit corporations that have done antipoverty training programs, or developed and sold curriculum materials to schools. Generally, teachers' unions have opposed the development of such arrangements.[21]

The contracts do not usually specify how the training shall be conducted, and this is the radical departure. Typically, the framework for school operations is structured to a high degree by the institutional form of the school. This form controls hiring procedures, curriculum materials to be used to attain specified ends, salary increase incentives, school hours, incentives to be offered students, and so on. In effect, school operations are process-centered: i.e., they focus more on how to get there than on whether the goal is obtained. The assumption is that if the "right" things are done, we can take results for granted. The contractor structure can be precisely the opposite. Hopefully, this new structure will stimulate contractors to develop new modes of operation that are results-oriented and produce the results.

This shift in educational emphasis has produced one predictable effect. In one of the first contracting experiments, an evaluator discovered that the teachers employed by the contractor had been giving their students exact questions and answers from the planned reading test in advance. In the ensuing controversy, the school district attempted to claim a refund from the contractor. The outcome of this dispute is unclear, although it obviously did not help the prestige of the innovation of performance contracting.[22]

Some of the details of a particular contracting arrangement may be of interest. In 1970 the Dallas, Texas, school district entered into a contracting arrangement covering several areas of student performance.[23] A number of steps occurred preceding the actual execution of the contract. The steps included determination and specification of what types of student improvement the district wished to "buy"; the solicitation of bids from a number of apparently qualified corporations; the collection, analysis, and final negotiation of bids covering three different items; and finally, the employment of another outside contractor (with educational measurement capability) to audit the contract output.

Among the performance criteria specified for various groups of students were:

a. In math and communications, the students would have to gain 1.4 grade levels in one scholastic year, as compared with the 0.5 grade levels this particular group of students had been gaining.

b. In achievement motivation, the contractor would have to reduce dropout rates in math and communication classes below those in the five most successful antidropout projects then being conducted throughout the United States.

c. In occupational training, the adequacy of the contractor's output would be judged by a committee of local employers.

The contractors' compensation will be on a penalty-incentive basis.

In the Dallas arrangement, one element is not typical for the usual business purchase contract. The Dallas system committed the contractors to employ regular Dallas teachers and personnel to do the actual instruction. The contractor will supply the materials and training, while the work is done by district employees. Obviously, such an arrangement will serve to diminish staff and teachers' union resistance to the proposal. Whether it also seriously diminishes contractor flexibility—by restricting certain types of personnel and incentive innovations—remains to be seen.

Measurement experts have pointed out that contracting arrangements pose vexatious problems of educational measurement that have not been adequately resolved.[24] For instance, any time a student takes a test, there is a good likelihood that his score will reflect not only his degree of learning but also his temperament on that particular day, plus his individual strengths in the exact material tested (if he has had to learn 100 spelling words, and has only learned 90, a 10-word test could conceivably cover just the 10 he does not know). Thus, one brief test of a student may be a relatively poor measure of his competence. The problem is compounded when the student is pretested and posttested, to see what happened between the beginning of instruction and the end. There could be a pattern of questions in the beginning test that artificially raised his score and a pattern of questions at the end that artificially lowered it. The results would show that he had lost knowledge in the program, though he might actually have gained knowledge.

In assessing entire educational programs (as opposed to individual students), problems of individual idiosyncrasies can be dealt with by testing a large number of students and determining their average level of performance. This technique allows for individual variations, since there is just as much chance of a student's doing unreasonably poorly as unreasonably well; thus, individual discrepancies average themselves out. However, some performance contracts compensate the contractor on the basis of *individual* student performance; such arrangements do not adequately cover this individual variance issue. Conceivably, the contractor could be paid for students that did not learn and penalized for students that did.

This is not to say that the measurement difficulties are insoluble. There are a number of correctives that can be applied individually or in combinations. For example, longer tests diminish the possibility of asking only what the student happens to know or the few things he failed to learn. However, the solutions will require reshaping of educational measurement techniques and will take planning, money, and time. It may be that going into performance contracting without sufficient development of appropriate measurements or sensitivity to measurement limitations can gravely limit the progress of this innovation.

Another issue that should be clearly faced is that performance contracting, as currently discussed, can at best directly affect only a minority of American school children. Most American school children stay in school and perform adequately at math and reading. The larger challenge facing schools is to help these students grow into effective adults. We are only beginning to develop measurements to assess such efforts, and no contractors have even begun to propose how to achieve such goals. So we have quite a way to go before contractors take over the main business of schools, since this main business is not yet very well defined. However, the possibility that the *example* of the contractors can pose new models for school conduct and develop a results orientation in schools is probably of more long-run importance than any effect they produce on individual children. After all, if flexibility and accountability work for the contractors, why not install it in all our schools?

## Voucher System

Educational voucher systems represent another effort to bring accountability themes into play in public education. One report, financed by the Office of Economic Opportunity, offered the following description of the idea:

> Under the proposed voucher system, a publicly accountable agency would issue a voucher for a year's schooling for each eligible child. The voucher could be turned over to any school (by the child's parents) which had agreed to abide by the rules of the voucher system. Each school would turn in its vouchers for cash. Thus, parents would no longer be forced to send their children to the school around the corner simply because it was around the corner. If the school was attractive and desirable, it would not be seriously affected by the institution of the voucher plan. If not, attendance might fall, perhaps forcing the school to improve.[25]

The report then went on to confront a basic argument against voucher proposals: parents are just too uninformed to make intelligent choices about their children's education; the matter must be left to the experts. In answering this argument, the report implicitly relied on much of the output research I have discussed:

> there is no evidence that "experts" really know any more than parents about the likely effects of specific schools on specific children. There is no consensus about what causes what in education, much less any scientific information to back consensus. This makes it hard to argue that the government should protect children from their parents' naivete by denying the parents choice about their children's schooling and imposing what the government experts happen to think "best."[26]

The proposed voucher plans assume that school boards or the state will continue to exercise certain licensing authority over the schools selling education for vouchers, but the licensed schools would include private as well as public schools. In effect, both private and public schools would be funded through the same source: vouchers received as a result of successfully competing with each other for pupils.

The parents' freedom of choice under voucher plans will naturally raise questions about school effectiveness. What information will they receive to make a choice possible? Once their children are enrolled, what information will give them the assurance that they should stay enrolled? Of course, such information can also be pertinent for parents using contemporary schools. The fact is, however, that contemporary parents ordinarily have few interschool choices, unless they are willing to (a) move to another school attendance area or district or (b) pay for private schooling. Given such a restricted choice, there is little incentive for an individual parent to seek accountability information; if he receives it, he cannot switch schools with the same freedom he changes stocks, trades his car, or retains a different lawyer. Conversely, voucher plans offer individual parents strong incentives to seek accountability information; they can do something with their knowledge.

At this moment, the voucher plans really represent concepts rather than plans. Voucher proponents admit that many of the objections against the plans are substantial. However, the proponents also point out that many of these objections may be corrected by careful development. One important objection has been that the plans might encourage parents to withdraw their children from interracial and interclass public schools, thus creating schools segregated by class and race. For just this reason, the objectors point out, voucher systems were tried in the South by groups that were fighting school desegregation. Voucher proponents contend that the proposed voucher plans can be designed to compel voucher schools to apply quota structures to bring about the maintenance of desegregated and heterogeneous schools. The proponents go on to point out that our current public school system did not appear all at once in its current form, arguing that the voucher approach should be given opportunities to refine and test their proposals in operating school districts.

There are probably no pure voucher arrangements in operation in American education at this time. However, a model voucher law has been seriously proposed to at least one state legislature, and the Office of Economic Opportunity has sought federal funds to finance one or more local school district developmental projects.[27] The office's fund-seeking efforts in Congress have been contested by diverse opponents. One periodical reported that

> the American Federation of Teachers got out a "coloring book" that left no doubt about its stand on the issue.[28] One picture in the book shows the Office of Economic Opportunity as a magician flanked by two grinning men labelled

"private schools" and "private enterprise" while a bewildered figure named J. Q. Public looks on. The caption reads: "and now for the next trick! Mr. Public's school system will disappear – only to reappear in the hands of these gentlemen!"

The assistant executive secretary of the National Education Association testified that vouchers promote "hucksterism," as a result of interschool competition for students. Some civil rights and liberal groups have opposed experimenting with the approach because of its resegregation potential, and because it might lend assistance to church-controlled private schools.

Despite this resistance, the concepts underlying the proposal are congruent with many American traditions about individual choice and with a growing trend toward school decentralization. Therefore, the concepts may still be tried. Even if they abort or are never tried in any pure form, their themes may still spur public interest in accountability approaches.

## Accountability in Operation: The Case of Head Start

If accountability develops greater momentum, we will see occasions where its application may lead to the reshaping or abandonment of an "unsuccessful" school program. In such cases, disputes will arise about the pertinence of the criteria used, the appropriateness of the evaluative activity, and the political implications of the evaluation. One example of such a dispute is already before us in the federal Head Start program.[29] A look at the developments in this dispute may help us see what lies ahead for school operations that are subject to accountability.

Head Start was begun in late 1964, when the United States Office of Economic Opportunity was seeking diverse ways of engaging in the war on poverty. It was proposed as a federally financed program to provide concentrated remedial education to the preschool children of disadvantaged parents. Presumably this focused program would prepare preschoolers to become more effective students by the time they entered school. Undoubtedly, one element assisting the birth and growth of the program was the fact that it did not directly attack or seek radically to revise any existing institution. It simply suggested an additional element to assist the institutions already in operation. At first it was planned to have a small number of summer programs for children about to enter school in the fall of 1965. However, the salability of the idea caused a flood of applications, and a decision was made to assist a large number of programs. Eventually, over $100 million was expended for the first programs in the summer of 1965.

The preschool concept underlying the program had apparent merit. It was supported by some research showing that preschool education programs for children from disadvantaged families might significantly diminish their learning handicaps. However, it was a far cry from a few experimental programs to the expedited development and launching of a nationwide program for tens of thousands of children. In reality, the six-to-eight-week 1965 summer program contained a high degree of local autonomy about how projects should be carried out. This meant the programs varied greatly in format and quality. Later, Head Start shifted to the funding of full-year programs, but similar local flexibility applied.

Eventually, the Office of Economic Opportunity created a subunit, the Office of Research Plans, Programs and Evaluations (ORPPE). One of the responsibilities of ORPPE was to audit local and national program efforts and maintain accountability to the national headquarters. While ORPPE was in operation, the national Head Start office began independent efforts to evaluate the program it was managing, ensure that it was well organized, and receive feedback. A series of conflicts arose between Head Start headquarters and ORPPE. Each of these units was planning and operating Head Start evaluations; each found shortcomings in the evaluations produced by the other.

For example, the Head Start unit contended that the ORPPE evaluation covered only a fraction of the program's goals, because it assessed only cognitive and not affective learning, e.g., vocabulary, recognizing letters of the alphabet, and developing self-discipline. Allegedly, the evaluation should also have considered other Head Start programs goals, e.g., health, nutrition, and parent involvement in the program. Therefore, the ORPPE evaluation was inadequate and should be disregarded, even though it found that the Head Start program did not produce important and/or lasting gains in its pupils for the criteria measured.

Conversely, ORPPE was dissatisfied with the evaluations produced for the Head Start national office. ORPPE contended that the tests used to evaluate pupils' gains were inadequate, that there were few follow-up tests (to see if any gains by the children were retained after they went on into school), and that the tests were not always applied to control groups so that useful comparisons could be made between Head Start and equivalent non-Head Start children. Without more refined data of this sort, ORPPE contended that it would not be wise to enlarge the Head Start program and that it probably required radical reshaping.

Throughout these persistent evaluation efforts, continuing discussions occurred between the staffs of the two OEO units. In these discussions, the Head Start staff members often tried to block or postpone evaluations with the plea that they "might lead to misleading negative results which could shake the morale of those associated with Head Start and bring unwarranted program cutbacks." Eventually, a major study authorized by the ORPPE did show the program in an unfavorable light. Inevitably, the study left some questions unanswered, and the answers it gave were sometimes subject to methodological criticism. Still, the study received widespread publicity and stimulated prolonged discussions about the effectiveness and appropriate aims of the program.

Two former members of the ORPPE office analyzed the Head Start experience and the implications of these evaluations disputes in an article for the *Annals of the American Academy.* They concluded that the major implication of the controversy was that new or substantially revised educational programs should be promoted in a *developmental* manner. By this, they meant that Head Start's major operating problems, which were the reason for the tensions surrounding evaluation and accountability, arose from the attempt to launch an ambitious program with insufficient prior development, planning, or research. The basic idea—to aim at very young children from disadvantaged families—made good sense. But there is a huge gap between endorsing such an idea and organizing a large-scale program quickly to set up and conduct innumerable preschool programs when the only equivalent programs had been managed in experimental, artificial settings.

Once the Head Start program was launched on a large scale, enormous pressures were generated to maintain the program as it began: innumerable localities had hired staffs and begun operations with particular assumptions. The national headquarters managing the program operated on similar assumptions. Many press releases were issued proclaiming the bright promise of the program. Ambitious goals were proclaimed to win public and Congressional support. The idea that an evaluation might conclude that the format of the program was unwise could be a programmatic and public relations disaster. Even if the evaluation endorsed the basic theme of the program—i.e., to help preschoolers—the equivocal publicity would seriously mar the program. Its credibility would be impaired, and inevitably pressures would arise to cut back the program until "the kinks were ironed out."

These considerations naturally raise the question: if accountability makes school programs susceptible to equivalent criticisms, how can we design and conduct programs that work? In other words, what procedures may be followed to produce school improvement if we make use of the implications of accountability? There is a useful example that we can consider.

## The Tutorial School

A school district in Los Angeles, California, is trying to develop a tutorial elementary school in which students teach students on a cross-grade basis, and teachers become evaluators, planners, and consultants rather than teaching classes.[30] The students will do all the teaching. The school is being developed under a five-year plan that makes full use of the principles of feedback and accountability. It is being developed by psychologists associated with the Systems Development Corporation (SDC), which in the past has primarily done defense work. This history has strongly influenced SDC's procedures for planning education change, so it is pertinent to consider this history first.

SDC was initially developed as a subsidiary of the RAND Corporation, which did systems analysis and evaluation work for the Air Force. SDC was a RAND division handling the development of training systems for the Air Force, such as procedures to train personnel to operate new electronic missile and plane detection systems. It usually had adequate funds available to do this work; all concerned agreed that it would be a disaster to put in a new multibillion dollar radar system and have it broken or misused by poorly trained personnel. Suppose some operator mistook a goose for a missile? The mistake might lead to nuclear disaster.

SDC's process of developing training systems made intensive use of feedback. For each new piece of equipment for which they had to devise a training procedure, they first built a simulator. This permitted SDC staff to confront trainees with realistic problems by feeding data into the equipment that simulated operational problems. SDC then trained the operators according to the best technique they could plan and subjected them to a test on the simulator. The new operators would almost always make some mistakes. SDC would analyze the feedback, try to identify the mistake, and revise the training methods to prevent its reoccurrence. Then the Air Force would assign a new group of trainees, and the revised developmental training cycle would be rerun with another simulation at the end. After several cycles of this sort, SDC would have a training system that produced trainees who handled the new equipment without serious mistakes. SDC would then train a group of regular Air Force trainers to using the new training system and later test the trainers' students on the simulator. If the results were satisfactory, SDC could then say they had developed and delivered a system that could be widely applied by the Air Force to train tens of thousands of men.

In 1966 two SDC professional staff members undertook to apply their feedback approach to the improvement of elementary school programs. Their first effort was described earlier in this book in the discussion of the reading program for Mexican-American pupils that relied on the teaching of concept words. In a sense, that program was also a test of the developmental approach itself; developmental feedback techniques were applied to find out if and why the children could not learn reading by the usual method and to see whether and why the various experimental techniques worked better.

The Mexican-American program had suggested to the researchers that tutorial arrangements—where students teach other students—had considerable promise as an innovation. They recognized that this was just an intuitive assumption, but they determined to use it as the theme of their next developmental effort. However, they recognized (somewhat unlike the Head Start program) that they really did not know how to run a tutorial school and that it would take them a number of years to get *one* effective tutorial school in operation. Then they translated their developmental aspirations into specific goals for the finished tutorial school:

1. Students will do the teaching, largely on a cross-grade basis.

2. Teachers will largely be out of teaching and into the business of consulting with students and other teachers and administrators.

3. The pupils will perform on objective tests as well as or better than comparable pupils from traditional schools.

4. The cost of routinely operating the new school will be no greater than in traditional schools.

5. Parents will play a significant role in school operations and policy-setting.

6. The developers will produce a manual describing how other schools can adopt their system.

Next, they identified an elementary school in a lower-income neighborhood that apparently was well managed, and not confronted with insurmountable problems. The assumption was that developmental work should be done in a realistic environment, but not in one that presented the most severe problems from the start, since there were already enough challenges facing the developers. They obtained the commitment of professional staff cooperation. The staff of the school voted unanimously (by secret ballot) to support the effort. Next, they met with parent groups to explain the program (promising them involvement and feedback) and to seek parent support for the program. They received a promise of support and then set about developing the program. (The development costs were underwritten by a long-term foundation grant). They assumed developing the program would take from five to seven years.

They determined to begin by having the kindergarten tutored by upper-grade classes and gradually to move the development ahead one grade a year, until it encompassed the whole school. During the process, they planned to monitor all operations constantly. Children would be tested to see how well they were learning, and observers would prepare reports on operations and later meet with teachers, administrators, parents, and researchers. As the program evolved, there were frequent meetings of committees and subgroups to discuss progress. New measures and tests were devised to see more precisely what results were occurring. An annual evaluation visit by an independent team of outside consultants was arranged. Their evaluation is made available to parents.

Inevitably, problems appeared as the program evolved. One of the greatest difficulties was getting teachers to talk to each other about the progress of their respective tutors and tutees. Without such cooperation, the effort would fail; the kindergarten teacher had to talk comfortably to the third grade teacher about how the third grade tutors were acting while they were tutoring in kindergarten, and the third grade teacher had to let the kindergarten teacher know what the third graders thought about the learning of the kindergarteners. However, such interteacher cooperation is a radical break with the general pattern of teacher performance. Many pieces of research have demonstrated that teachers usually are remarkably reluctant to discuss classroom techniques with each other. Some researchers have attributed this to the inadequate character of our present knowledge about classroom teaching; the weak knowledge base makes teachers feel awkward about revealing their insecurities.

In any event, the SDC researchers undertook to develop means of answering this communication problem. Various committee patterns and other communication stimulators are being tried. Concurrently, persistent evaluation and revision continues in many other elements of the program, always directed toward identifying more effective methods and enlarging on their potential. At this time, the developmental project is still underway. But the outcome of the particular effort is less important than its significance as a model of educational development at work. As we see, developmental efforts follow a certain general pattern: a desire to develop some idea or research-based hunch; an early commitment to definite, definable goals; a determination to proceed bit by bit, starting on a small scale; a willingness to spend funds on collecting feedback and revising the system being developed; the acceptance of feedback and evaluation; an understanding that developing the system will take time and must proceed through a series of steps; the location of the development in a realistic, but still manageable environment; the eventual production of some manual or plan so the developed product can be used elsewhere; and the assumption that the developed product will eventually be used on a large scale and must be designed to facilitate such use. Almost all these principles are alien to educational innovation today, but if accountability produces more interest in developmental innovation, it will have a greater impact on education.

## Footnotes

1. Raymond J. Chambers, *Accounting, Evaluation and Economic Behavior* (Englewood Cliffs, N.J.: Prentice-Hall, 1966), p. 374.

2. The office also has later reports in preparation. See also the reports of the National Advisory Council on the Education of Disadvantaged Children, particularly *Title I ESEA: A Report and a Look Forward–1969*, Fourth Annual Report (Washington, D.C.: Government Printing Office, 1969).

3. Robert J. Dentler, "Urban Eyewash: A Review of Title I/Year II," *Urban Review* 3 (February 1969): 32-33.

4. U.S. Office of Education, *Federal/State Task Force of Educational Evaluation; An Overview* (Washington, D.C.: the Task Force, 1971).

5. U.S. Office of Education, *Do Teachers Make a Difference?* (Washington, D.C.: Government Printing Office, 1970).

6. National Assessment of Educational Progress. *Science–National Results, Report 1; Citizenship–National Results, Report 2; Writing–National Results, Report 3* (Washington, D.C.: Government Printing Office, 1970).

7. Frank B. Womer & Marjorie M. Mastie, "How Will National Assessment Change American Education," *Phi Delta Kappan* 53, no. 2 (October 1971): 118-120.

8. Educational Testing Service, *State Educational Assessment Programs* (Princeton, N.J.: Educational Testing Service, 1971), p. ix.

9. Pennsylvania State Department of Public Instruction, *Proceedings, First Meeting of State Advisory Committee on the Assessment of Educational Quality* (Harrisburg, Pa.: State Department of Education, 1968); Henry S. Dyer, "The Pennsylvania Plan," *Science Education* 50 (April 1966): 242-248. See also Educational Testing Service, op. cit.

10. Pennsylvania State Department of Public Instruction, *Phase I Findings* (Harrisburg, Pa.: State Department of Public Instruction, 1969).

11. University of the State of New York, State Educational Department, *New York State Pupil Evaluation Program* (Albany, N.Y.: State Department of Education, 1966).

12. California School Assessment Act of 1968, Education Code § § 12851–12853. Repealed 1969 by § § 12852-12853 are now covered by Education Code § § 12848-12849.

13. C. Phillips Kearney & Robert J. Huyser, *The Michigan Assessment of Education, 1969-70: The Politics of Reporting Results* (Paper delivered at the Annual Meeting of the American Education Research Association, New York, February 1971).

14. Ibid.

15. Educational Testing Service, op. cit., p. xi.

16. Educational Testing Service, op. cit., p. xvi.

17. United Bronx Parents, *Various Training Materials for Parents* (United Bronx Parents, 791 Prospect Avenue, Bronx, N.Y. 10455). See also Ellen Lurie, *How to Change Schools* (New York: Random House, 1971) (Mrs. Lurie is research director for the United Bronx Parents); Edward Wynne, "A Review: Various Training Materials for Parents," *Phi Delta Kappan* (January 1969): 294-295.

18. U.S. Office of Education, "Poor People's Demands on Education," mimeographed (Washington, D.C.: Office of Education, 1968).

19. *New York Times,* 19 March 1971, p. 25.

20. Howard O. Merriman, *The Columbus School Profile* (Columbus, Ohio: Columbus School District, 1970); Luvern L. Cunningham & Raphael O. Nystrand, *New Forms of Citizen Participation in School Affairs* (Washington, D.C.: The Urban Coalition, 1969).

21. James Welsh, "D.C. Perspectives on Performance Contracting," *Educational Researcher* 21 (October 1970): p. 1.

22. Ibid.

23. Nolan Estes & Donald R. Waldrip, "Issues In Implementation," *Proceedings of the Conferences on Educational Accountability, Washington, D.C., and Hollywood, California, March 1971* (Princeton, N.J.: Educational Testing Service, 1971).

24. Roger Lennon, "Accountability and Performance Contracting" (address to the American Education Research Association, New York, February 6, 1971).

25. Center for the Study of Public Policy, *Financing Education by Grants to Parents.* Prepared under Grant GC 8542 from the Office of Program Development, USOEO (Cambridge, Mass.: March 1970).

26. Ibid, p. 5.

27. California Legislature, Senate, Committee on Education, "Voucher Systems and Contractor Proposals, Proceedings of Hearings," mimeographed, 12-13 January, 1971.

28. James Welsh, "Perspectives: The OEO and Vouchers," *Educational Researcher* 22 (June 1971): 5.

29. Walter Williams & John W. Evans, "The Politics of Evaluation: The Case of Headstart," *The Annals of the American Academy* 385 (1969): 118-132.

30. Ralph J. Melaragno & Gerald Newmark, "The Tutorial Community Concept," in James W. Guthrie & Edward Wynne, *New Models for American Education* (Englewood Cliffs, N.J.: Prentice-Hall, 1971), pp. 98-113.

# 6
# Outsiders and Insiders: The Public and School Macrochange

> People or groups participating in [precedent breaking events] experience some shattering of the existing social and cultural order to which they are bound. Hence . . . they become more . . . ready to respond to people who are able to present to them new symbols which could give meaning to their experiences in terms of some fundamental cosmic, social, or political order, to prescribe the proper norms of behavior, to relate the individual to the collective identification, and to reassure him of his status and of his place in a given collectivity.
>
> S. N. Eisenstadt

If large-scale accountability does develop within American education, it will be an instance of macrochange. That is, the changes that occur—and the way they occur—will be radically different from typical school innovations. In such a case, the relationship between the public and the macrochanges may contrast sharply with the typical role played by the public in school change. To understand the relationship between the public and accountability change, we must look at school macrochange rather than more frequent and minor innovations.

This means a historical survey: by definition, macrochange rarely occurs; to see several instances, we have to look over long periods of time. This need not be a disadvantage; sometimes we can get a better perspective on a class of phenomena if some of its incidents are farther away. As our instances, I have selected the common school movement of the first half of the nineteenth century; the progressive education movement between 1895 and 1940; the post-

Sputnik curriculum reforms between 1955 and 1965; and the school desegregation and compensatory education programs starting in, perhaps, 1945 and continuing through the present. In all these instances, persistent and widespread public demands on education eventually produced important changes in the day-to-day operation of local schools throughout the country. Perhaps there are some parallels between the current accountability situation and these historic episodes.

At this point, someone may reasonably raise the following issues: What does the public actually have to do with running the schools anyway? Are they not run by administrators trained in schools of education (and more and more restrained by teachers' unions), with the legitimization of school boards? How can the public be connected with important innovations? Indeed, where the public is involved in school change, does it not typically act as a brake? For example, a 1966 Gallup poll showed that school board members were hostile to innovations such as a nationally standardized high school test that also smacked of accountability.[1] These points represent a certain truth, but let us first scan the history and then come back to the questions.

## The Common School Movement

In the first half of the nineteenth century, the traditional governing classes in many American states were faced with a serious challenge. Jacksonian Democracy and the forces inherent in the American Revolution had generated a powerful push toward universal male suffrage. Simultaneously, successive waves of low-status immigrants threatened to engulf the existing social order. For example, in Boston in 1834 conflicts were rife between lower-class Irish and anti-Irish groups. One outburst resulted in the burning of an Ursuline convent by an anti-Irish, anti-Catholic mob.

Reform oriented politicians, from the governing middle and upper classes, concluded that widespread public education might temper these disturbing influences.[2] One such politician and lawyer, Horace Mann, resigned from the Massachusetts legislature in 1837 to become first secretary to the newly established state board of education, which he, as a legislator, had helped create.

Mann's formal authority as secretary was slight; but he believed that his office might give him an important platform. When he accepted the appointment, he noted in his diary that the law provided only that he was to "collect statistics, diffuse information, and arouse and guide public sentiment in relation to the practical interests of education." He concluded: "I must be a fluid sort of man, adapting myself to tastes, opinions, habits, manners, as far as this can be done without hypocrisy or insincerity, or a compromise of principle."[3] Today, we might call him a change agent.

One of his first acts was to undertake a statewide speaking tour to generate public support for his proposals for enlarging educational opportunity. His speeches bluntly stated his general principles:

> The mobs, the riots, the burnings, the lynchings, perpetrated by men of the present day, are perpetrated because of their vicious and defective education. We see and feel the ravages of their tiger passions now, when they are full grown; but it was years ago when they were whelped and suckled. And so too, if we are derelict in our duty to this matter, our children in their turn will suffer. If we permit the vulture's eggs to be hatched, it will be too late to take care of the lambs.[4]

Again, in a widely distributed article, Mann said of the disorderly Irish immigrants and laborers:

> It must be manifest to every forecasting mind, that the children of these people will soon possess the rights of men, whether they possess the character of men or not. There is a certainty about their future political and social powers—while there is a contingency depending on the education they receive—whether these powers be exercised for weal or woe.[5]

Mann and his allies contended that state laws must be passed compelling each community to maintain free public elementary schools open to all. These would be called "common schools." Mann observed that "the common schools would be so fine that no one would wish to send their children to private school." In part, the reformers deliberately aimed at teaching students by mixing different groups together.

Over the years, the school reformers were active in many northern states. In 1805 Mayor De Witt Clinton of New York became an organizer and president of the Free School Society (later the Public School Society). He remained its president for over twenty-five years, including the four years he spent as state governor. As governor, he sent many messages to the legislature to support public school legislation.

Thaddeus Stevens, then a Pennsylvania state legislator, led a fight to pass common school legislation in the state. After the legislation was passed, an effort was made to repeal it. In 1835 Stevens delivered this defense of the law to his fellow legislators:

> If an elected Republic is to endure, every elector must have sufficient information not only to accumulate wealth and take care of his pecuniary concerns, but to direct the legislature, the ambassadors, and the Executive of the Nation—for some part of all these things, some agency in approving and disapproving them, falls on every freeman. If the permanency of our government depends on such knowledge, it is the duty of Government to see that the means of information be diffused to every citizen.[6]

The repeal attempt failed. In 1864, with a long political career behind him, Stevens wrote to a lady who had written him about this earlier effort, "When I review all the measures in which I had taken part, I see none in which I take so much pleasure, perhaps I may be excused for saying pride, as the free school system of Pennsylvania."[7]

Meanwhile, Mann found potent political allies in Massachusetts. Governor Edward Everett, for example, made the following speech in 1839:

> We must have officers unqualified for their duties; or we must educate a privileged class to monopolize the honors and emoluments of place; or we must establish a system of general education, as will furnish a supply of well-informed, intelligent, and responsible citizens, in every part of the country, and in every walk of life, capable of discharging the trusts which the people may devolve upon them. It is superfluous to say which of the three courses is most congenial to the spirit of republicanism.[8]

The middle-class reformers frequently received concurrent support from the lower echelon. For instance, a report by the Philadelphia Workingmen's Committee in 1830 contended that "the original element of despotism is a monopoly of talent, which consigns the multitude to comparative ignorance, and secures the balance of knowledge on the side of the rich and rulers . . . . the means of equal knowledge (the only security for equal liberty) should be rendered, by legal provision, the common property of all classes." The report also criticized the existing school arrangements: "The [state-supported schools for paupers' children] are irresponsible institutions, established by individuals, from mere motives of private speculation or gain, . . . and frequently without the requisite attainments and skills."[9]

The reformers understood that their task required a powerful communication and persuasion apparatus. In Massachusetts Mann founded the *Common School Journal,* and as secretary of the state school board, he also authored fourteen annual reports to the board. The reports were powerful propaganda documents. In 1842 eighteen thousand copies of one of his reports were distributed in New York State. One of his pro-education Fourth of July orations had twenty-seven thousand copies distributed. In addition, education historian Elwood Cubberly notes that "hundreds of School Societies, Lyceums, and Educational Associations were organized throughout America; many conventions were held, and resolutions favoring state schools were adopted; many 'Letters' and 'Addresses to the Public' were written and published."[10] Michael Katz, an historian who has mixed feelings about the movement, still concludes that "for about two decades at mid-century, the men in communities busiest with their own complicated affairs, extended immense amounts of time and effort in their commitment to improve and extend public education."[11]

The educators of the time greeted the movement with mixed feelings. Many of its most prominent leaders were not educators, but politicians; of fourteen key common school reformers, eleven had held elective office, and nine had been lawyers. Only one of the fourteen had been a career teacher.[12] In addition, powerful and innovative personalities like Mann inevitably had ideas of their own about how schools should be improved. However, his proposals were often seen by educators as inappropriate lay intrusions. In his "Seventh Annual Report" in 1834, Mann questioned the widespread use of flogging in the publicly supported Boston schools. The schoolmasters countered this with their "Remarks on the Seventh Report to Mr. Mann." The secretary, who was notoriously persistent, issued a "Reply to the Remarks." The schoolmasters came back with "A Rejoinder," but Mann had the last word with his "Answer to the Rejoinder to the Reply to the Remarks on the Seventh Report."

In his diary, Mann observed that "Most teachers have been activated by the account of the best schools abroad [contained in the Seventh Report]. Others are offended at being driven out of the Paradise which their own self-esteem has erected for them."[13]

After prolonged effort, the movement obtained substantial success: between 1825 and 1850, most of the northern states passed laws compelling localities to support common schools. A major step in developing our current school system had been concluded.

## The Progressive Movement

In the late nineteenth century, public schools were faced with a number of new and demanding challenges: rising waves of foreign language immigrants; crude political domination of teacher hiring and money management in the big cities; and uncontrolled and disorganized growth. A tide for educational reform began to develop concurrently with the movement for larger political reform throughout the United States. The conjunction of these pressures for school and social reform fathered the progressive education movement.

Lawrence A. Cremin, the historian of the movement, contends that it was born in 1892. At that time, *The Forum,* a muckraking periodical, financed a six-month-long, thirty-six-city school tour by Joseph M. Rice (some of whose work we discussed earlier). After talking to twelve hundred teachers and making countless observations, Rice concluded that he had seen a procession of "political hacks hiring untrained teachers who had blindly led their innocent charges in singsong drill, rote repetition, and meaningless verbiage. The public must save the public schools."[14]

Rice's charges provoked a strong response from school administrators. The *Journal of Education* characterized Rice as a young man who had "proved, beyond cavil, that he is merely a sensational critic." *Schools* called the article "cheap criticism and charlatanism by an alleged expert." Rice followed up with continuing investigations, including "The Futility of the Spelling Grind," published in the *Forum* in 1897. He demonstrated, by testing sixteen thousand children in many schools, that beyond a certain minimum amount of time, there was no important correlation between the length of time devoted to spelling drills and students' capabilities as spellers. This analysis, as we know, did not help his standing with educators.

Other reform forces active at the time began to shift their interest toward education. In New York City the Federation of Good

Government Clubs was concerned with promoting general civic reform. The Women's Auxiliary of Club E of the Federation took education as a priority issue and organized itself as the Public Education Association in 1895. The association has since played a persistent role in promoting school reform in the city.[15]

Muckrakers and social reformers came into the movement from many directions. In *The Battle with the Slum* (1902) Jacob Riis argued:

> Do you see how the whole battle with the slum is fought out in and around the public school? The kindergarten, manual training, the cooking school, all experiments in their day, cried out as fads by some, have brought common sense in their train. When it rules the public schools in our cities . . . we can put off our armor, the battle with the slum will be over.[16]

Similarly, Jane Addams, in *The Spirit of Youth,* argued for further reforms to make schools more responsive to the needs of the times.

Lawrence Cremin has observed that "progressive education began as part and parcel of that broader program of social and political reform called the Progressive Movement. . . . it viewed education as an adjunct to politics in realizing the promise of American life."[17] John Dewey, a philosopher temporarily turned educator, became its major spokesman. The movement developed a myriad of goals. One was to make the schools less political and more professional to meet the demands of the times. Another was to stimulate the schools to prepare their students better to participate in a democratic society. Dewey proposed to solve this problem by "transforming" the school:

> In place of a school set apart from life as a place for learning lessons, we have a miniature social group in which study and growth are incidents of shared experience. Playgrounds, shops, workrooms, laboratories not only direct the natural active tendencies of youth, but they involve intercourse, communication, and cooperation—all extending the perception of connections . . . . Under such conditions, the school becomes itself a form of social life, a miniature community and one in close interaction with other modes of associated experience beyond school walls.[18]

The movement won an important victory in 1918 with the issuance of the report of the National Education Association's Commission on the Reorganization of Secondary Education. The report—by an establishment group—urged the adoption of many of the progressives' child-centered and relevance-oriented principles. It symbolized a break from the previous tradition of narrower academic goals. The Progressive Education Association was founded in 1919 to advance the humanizing goals of the movement. The association's principal founders were a combination of liberal lay leaders and private school headmasters. In 1926, Dewey agreed to become its honorary president; however, every operating president of the association from 1920 to 1932 was, at the time of election, a private school headmaster.[19]

The association supported diverse school reforms, but its upper-middle-class perspective affected its priorities. Representatives of low-income groups withdrew from its efforts, contending that the association did not focus on the concerns of their parents. Many of the association's members were also hostile to the developing test movement; they argued that tests favored intellectuality over creativity. They railed against "the tyranny of the intellect."

While these debates went on, Dewey's name and *Progressive Education,* the association's journal, gained it wide recognition. The association's prestige grew, and its version of reform became widely accepted. With success came new dangers, as more and more professional educators found it advantageous to join. In the 1930s, according to Cremin, the association had become the "educational bandwagon" of the period, and, by becoming overprofessionalized, had separated itself from the politically progressive forces of the times.

A few progressive educators, based in colleges of education, did make an effort to return to politics in the tumultuous 1930s.[20] However, they did not think in terms of alliances. For example, in 1932 George Counts wrote *Dare The Schools Build a New Social Order.*[21] Shortly afterward, Counts attempted to have the Progressive Education Association issue *A Call to the Teachers of the Nation.* The *Call* urged teachers to seek and use power "in the interests of the great masses of people." While the association toyed with endorsing such approaches, it did not commit itself. In 1933 Counts and his allies founded their own periodical, *Social Frontier,* to carry the message that teachers should save society. Unfortunately, *Social Frontier* was unable to specify exactly what teachers as a group could do at a time of social crisis, unless they worked closely with other social forces. But the social reconstructionists had few ties with other important social forces, and their style did not assist them in this matter. One historian observed that in 1936, at the moment that the Roosevelt administration was changing the national economy and making important legislative progress, *Social Frontier* was totally ignoring these concrete episodes. For example, the periodical made no mention of the Wagner Act, the Banking Act, or the Social Security Act. The reconstructionists' efforts largely expired in the late 1930s, although some of their messianic perspectives for education may still be sensed today.

The Progressive Education Association itself eventually dissolved in 1955, although the zenith of its influence had passed before World War II. On the school front, the progressives had won an impressive rhetorical victory. Their vocabulary had become an essential part of the language of public education. However, Cremin, a sympathetic observer, is far less sanguine about their concrete effects on classroom practices. He observes that:

> What the progressives did prescribe made inordinate demands on the teacher's time and ability. "Integrated studies" required familiarity with a fantastic range of knowledge and teaching materials; while the commitment to build upon student's needs and interests demanded extraordinary feats of pedagogical ingenuity. In the hands of first-rate instructors, the innovations worked wonders; in the hands of too many average teachers, however, they led to chaos.[22]

This suggests that there was a persistent and enlarging gap between the aspirations of the progressives and their real accomplishments. The gap is understandable, because, as Counts and Rugg, two leading educational progressives, observed:

> in retrospect, after thirty years of curriculum-making in (the progressives') laboratory schools, one of the most regrettable wastes lies in the lack of definite information concerning the results of these fine dynamic types of education. After a quarter century of work, there are almost no measured records of outputs of these schools. In only rare instances have these laboratory schools set up machinery for obtaining eye-witness accounts and measured records of innovations in the content and organization of the curriculum.[23]

In short, they made no provision for feedback.

## Post-Sputnik Curriculum Reforms

Until the 1920s the high school curriculum had been designed essentially to prepare youths for college, on the correct assumption that most high school students were college bound. As high school enrollment grew with the enlargement of schooling, this assumption no longer held. One important effect of the progressive movement was to stimulate educators to revise the high school curriculum. The National Education Association's 1918 report on the reorganization of secondary education, which I referred to earlier, was one aspect of this pattern. However, by the 1950s a new situation had arisen: the high school students of that time, in a more prosperous society and with better-educated parents, aimed to go on to college. They were usually admitted, but within the colleges dissatisfaction arose over their lack of preparation.

This dissatisfaction was voiced in increasing complaints about "progressive education principles," and lax educators. Historian Arthur Bestor and Admiral Hyman Rickover, the nuclear engineer, were among the prominent critics.[24] Rickover, in particular, emphasized the national security implications of "soft" education. Concurrently, university-based physical scientists undertook to promote the public school curriculum reforms they thought were needed.[25] In 1956 they founded the Physical Science Study Committee, which was funded by the National Science Foundation. The committee's goal was to develop and disseminate the new physical science curriculum materials. Though schools were their eventual target, the committee first sought the support of scientists: for instance, at a 1957 planning conference, only five of the forty-eight participants were professional educators.[26]

In October 1957 Russia's Sputnik, the first man-made satellite, circled the Earth. This dramatic event seemed to confirm all the fearful predictions of American intellectual ineptitude. It triggered a strong drive to "harden" the school curriculum. General public support quickly intensified, partly due to persistent and sympathetic publicity in the media. In addition, within a month of the Sputnik orbit the National Defense Education Act was introduced in Congress. The act was intended to supply funds to further science courses and generally improve the quality of high school education, and the ensuing debate revealed a great deal of congressional suspicion toward educators.

At the hearings on the act, one witness quarreled with Congresswoman Edith Greene, who had attempted to defend the judgment of educators: "There is no institution so hallowed," he said, "that it cannot be judged by other people. Whenever you get to the point where you let the individuals in a given calling or profession be their own judges, you're in for trouble."[27] Admiral Rickover's remarks may not have convinced Congresswoman Greene, but they did affect the other representatives; the admiral was invited to testify far longer than any other witness. Eleven months after Sputnik, the president signed the act.

In its first year of operation, the act made $110 million available to schools. This compares to the $10 million used by the Physical Science Study Committee in its first four years. However, the committee got a measurable impact from their dollars, because of public appeal, flexibility, and prestige. For example, 40 percent of the students taking the College Entrance Examination Boards test in physics in 1965-66 had taken a course developed by the committee.[28] It is harder to say what the act accomplished. Its evaluation provisions were so weak that the evaluators could safely say only that the money was spent for educational needs. However, there is general agreement that the high school curriculum has hardened somewhat during the past fifteen years and that high school graduates come to college better prepared, especially in the sciences. For example, between 1948-49 and 1962-63, there was an increase of 595 percent in new mathematics courses offered by schools.[29] Some commentators, however, have contended that the exclusion of educators from planning has resulted in a curriculum that excessively emphasizes cognitive values; a counterreaction may be evolving.

## Civil Rights and Poverty

In 1909 a group of American black and white liberals met in New York City and determined to form an organization to seek fuller equality for American blacks. The organization called itself the National Association for the Advancement of Colored People. It committed itself to the eventual full integration of blacks into American life, as opposed to the separatist doctrines then being espoused by some black spokesmen such as Booker T. Washington. Since the political strength of blacks was weak, the association's strategy evolved toward a continuing campaign of publicity and carefully chosen litigation. The theme underlying the campaign was that the segregation of blacks and denial of their rights constituted unconstitutional conduct.

By the late 1930s, changes finally began to occur as the Supreme Court, in a succession of decisions, outlawed Southern practices that effectively denied the ballot to blacks and began to look more carefully at school segregation practices. By the 1940s, Supreme Court decisions had prohibited segregation in state-supported colleges and graduate schools.

Concurrently, an increasingly sophisticated black and white population was beginning to emerge throughout the country. Gunnar Myrdal's *American Dilemma,* published in 1944, was an eleven-hundred-page definitive study of racial discrimination. It concluded with the proposition that, despite the apparent American acceptance of racial discrimination, our society simultaneously had a widespread, implicit commitment to an "unwritten constitution," which guaranteed all citizens full legal equality. Myrdal suggested that this theme of underlying decency would gradually serve as the intellectual key to diminishing and extinguishing the bonds of segregation.

In 1952, a series of cases testing public school segregation were brought before the Supreme Court by the NAACP. The cases raised two significant educational research questions: the effects of school segregation and the possible effects of desegregation. The court asked the Solicitor General's Office for hard data on the probable consequences of their decision on school operations.[30] The government could not supply the court with any useful data. Psychologist Kenneth B. Clark did submit a memo, as part of the NAACP case, that summarized the meager research touching on segregation and education. The memo was cited in a footnote to the judges' eventual decision; it was the first use of social science in a Supreme Court decision. In 1954, in *Brown v Board of Education*, the court unanimously decided that segregation was unconstitutional, and a denial of equal protection of the law. It ordered the segregated schools to desegregate with "deliberate speed."

The proponents of change were now faced with the problem of policing desegregation, since the *Brown* decision was only binding on the particular schools in the case. But what could they do about the thousands of other segregated schools not in the case? First they needed to find out what was happening, but the U.S. Office of Education, despite the persistent public concern with these issues, kept no data about the extent of segregation or desegregation.

Within a month after the decision, an agency of the Ford

Foundation funded the Southern Educational Reporting Service to collect, analyze, and publish accurate monthly statistics about the extent of Southern school segregation and desegregation. Over the next ten years, the service received $1.8 million from the foundation to finance this task.[31]

In the first years after the *Brown* decision, the issue of Southern desegregation was surrounded by enormous controversy. A number of border states complied quickly and with little tension. But, as one author put it in 1957, the Deep South said, "Never."[32] Thus, though the indices of desegregation for all the Southern and border states practicing de jure segregation were encouraging, the indices for just the former Confederate states were apparently discouraging. In 1964-65, ten years after the decision, the percentage of children integrating public schools in the former Confederate states was only 2.2; in 1965-66, it was 6.1.[33]

These desegregation efforts were not particularly facilitated by the school administrators involved. There is no suggestion that their views were especially racist. However, one nine-city survey concluded that "The school board must face this demand for desegregation with very little help available to it. The school board cannot depend on the superintendent, whose orientation is an invitation to extensive controversy."[34]

Through the years after *Brown* desegregation supporters continuously sought to mobilize public concern, both in and out of the South. Many dramatic episodes on television newscasts, such as black children being mobbed and stoned, helped portray their story. Simultaneously, the evolution of potent, charismatic leaders such as Martin Luther King, the persistence of the courts, and the widespread determination of individual blacks all had an impact.

Some opinion poll statistics show the shift of public opinion about these issues.[35] In 1942 only two out of five whites regarded blacks as equals; almost four out of five did in 1956. Between 1942 and 1963, the proportion of white Americans who favored racially desegregated schools rose from 30 to 63 percent. The proportion of white Southern parents who stated that they would not object to their child attending class with a "few" black children rose from 38 percent in 1963 to 62 percent in 1965. These substantial changes may demonstrate Myrdal's theory of the unwritten constitution; an off-the-cuff racist opinion in a poll or casually considered is one thing, but deliberately supporting a clearly repressive policy is another. The task of the desegregationists was to show the public the ultimate implications of their unconsidered opinions. Essentially, they succeeded.

Support emerged for legislation to enforce the *Brown* decision by denying federal aid to segregated districts. This provision was contained in Title VI of the Civil Rights Act of 1964. That same act authorized the *Equality of Educational Opportunity Survey* (known as the Coleman Report), so that the Office of Education could actually find out what was happening.

Controversies inevitably arose around the enforcement of Title VI and varying interpretations of what constituted compliance with the law. However, the data makes it clear that Southern school segregation patterns based on Jim Crow laws have largely ended. In 1968-69, over 20 percent of the children in public schools in the former Confederate states were integrated.[36] The current percentage is unquestionably higher. (Remember, there is no reason it should attain 100 percent; many pupils simply do not live near members of other races.)

As the civil rights movement proceeded, the national government found its concerns directed at the general issue of poverty in a comparatively affluent society. President Johnson, following President Kennedy's lead, authorized legislation to conduct a "War on Poverty." The Economic Opportunity Act was passed in 1964 to carry out this effort. Inevitably, it included a number of measures relating to education for impoverished youths. Rather than changing or enlarging existing school programs, the antipoverty administrators and legislators, who were comparatively free from educator pressures, attempted to develop supplementary or independent educational programs. Thus, they organized the Job Corps, which trained disadvantaged youths at new federally managed or financed residential centers, and financed Head Start, which provided funds to agencies (often public schools) to conduct preschool programs for children from poor families.

The haste and strategic uncertainty underlying the operation, led to inevitable confusion. While the Head Start program was relatively popular, within a year the six-week summer program was generally abandoned in favor of promoting year-round Head Start programs to give more intensive help to fewer children. Nevertheless, controversy continues over whether the program is achieving its goals and, indeed, what its goals are.

The Job Corps, too, ran into trouble as the complex logistic and organizational problems of the hastily built enterprise began to appear. A high proportion of the Corps members were trained at so-called urban centers managed by private contractors. The following language, from an evaluation of these centers by the General Accounting Office, is pertinent:

> The vocational programs at the urban centers were structured to provide vocational training in a number of areas. Although at the time of our review, Job Corps was in the process of establishing uniform teaching objectives for vocational areas in many urban centers, it had not prescribed uniform criteria for graduation from either men's or women's centers. Therefore, such criteria were established by each of the centers. About 40% of the Corps members terminated from the Centers reviewed were classified as graduates. There was no assurance that the criteria established by the centers were comparable. Moreover, the centers did not always adhere to the criteria established and, in some instances, did not maintain the records necessary to determine whether Corps members had met the criteria. Consequently, a number of Corps members were classified as graduates, although they had not developed the attributes for employment in the area of their vocational training.[37]

The poverty and civil rights concerns of the times also spilled over into the U.S. Office of Education and brought about the passage of the Elementary and Secondary Education Act of 1965. The act (see chapter 5 for a discussion of its evaluation provisions) provided over $1 billion annually to schools with high concentrations of students from low-income families to help the schools offer compensatory education to the disadvantaged pupils. The new programs were usually conducted as extensions of the traditional school program. Continuing civil rights agitation and these patterns of legislation eventually stimulated the Northern stage of the civil rights movement. Unlike the Southern phase, the goals of the Northern effort were the product of only a brief refinement process. It proved impractical simply to adopt the Southern goal of desegregation: it is one thing to abolish laws that compel segregation; it is another to pass new laws—in unimagined modes—that compel integration where races are geographically remote.

Lacking a clear, traditional goal, and under intense pressure for results, the Northern civil rights movement has passed through several stages. Many of these stages have existed and now exist simultaneously. We have had stages such as *black power within neighborhoods*, e.g., the New York City dispute over school decentralization; *traditional political power to blacks* through the electoral process; *black power through defiance and perhaps violence,* e.g., the Black Panthers and the Watts riots; and *desegregationist activities* where they are practicable, e.g., school desegregation via bussing in communities such as Berkeley, California. The success of all these measures has been slow and uncertain, though blacks can clearly elect black candidates where they have the numbers. However, elections often do not represent quick, dramatic change.

Our society is far too close to these complex developments for any conclusive evaluation to be made. Still, some discussion of the educational significance of the changes is necessary. In the South, the desegregationists have made important progress toward their goal (part of a widespread change process). As a result of these successful desegregation efforts, will their children learn better? One cannot say definitely, but there are some research findings supporting socioeconomic desegregation as a mode of improving schooling. It's also not irrelevant that the themes of the desegregationists are similar to those of the nineteenth-century common school movement: formation of a "common" school. In some ways, then, historical precedents also support the logic of their goals.

In the North, the issue of schools and race is not so clear. Money is being spent, and some things are being tried, but the urgent pressure for results is not always productive. In addition, as black researcher Kenneth Clark implied, the whole effort is affected by the need to deal with the pathology of the ghetto. For example, the phrase "local control" is a highly satisfying rallying cry. But while we can define a desegregated school simply by counting pupils from different races, definition of a locally controlled school is much more problematic. Does it mean all black staff? Does it mean particular administrative arrangements? What is a locality? What is the relationship between the locality that uses funds and other localities that supply part of the funds? Thus, emotionally satisfying strategies have been adopted that may be poor foundations for long-range gains.

The education program of the OEO and Title I have both had mixed effects. They have demonstrated that we know very little about improving education and that more money may not be the major need for pupils from either poor or better-off families. Though their total proportion of research and evaluation expenditures has not been extremely high—perhaps 2 or 3 percent of all their funds went into such efforts—it is much higher than in traditional education patterns. Thus, the combination of these new research investments and the limited success of the new programs has given a special impetus to evaluation and feedback approaches in general. (After all, the new programs, which did not evaluate well, are not so different than the old, unevaluated ones.) Apparently, Head Start helped give a strong boost to early childhood education in general, though the educational value of such costly programs for nonpoor children is problematic.

## A Recapitulation

The basic process of educational macrochange is an important theme in this book. Therefore, let us try and extract some general principles from the preceding episodes. I will list a series of topics, and discuss the events and principles that seem pertinent.

### Lay Leadership

Lay leaders—politicians, journalists, judges, admirals, scholars, civil rights spokesmen, and scientists—played a critical role in these changes. The laymen were not always right: the principal segregationists were also laymen. However, their record is still impressive.

But this conclusion conflicts with the lead remark in the chapter, that lay leaders often do not seem to play a large or constructive role in contemporary school management. How can that be explained? I suggest that the distinction is between leadership in times of tranquility and leadership in times of tension and changes, i.e., between microchange and macrochange. For example, in World War II, one military unit had two sets of noncommissioned officers; one set served when the unit was encamped and out of combat, the other set assumed authority when the unit went into action; the commander and, presumably, the men understood that different skills were needed for combat leadership and for day-to-day encampment. Both were essential to maintain the unit, but they were different.

Similarly, citizens who "intervene" in microchange and oppose or push minor innovations—e.g., new reading systems or ungraded classes—are often not of the same caliber as those who lead desegregation campaigns, plan national surveys, develop settlement houses, or direct the common school movement. Even the lay followers of these major leaders are of a different stature than the microchangers. To put it another way, assume a school system where an administrator has attained an advanced degree and successfully passed from teacher to principal to assistant superintendent to superintendent. There are important talents implied in this progression, but they are focused on system maintenance, not system change. It is unlikely that such internal leadership can promote important change without powerful lay stimulation.

But let me explain why day-to-day citizen concern with schools is often unconstructive. The simple truth is that most school policy debates are conducted at a rather low conceptual level. For instance, they often focus on whether the school budget should be increased by 2 or 4 percent in order to change or maintain a pupil-teacher ratio or pay for a new building. Debates arise on the pros and cons. However, the research we have surveyed has not yet found a very important relationship between such changes and pupil learning; in other words, if the budget were not raised, and the ratio shifted from 30:1 to 32:1, there's no evidence (and this is one of the most researched questons in education) that it would make a great difference. Of course, the public does not know of the research, but they feel they are not being given a full picture. They are right.

On the other hand, in the macrochange debates we can see that important issues were in the open and were clearly stated: what kind of a country do we want; what does our constitution mean; shall we have uninformed voters; how shall immigrants become part of America? In the long run, such issues and statements elevate and intensify the overall level of public debate. People are forced to think things through.

However, the more typical pattern of obfuscation and nondisclosure means that usually the real issue is not before the public. Hence the notoriously low proportion of voter turnout in most school board elections. This pattern is not necessarily displeasing to administrators or elected school board members, since they have been socialized to such an environment. But in exchange for this quietude (Don't rock the boat!), they must accept comparative dormancy, plus the underlying ignorance and suspicion of the general public. Then, when some issue does excite the public, two currents arise: latent hostility is translated into open anger, and powerful new lay leaders are forced to intervene and turn the crisis into constructive change. Conservative administrators then say: "Look how nasty these people are. Weren't we wise to try and keep them out?" They said it about Mann, Rice, Riis, King, Rickover, the Supreme Court, etc. The attitude is nicely exemplified by the title of an article in a school administrators' periodical: "How to Start and Stop Citizens' Committees."[38] One section of the article was called "How to Get Rid of a Committee." More farsighted administrators may say something else about citizen involvement: "We're finally getting the reserves and help we need, as well as having the problem clearly aired. Now we can get on with the job."

In sum, I suggest there are three levels of public opinion about education: (a) the opinion of the typical school board member and his associates—mildly benign and supportive; (b) what I call the latent but mutable opinion of most members of the public—suspicious, but withdrawn; and (c) the farsighted opinion of major public leaders and thinkers, which can often become public opinion through the course of events and the conduct of the leaders. It is this third level of public opinion and leaders that is the force for constructive education macrochange. This third level is represented by the leaders of the Southern civil rights struggle, who, when three out of five white Americans thought blacks were inferior, sensed that these were not "hard" numbers. But men who are motivated by an underlying fear of the public will not attain this level of perception.

### Time

Education macrochange takes time. The common school reformers, the progressives, and the desegregationists all took from twenty-five to fifty years to move from some identifiable beginning point to culmination. The curriculum reformers moved faster, but they were not so much starting anew as reviving older education themes that had never completely expired. But the time lag should not surprise us. Education comprises over 2 million teachers and administrators and 50 million students, and consumes over 8 percent of our gross national product. This vast system is understandably slow to change.

One cause of the delay is that the development of an effective change strategy is a complex matter. The NAACP did not immediately know it wanted to start court suits against school desegregation. Mann and his allies engaged in continuous refining – developing the concept of the normal school or teacher's college, studying European education patterns, etc.–as they promoted their goals. It is possible that the progressives' main problem was that they never took the time to settle on a focused strategy to implement their rhetoric and stimulating ideas. This problem may also be troubling Northern blacks.

The need for persistence is also supported by experience abroad. Charles Silberman, discussing the infant school reforms in England, contended that they had been in the process of development for perhaps fifty years. Even with this developmental time, Silberman concluded that in 1970 the reforms were in full operation only in perhaps 25 percent of the schools where they could be applied. All concerned believed this incremental process had greatly strengthened the quality of the reforms. One researcher said, "It has perhaps helped that the English reforms came more slowly than [the progressive movement] in the United States."[39]

When successful, changes tend to follow the S curve usually associated with innovation dissemination. That is, there is a long period of slight change (while development, planning, and persuasion is underway) and then, as in Southern desegregation, a relatively sudden burst of wide change adoption. Finally, the few remaining nonadoptors eventually come in. One economist, talking about successful economic development, put it this way:

> It is essential to recognize the time it takes to test the knowledge acquired, or thought to be acquired. How often can the failure of so many large-scale agricultural projects, the high cost of so many industrial projects be traced to the impatience with the length of time it takes to accumulate the necessary knowledge? . . . . There is evidence that projects that start small, and feel their way by experiment grow faster, become bigger, and create more income and employment than projects that start too big from the beginning.[40]

## Strategy

A major challenge for any change movement is to develop definable, constructive, and generally acceptable goals, such as: pass a law requiring localities to provide free elementary education to all; prohibit de jure school segregation; have all high schools offer a physics course covering certain topics; etc. Careful definition of goals permits all the scattered followers to work toward the same end, and to tell whether they are getting there. At the same time, it is a vital recruiting tool. One reason supporters join up is that the leaders seem to know what they are doing. Probably one cause for the end of the social reconstructionists in the progressive education movement was that no one could see where they were going; in the longer run such imprecision corrodes recruitment and support.

Definition presents both intellectual and emotional problems. Intellectually, the determination of appropriate goals is a complex task: what concrete, recognizable step will be worth a long campaign? Emotionally, there is always a tendency to abandon one remote, arduous goal and pursue a new, more promising prospect without considering whether progress toward the new goal will really be faster or whether the goal is better defined. For instance, while Mann was secretary to the board of education in Massachusetts, he was under constant pressure to become involved in the abolitionist movement, another great issue of the times. However, despite his abolitionist sympathies, he refused; he felt such public commitment would seriously weaken his effectiveness as an education reformer, because in that movement he also had to work with antiabolitionists. After fourteen years, however, he was satisfied that the major work had been done, and he left his position as secretary to run for Congress. There he undermined his budding political career by deliberately taking a firm abolitionist position.[41]

### New Institutions

The reformers sought or created institutional bases for their continuing effort: the Massachusetts State Board of Education, the NAACP, the Progressive Education Association, the Physical Science Study Committee, the Office of Economic Opportunity. These bases were removed from the control of traditional schoolmen and got their funds from other sources. The maintenance of these independent bases was essential to their enterprises.

### Publicity

The reformers usually included skilled, tenacious, perceptive, and eloquent spokesmen, such as Mann, Rice, and Rickover. In many ways, they were essentially publicists. They often crossed lances with traditional schoolmen, appealed to the public for support, and did not come out losers. The movements often created or captured their own periodicals, for feedback and propaganda purposes: *The Common School Journal, The Forum, The Southern Education Reporting Service,* Mann's fourteen annual reports, the NAACP journal *The Crisis,* and *The Progressive Educator.*

In addition, in our own time, the Southern desegregationists made skillful use of television, via demonstrations that dramatically portrayed the character of their repression. But while school desegregation can be simply characterized, it is difficult to dramatize a locally controlled school in the media. So the character of the proposed reform can affect its visibility and, ultimately, its public support and success.

## Footnotes

1. Gallup International, *School Board Members' Reactions to Educational Innovations* (Princeton, N.J.: 1966).

2. Sources for this discussion are: R. Freeman Butts & Lawrence A. Cremin, *A History of Education in American Culture* (New York: Holt, Reinhart & Winston, 1953); Ellwood P. Cubberley, *Readings in Public Education in the United States* (Boston: Houghton Mifflin, 1920); idem, *Public Education in the United States* (Boston: Houghton Mifflin, 1934); David B. Tyack, *Turning Points in American Educational History* (Waltham, Mass.: Blaisdell Publishing, 1967); L. H. Tharp, *Until Victory* (Boston: Little, Brown & Co., 1953); Michael B. Katz, *The Irony of Early School Reform* (Cambridge: Harvard University Press, 1968).

3. Tyack, *Turning Points,* p. 124.

4. Tharp, *Until Victory,* p. 143.

5. Ibid., p. 148.

6. Cubberley, *Public Education,* p. 155.

7. Ibid., p. 195.

8. Tyack, *Turning Point,* p. 155.

9. Cubberley, *Readings,* p. 560.

10. Cubberley, *Public Education,* p. 167.

11. Katz, *Irony,* p. 36.

12. Tyack, *Turning Points,* p. 125.

13. Tharp, *Until Victory,* p. 203.

14. Lawrence H. Cremin, *The Transformation of the School* (New York: Vintage Books, 1961), p. 6.

15. Sol Cohen, *Progressives and Urban School Reform: The*

*Public Education Association of New York City* (New York: Bureau of Publications, Teachers College, Columbia University, 1964).

16. Jacob A. Riis, *The Battle with the Slum* (New York: Macmillan Co., 1902) pp. 404, 410.

17. Cremin, *Transformation,* p. 88.

18. J. Dewey, *Democracy and Education* (New York: Macmillan Co., 1916), p. 416.

19. Patricia Albjerg Graham, *Progressive Education: From Arcady to Academe* (New York: Teachers College Press, 1967), p. 56.

20. C. A. Bowers, *The Progressive Educator and the Depression: The Radical Years* (New York: Random House, 1969).

21. George S. Counts, *Dare the Schools Build a New Social Order* (New York: John Day, 1932).

22. Cremin, *Transformation,* p. 348.

23. Harold Rugg & George S. Counts, "A Critical Appraisal of Current Methods of Curriculum-Making," in *Curriculum-Making: Past and Present, Twenty-Sixth Yearbook of the National Society for the Study of Education, Part I* (Bloomington, Ill.: Public School Publishing Co., 1926), pp. 438-439.

24. Arthur Bestor, *Educational Wastelands* (Urbana: University of Illinois Press, 1953); Hyman Rickover, *Education and Freedom* (New York: E. P. Dutton, 1959). Speeches between 1956 and 1958.

25. Paul E. Marsh & Ross A. Gortner, *Federal Aid to Science Education, Two Programs* (Syracuse, N.Y.: Syracuse University Press, 1963).

26. Marsh & Gortner, *Federal Aid,* p. 32.

27. U.S. Congress, House, Committee on Labor, *Hearings on H.R. 10381, H.R. 10278 (and similar bills),* Part 2, 85th Cong., 2d Sess., 1958, p. 979.

28. Raymond E. Thompson, *A Survey of the Teaching of Physics in Secondary Schools;* William Kastrinos, *A Survey of the Teaching of Biology in Secondary Schools;* Frank J. Fornoff, *A Survey of the Teaching of Chemistry in Secondary Schools* (all, Princeton, N.J.: Educational Testing Service, 1969).

29. Kimball Wiles, "Contrasts in Strategies for Change," in *Strategies for Curriculum Change* (Washington, D.C.: Association for Supervision and Curriculum Development, 1965).

30. Catherine Caldwell, "Social Science as Ammunition," *Psychology Today* 4, no. 4 (September 1970): 38-44.

31. *Southern Education Report,* June 1969.

32. John Barlow Martin, *The Deep South Says Never* (New York: Ballentine Books, 1957).

33. Abbott L. Ferriss, *Indicators of Trends in American Education* (New York: Russell Sage Foundation, 1969).

34. Robert L. Crain, *The Politics of School Desegregation* (Garden City, N.Y.: Doubleday & Co., Anchor Books, 1969).

35. Thomas F. Pettigrew, "Racially Separate or Together," *Journal of Social Issues* 25 (1969): 43-69.

36. Ferriss, *Indicators,* p. 204.

37. U.S. Congress, Senate, Committee on Labor & Public Welfare, House, Committee on Education and Labor, *Report by the Comptroller General of the United States, Review of Economic Opportunity Programs,* 91st Cong., 1st Sess., 1969.

38. Otis A. Crosby, "How to Start and Stop Citizens' Committees," *Nations Schools* 75, no. 5 (November 1965): 50, 51.

39. Silberman, *Crisis,* pp. 211, 283.

40. W. F. Stolper, *Planning Without Facts* (Cambridge: Harvard University Press, 1966), p. 11.

41. Tharp, *Until Victory.*

# 7

# Mass Media: Poor Reporting

Newspapers need not become graduate schools, but neither should they produce the kind of shabby analysis they do of city budgets and school reading scores.

Gerald Grant[1]

The mass media—particularly newspapers and magazines—are the major means of presenting the public with nonintuitive feedback about schools. As suggested by Figure 1, this proposition simply states a commonsense principle: adults learn about most new developments relating to indices and statistics through their newspapers and magazines; television is not well adapted or oriented to present new nonintuitive indices, and adults are not generally likely to take school courses focusing on these issues.

It is true that there is a substantial number of popularly written books promoting education reform. However, almost none of this literature—with the notable exception of Charles Silberman's *Crisis in the Classroom*—gives serious attention to the question of output accountability. But even if books did affect public perspectives toward accountability, the new perspectives would fade quickly, if the daily press did not reflect them in the issues it reported or in the questions asked by reporters or editorial writers. So let us attempt to assess the character of press interest in accountability to see where it is and where it may go.

## Basic Press Patterns

Essentially, American newspapers are not especially interested in school accountability via output data. For example, there is a national Education Writers Association, with over 600 members, nearly half of whom are active writers, principally reporters. The association holds an annual conference, publishes a periodic newsletter, distributes a clipsheet of stories or articles, and attempts to raise the standards of education reporting. However, the writers are apparently indifferent to accountability. In general, their stories focus on short-range, conflict-oriented education issues (often of a peripheral nature). When they examine questions in greater depth, the matter of supporting statistics or the lack of such statistics is still usually slighted. In 1971 the association gave awards for the following eleven stories on elementary or high schools.[2] Their perspectives are suggested in their titles.

"Black, White Students Swap Visits"

"The Old South Tries Again" (independent schools to avoid desegregation)

"Los Angeles Fights School Vandalism"

"Can People Power Save the System" (school decentralization)

"Parent Participation Means Parent Power"

"From 'Desert of Despair' to Oasis of Learning" (through changed school policies)

"Teachers Aides Spur Youngsters to Learn Faster"

"The Welcome Mat Isn't Always Out" (use of school volunteers)

"Tutors Give Young a Helping Hand" (to education)

"When Citizens Get Involved In Their Schools"

"Boom in Mail-Order Schooling Marked By Dubious Practices"

In addition, eighty-four articles in the association clipsheets between 1968 and 1971 were randomly selected and analyzed.[3] Only four of these exemplary articles made serious references to statistics. Two of the four discussed the wide-ranging controversies about school use of IQ scores and the issue of nature versus nurture. A third was an informative presentation about the effect of school desegregation on student learning. The fourth article, about P.S. 192, a ghetto elementary school in New York City, is reproduced below:

*Principle Overcomes All Disadvantages*
*to Elevate Standards in Harlem*

A strange thing is happening in P.S. 192 in New York's Harlem. The children are reading and writing and doing arithmetic as well as, or better than, children in any public school in America.

The experts are astonished. There just seems to be no reason why the children in P.S. 192 are not one to three years behind grade level as children are in ghetto schools in other large cities.

In fact, P.S. 192 should be worse off than the average ghetto school.

It is overcrowded. It is in an area infested with narcotics addicts, criminals and desperately poor families. The enrollment is equally distributed among Negroes, Puerto Ricans and recent arrivals from the Dominican Republic.

There are formidable language problems. The children come to school hungry. All other factors blamed for the continuing decline of American urban education are present.

The difference is Dr. Seymour Gang.

This soft-spoken, soft-looking man was made principal of P.S. 192 six years ago, some say as "punishment" for being an embarrassingly accurate critic of the New York school system.

His exile has proven to be even more embarrassing to the Board of Education and the administration of the system.

*Standard Set*

When he started at the school, the usual pattern prevailed. The children were far behind in the basic skills and were falling further behind the longer they stayed in school.

"Basically," he explained, "it's simple. I just told the teachers and the parents right off that their children were going to perform at grade level and that I was not going to listen to any excuses for them not performing at grade level."

Dr. Gang spoke as he plunged along through the school corridors going from one classroom to another. He spends from 9 A.M. until 3 P.M. in classrooms. Paper work gets done from 3 P.M. until 8 P.M.

"We don't have any talking typewriters, or computers here," he said. "We just insist that every teacher teach and that every child learn."

He strides through an open classroom door.

"Hi, Miss Alpert," he says to the young teacher. "You look pretty today. Doesn't Miss Alpert look pretty today, children?"

*Teachers Screened*

There is laughter and waving and "hiya, Dr. Gang." He stays half an hour, listening to the teacher and occasionally explaining a point in the lesson with a joke or a story. His presence has brought a quality of excitement to the classroom.

Out in the corridor again, he continues:

"It was tough in the beginning. We got a lot of nonsense from downtown."

Dr. Gang said he had "booted out" teachers who would not or could not produce what he demanded: grade level performance. He rejected others sent to the school by the administration.

"I decided I would rather have a vacancy than a poor teacher or a teacher who doesn't understand what we are up against here," he said.

Gradually teachers interested in what was going on at P.S. 192 began coming to see him.

The school administration fought for a time. Principals could not be permitted to take over responsibility for assigning teachers. There would be chaos.

But Dr. Gang had won the confidence of the parents and others in the neighborhood. They promised to back him with any pressure needed.

*"Parent Power"*

As you walk through the school, there is clear evidence of what Dr. Gang calls "parent power." Adults help teachers herd children into classrooms, supervise play outside and quietly are helping out in corridors and classrooms all through the four-story building.

"The key is reading," he said. "We broke up classes and did a lot of shifting so we could free some teachers to work only with our poor readers in small groups.

"We converted closets, dressing rooms and every space we could find into special reading rooms. These teachers are great. They work hard and they work long hours and they believe in these kids."

A bell rings and the children pour from classrooms into the corridor. A tiny Negro girl runs to him and takes his hand.

"Hello, Glorie. How are you today?"

She says nothing, but smiles. He reaches into an inside coat pocket and brings out a pretzel stick. The child accepts it eagerly, grins at him and leaves.

As he walks through the busy halls, more pretzels are handed out, children are picked up and hugged, heads are patted and there are smiles and waves and greetings all around.

He puts an arm around a middle-aged graying woman. "This is Millie," he says. "Greatest third-grade teacher in the history of the world."

She tries to cut off a smile. "Oh, go away. Don't you have anything better to do?"

"That teacher," he said later, "told me she never had a chance to really teach before. You have to let them teach. A big part of a principal's job is getting things off teachers' backs so they can teach."

A young Negro boy named Mike is waiting for Dr. Gang when he enters his office. The boy is thin, his clothing shabby, and he speaks with a serious stammer.

Dr. Gang speaks with the boy at length and walks to the door with him.

"You got any money?" The boy shakes his head. Dr. Gang pokes around in a worn wallet and pulls out three dollar bills.

"Get yourself a place to stay tonight and come back here at 2 o'clock tomorrow. If I'm not here, you wait. All right? We'll take care of things tomorrow."

Mike leaves and Dr. Gang tosses a pencil into a wastebasket. "Bastards," he says softly.

Mike left P.S. 192 a year ago, Dr. Gang explained. His parents have deserted him and he sleeps at the homes of friends or any place he can find.

The junior high school he transferred to decided he was a "troublemaker" and he was told not to come back.

"They will keep him on the rolls, see, and if something comes up, they will just say he's a truant and have him arrested. Beautiful, right? Does anybody give a damn? Do you give a damn?"

Because Dr. Gang does "give a damn," his school is a bright spot in the bleak landscape of failure and despair that is American urban education.

In the public schools of the cities visited and of many other cities for which statistics are available, the children—particularly the poor children—are being cheated, abused and neglected.

Many emerge from 12 years of public education academically crippled. They go into the adult world with the reading and arithmetic skills of small children.

More than a third drop out from 10th grade to graduation—thousands never reach 10th grade.

Countless thousands attended classes in buildings more than 50 years old—drafty, non-fireproof buildings scarcely fit for habitation, much less education.

Crowding and large class sizes are commonplace.

Segregation—racial, economic and social—is severe and increasing.

There are not enough books and materials, not enough teachers and not enough money.

And the bitter result of all of these things is that the children are not learning.

All across the country thoughtful persons are saying that the schools need a massive infusion of money, more and better-trained teachers and a host of other things.

But what the schools need most of all is for more persons to "give a damn" about what happens to the children.[4]

As one can see, the question of whether the children in P.S. 192 are learning better than similar students in other schools is the crux of the article. The article does say "the children are reading and writing and doing arithmetic as well as or better than any other school in America." But no statistics or education researchers are cited to back up that crucial point.

The reading score assertion in the article is provocative, but is it correct? The students in the best schools in America are sometimes reading, on the average, two or three years ahead of national norms. On the other hand, ghetto school children are sometimes two or three years behind. Thus, the literal language of the article "as well as *any* other school" would mean that the P.S. 192 children are four to six years ahead of their ghetto counterparts. Is this what the article intends?

The assertion raises further questions. For instance, is it possible that the P.S. 192 students, even though they are minority groups, are not "typical" ghetto children; perhaps some subtle self-selection process has affected who comes to P.S. 192 and who chooses to stay. At least some ghetto school administrators have told me that more-motivated families, over time, tend to drift into the neighborhood of the better-reputed schools, while the less-organized families drift out, because of the performance pressures the schools put on their children. But that is a matter for careful socioeconomic studies, not administrative speculation.

Finally, as the preceding sections of this book have made evident, output measures are subject to numberless interpretations and, sometimes, manipulations. If any corporation contended its profit rate was several times higher than that of its competitors, perhaps the first people we would question would be its accountants—even though business accounting practices are fairly well defined. In the case of schools, the matter of superior performance may be reported without even a discussion of data interpretation or credibility—even though school output statistics are far less developed than accounting practices.

None of this is said to criticize the principal or his school; it may be a fine operation. But even while admiring the energy and dedication of the principal and staff, it is necessary to have expert assistance to appraise the results. Without such counsel, a reporter cannot really offer a nonintuitive appraisal. Of course, the misleading effects of such articles extend beyond the P.S. 192 situation. Such articles generally encourage other school administrators and reporters to accept loose assertions and uninformed appraisals in other education controversies. In sum, only one of the eighty-four randomly selected clipsheet articles directly dealt with output, and that article was not well focused.

These conclusions about the overall nature of educational reporting are not too surprising, especially if we examine data about who the education reporters are. One recent survey of the membership of the Education Writers Association disclosed that 47 percent of the reporters had been undergraduate majors in journalism or English and another 17 percent had no undergraduate degree.[5] Among the undergraduate degree holders, only 2 percent had majored in sociology or social science, and other 2 percent majored in education. The others had degrees in a wide variety of disciplines: political science, history, psychology, etc. There is also considerable turnover among education reporters; over 50 percent of the members had been education reporters for less than five years. This pattern of brief experience and prose-oriented training does not equip the reporters to see or report education events in nonintuitive terms.

## Some Examples

In general, the press is interested in making achievement score data available to the public. The New York City reading scores were first made public as a result of the questions of a *New York Times* reporter. The following excerpts from a *Washington Post* editorial of 18 April 1967 are reflective of newspaper positions on this matter:

The Silent Disaster

The collapse of public education in Washington is now evident. Reading scores reported in this newspaper show that fully one-third of the city schools' pupils have fallen two years or more behind their proper grade level. These scores mean that more than 40,000 children, still going to school every day, are being prepared for careers as illiterates. For one-third of its children, the Washington school system does not work. The wretched outcasts of the basic track demonstrate precisely how little a child can learn in these classrooms; the average reading score for the ninth grade basic track is at the third-grade level. The School Board owes it to the public to release the class achievement scores, school by school. The variations in these scores will show that the blame for bad schools cannot be assigned to the children, or to the neighborhoods.

The more important shortcomings of media coverage of school accountability issues arise over interpretive reporting. The policy questions presented by the scores are different from school issues which newspapers have considered in the past. It often appears that reporters have missed the point. The following article from the 25 November 1969 *New York Times* is typical:

Pupils' Progress Not Tied to Funds, Report Says

Little correlation has been found between the amount of money spent on a child in a predominantly Negro and Puerto Rican school and his rate of achievement, according to a study of New York City public schools conducted by the First National City Bank.

This "raises the question of whether or not continued indiscriminate funding 'will' in and of itself necessarily increase educational output proportionately," the report said.

It was published in a 42-page, illustrated volume distributed yesterday at a luncheon in one of the bank's private diningrooms in its building at 399 Park Avenue.

The study, which concentrates more on analyzing problems than on suggesting remedies, is the fourth in a series of research reports on the metropolitan area prepared by the First National City Bank. One executive described it as the bank's "contribution" to the city. Another put it this way: "What's good for New York is good for the bank."

According to the report, the per-student costs in 150 of the city's schools where 90 percent or more of the enrollment was black or Puerto Rican in the 1967-1968 school year ranged from $529 to $1,560. The figures take into account all the school's expenditures, from teachers' salaries to school equipment.

But whatever the per-student cost, the improvement rates of students on standard reading tests were about equal in these schools, according to the report.

The study was completed before Election Day, but was not released until now so that its findings could not be used for political purposes.

It found that predominantly Puerto Rican schools appear to have about the same scholastic scores as predominantly black schools.

Last year, fewer than half of the pupils in the city's schools were reading at or above their grade level, as defined by standard nationwide tests. Slightly more than one of every three fifth-graders was reading one or more years below grade-level. One in seven was reading two or more years below grade-level.

As in the rest of the country, children from predominantly white middle-class neighborhoods scored better on reading tests than children from lower social and economic levels.

The report described in the article is a competent analysis, attractively presented.[6] The article does not discuss the reaction of school officials, politicians, or community figures to the report. It appears that the reporter went to the luncheon, perhaps examined the report, and wrote the article. But the report implicitly raises profound questions about the largest budget item for the largest municipal budget in the world. The article ignores these questions. There were no follow-up articles on the matter.

Naturally, one might wonder how much news potential is in school accountability anyway: where is the action? The following two articles are not typical. Still, they suggest how aggressive interpretative reporting can transform apparently mundane issues into news.

Nixon School Report a Challenge
by William K. Stevens

The thinking that undergirds the educational reform message sent to Congress by

President Nixon on Tuesday challenges the conventional view on how to improve the nation's schools.

That view holds that if more money is poured into the schools, education is bound to get better.

The counterthinking holds that in schools as they presently exist, broadly stated, there is no cause-and-effect relationship between how much money is spent and what a child learns; that other factors—many of them unknown—determine what and how children learn.

It is further argued that many schools are failing in their mission despite higher expenditures, and that the key to better education must therefore lie elsewhere than in mass infusions of funds.

These views grow directly out of the conclusions of an extensive social science study, the 1966 Coleman Report, named after its chief author, Dr. James S. Coleman, a professor of social relations at Johns Hopkins University.

The President's message "says a lot of things I might have said myself," the 43-year-old Dr. Coleman said yesterday in a telephone conversation.

The Coleman Report was identified in a telephone interview this week by Daniel Patrick Moynihan, counselor to the President, as having provided the intellectual underpinnings of the education message.

In the message, Mr. Nixon proposed to hold the line on Federal funds for elementary and secondary education while stepping up efforts to reform the means of instruction. His proposed National Institute of Education would take the experimental lead in those efforts.

Dr. Coleman, who became intrigued with the workings of public education when he undertook a sociological study of 10 high schools in Illinois in 1957, was commissioned by the United States Office of Education in February, 1965, to conduct an Equality of Educational Opportunity survey.

The survey was mandated by Congress as part of the Civil Rights Act of 1964.

"Our job was to design a survey that would test conceptions of educational opportunity," Dr. Coleman said. "One of these had to do with the differences in inputs (such as money) between schools as they related to differences in the effectiveness of schools."

"We expected to find some fairly straightforward relationships between school inputs and pupil achievement."

However, the results turned out to be a surprise.

After surveying nearly a million pupils in 6,000 schools in the fall of 1965, the Johns Hopkins team found that family background and social environment were the basic determinants of how well a child did in school.

The team found that whatever the amount of money spent on a given child, the schools as currently operated were unable to modify significantly the intellectual patterns established in the home.

In the case of a slum child, for example, this meant that his chances of learning to read were quite limited, even though large amounts of money might be devoted to his education.

When published in July, 1966, the findings were greeted among conventional educators by attitudes ranging from indifference to hostility. Many others in the academic community were fascinated by them.

In the Cambridge, Mass., community, the Coleman findings became a magnet to physicists, lawyers, doctors and engineers—men who ordinarily paid little attention to such matters.

"Word got around that no one knows much about education; that it was not easy to understand, but hard," recalled Mr. Moynihan, who as director of the M.I.T. Harvard Joint Center for Urban Studies set up a small seminar in late 1966 to re-examine the Coleman Report.

"The whole subject (of schooling) had been moribund because it had been thought to be easy; and guys who run on a fast track are not interested in something easy. But by the end of the academic year, our seminar had grown to about 75 professors—became a conference, really. We had the whole top floor of the Harvard Faculty Club."

The upshot of this intense re-examination by top-flight academics was vindication for the Coleman Report. An 800-page re-evaluation upholding the Coleman conclusions, written by Mr. Moynihan and Frederick Mosteller, a Harvard mathematician, is to be published next fall.

Critics of the President's education message hold that it is a handy rationalization for Mr. Nixon's drive to reduce Federal expenditures generally.

But Dr. James E. Allen, Jr., the United States Commissioner of Education, whose concern about the financial plight of schools is well known, supports the basic thinking in the message, although he adds a substantial qualification:

"You can't put children in a deep-freeze while you experiment," he said in a telephone interview. "You've got to keep the system going, and this costs more money."

But he recalled that in New York City in 1961 it was predicted that if school expenditures were doubled within eight years, the pupils' reading deficiencies would disappear. Expenditures doubled in six years, but the reading scores continued to drop.

The conclusion he draws from that experience dovetails neatly with the Coleman challenge to the conventional view: "Doing more of the same thing hasn't proved to be the answer in the schools," Dr. Allen said.[7]

* * * * *

### Principals Face an Acid Test: The 'Pay for Performance' Plan
by John P. Corr

The public school principals were assembled Tuesday to hear about a new salary system that would require them to do their jobs properly if they wanted salary increases. Most of them disliked the idea. They would rather continue to get automatic pay raises whether they are any good at their jobs or not.

In the midst of the uproar centering on the Simon Gratz High School expansion, the announcement of the new system received insufficient attention.

It is one of the most important recent developments in American urban education. It could make basic changes in the way that schools are run and the kind of people who are hired to run them.

It introduces to education the "pay for performance" principle that is basic to almost every other American enterprise, with the exception of government.

The principals, or most of them, resented the idea that anyone would presume to evaluate the degree of difficulty of their jobs and suggest that they be paid accordingly.

Also, they resent the idea that they should be required to meet specific goals, even if they have a hand in setting the goals.

It must be noted that not all principals are against the plan. The good ones, like Walter Scott of West Philadelphia High School and Marcus Foster of Gratz are too busy doing a good job to worry about whether they are being evaluated.

Superintendent of Schools, Dr. Mark R. Shedd, asked the management consulting firm of Edward N. Hay and Associates to study the administrative set-up of the school system and try to make some sense out of the bureaucratic Disneyland.

Representatives of the firm, particularly its brilliant young researcher, Bernard Ingster, then touched off a severe epidemic of anxiety syndromes by asking people what they were doing during the work day.

The researchers then compared school jobs to similar jobs in industry, government and other large school systems, computed competitive salaries and recommended a new salary set-up for the principals.

The real fun begins next July when Hay will describe the jobs of superintendents, directors and other administrators and say how much these people would be earning for doing the same thing elsewhere.

The administrators, of course, will raise the same cry as the principals are raising: "Nobody can evaluate my job."

The heart of the new pay plan for principals is the matter of setting goals. These would be set at the beginning of the year by the principal, his supervisor, representatives of parents and curriculum specialists.

For example, goals might include a specific degree of increase in pupils' ability to read as compared with national norms, or a reduction in the number of racial incidents in the school or more parent interest as reflected by visits to the school or increased attendance at home and school meetings.

The principal would have considerable say in determining which goals are realistic.

Then, at the end of the year, the principal's performance is measured by how well the school moved toward its goals. If the goals are exceeded, the principal could earn a pay raise which would exceed the annual raises now being given, which amount to about 6 percent per year.

However, if the principal is not getting anything done, it will be harder for him to talk his way out of it. No improvement; no raise.

The new system would start with a reclassification and a raise for all of the principals. Now, principals are paid according to the number of pupils in their schools, and schools are classified, by enrollment, as either A, B or C schools.

The new plan divides the 275 schools into seven groups according to the complexity of the job of operating the school. Principals of schools in Group One would be paid a minimum of $11,590 and a maximum of $16,232.

Since the range for the most difficult schools is $15,346 to $21,480, the principals in the top classification could earn less than a colleague in the lowest unless he moved from the minimum toward the maximum.

The way to move is to achieve the goals. Doing so, results in a competent rating and a 5 percent increase. Exceeding the goals brings a commendable rating and a 7 percent raise.

A few will do such an exceptional job that they will be rated "distinguished" and could earn as much as a 10 percent raise and could, in time, exceed the stated maximum for their classification by as much as 8 percent.

If a principal continues to miss being rated even competent, the report indicates he should not be a principal. If he remains at the competent level, he will never earn more than three-fourths of the maximum salary for his classification.

Hay reported first on the principals because that job is considered to be pivotal in the school system and will become increasingly crucial as Dr. Shedd's plans for decentralization progress.

Dr. Shedd came to town with bold plans for improving the schools here. Central to these plans were decentralization and accountability.

First, he believes that people must become involved in their schools if the schools are to be improved. Schools must tap the strength and resources of the communities they serve, he said, and to do this, the communities must be given a say in what goes on at the schools.

The second side of the coin is accountability. If principals are going to be given more autonomy and more control over what goes on in the schools, there must be a way to decide whether they are doing a good job.

Are the children learning at the same rate as others? Can he hold onto good teachers? Does he get the community to work for the school? Is there control without oppression in the school? Does he keep adequate records?

Now Dr. Shedd is at last faced with something more than writing a speech about accountability. The principals and the administrators—especially the drones—are going to fight him. Some of them are in their jobs because of years of inter-system maneuvering and they will use alliances established during these years to attempt to undermine and discredit Dr. Shedd.

For many reasons, this would be the easiest time for him to take his first step backward, make some deals and keep the peace.

So, a lot of people, particularly in the school system, on the school board and among those in the country who taste the winds of educational change, are waiting to see what he will do.

They wait to see if he can make this unique plan work. And they wait to see if this young superintendent is tough enough to beat the system and back up his speeches with action.[8]

## A Case Study

The following materials are largely self-explanatory. They comprise two case studies, demonstrating some of the misconceptions and challenges that arise from the issue of school accountability.

First, on reading scores, a *New York Times* editorial of 13 January 1971:

Solving the Reading Puzzle

The results of reading tests recently administered by the city's public schools raised more questions than they answered. The bright spot shown by these statistics is the marked improvement of reading ability in the second grade. The city's second-graders as a group now register slightly above the national norm, while all other grade levels lag behind.

The overall picture is so dismal because this lag worsens from grade to grade. Almost two-thirds of New York's children from second through ninth grade read behind the national norm. For the one pupil out of every ten who is three years behind in this essential skill, the whole educational venture thus turns into a dead end.

To what extent can different teaching methods, better materials or changes in the training and deployment of teachers be credited with the second grade's gratifying success? Is it possible to identify gains resulting from better relations between teaching staff and parents, or between regular teachers and para-professionals? It is equally important to pinpoint specific reasons for the appalling failures. The use of ethnic patterns as an alibi is rendered unacceptable by the very fact that the same patterns exist in the successful lower grades.

The first priority for research is to concentrate not on educational theories but on observation of successful action in the field, with a view to making the success contagious. In such efforts, school administrators, teachers and teacher-training institutions can cooperate most fruitfully. The challenge now is to turn the success of the second-grader into a foundation for rising accomplishments all the way up the educational ladder.

Next, a letter (provoked by the editorial) from the author of this book to the *Times* editor on 14 January 1971:

Your January 13 editorial attempted to analyze the results of the reading tests released by the city schools. The editorial displayed a distressing lack of sophistication about a critical education issue. The first thing to consider is that one of the most important factors affecting school reading scores is the home background of the students concerned. Repeated research has shown that family attitudes and experiences concerning school and learning have a large impact on how well students learn in school—and how well they do on reading tests.

This is not to dismiss the school's responsibility to teach all students; however, if any attempt is made to appraise the test results, it is essential that such socioeconomic data be available for the appraisal process. Without such data, for example, scores might go up (because the types of students attending school have changed) while the teaching is actually lowering in quality. Conversely, teaching could be improving, and scores moving in the other direction, because of external factors difficult for school personnel to affect. Of course, precise socioeconomic data of this type is not collected now by the schools for evaluative purposes. The most important fact about the current reading scores is not so much their annual movement up or down, but the gross inadequacy of such data, as presently collected, for all serious evaluative purposes. This inadequacy is no accident. School administrators throughout the country have persistently followed a policy of failing to collect adequate data of this sort. This has made it impossible for technically competent persons to make serious assessments of what is being done right or wrong, and who deserves praise and who deserves blame.

Any judgments made on the basis of the current data is simply a tea-leaf interpretation. Apart from the lack of adequate data, a survey I made two years ago in the city convinced me that the scores are further faulted by leaking of test questions at lower levels, and other evasions practiced by administrators and teachers.

I doubt that these practices have stopped. In sum, the scores are practically useless for most administrative purposes. They do not have enough precision to permit anyone to conduct a serious analysis, or offer any important prescriptions. I'm not surprised the schools don't admit this fact. However, I am disappointed that the *Times* was sucked into the game, and attempted to use these mythological scores for constructive purposes. Any well qualified statistician would say that we need far more information than is currently available before we attempt any analysis of this problem. The real story is: why isn't the necessary information collected? Why don't you ask that question—and keep at it? That might do some good. In asking the question, it wouldn't be a bad idea to talk to some ed researchers and statisticians (not just school administrators) who really know something about reading scores and school evaluation.

The letter received a formal acknowledgment but was not published. On 3 April 1971 the following article began on the first page of the *Times:*

Actual Tests Used To Prepare Pupils for Reading Exam
by Leonard Buder

Pupils in at least two Brooklyn elementary schools were coached for the citywide reading tests given here on Thursday by being drilled on material taken directly from the tests or based on them.

At one school, P.S. 178, two teachers copied sections of the vocabulary section of the test for their grade—including the actual test illustrations—and used the material to prepare their pupils for the examination.

An acting assistant principal at the same school also showed 15 words from the vocabulary section to teachers at a workshop she conducted and told the teachers to use these words "in teaching situations" with their pupils. The workshop was attended by new teachers from P.S. 137 as well as P.S. 178.

At another school, P.S. 327, pupils were given advance exercises that contained paraphrased versions of all eight examples in the reading comprehension section of the test used in the third and fourth grades.

A reading coordinator at the school said yesterday that she and another coordinator did this intentionally "to cause a stir" and focus attention on citywide tests because they regarded the tests as "unfair" and "inaccurate," particularly for disadvantaged pupils.

She said that they intended to disclose their scheme when the results were made known later this spring and the school's pupils "hopefully would score 100 per cent." Last year's test showed that the average fifth-grader at P.S. 327 was two years behind in reading comprehension.

At P.S. 137, some teachers have also charged that they were given practice material by a school administrator that contained words that appeared on the actual test. One such sheet, alleged to have been distributed to teachers, contained 32 words—30 of which were mentioned in the test.

The principal of P.S. 137 earlier this week denied any allegations of improprieties in connection with the test. Yesterday he referred inquiries to the district office, where officials refused to make specific comments at this time.

The principals of the other two schools—P.S. 178 and P.S. 327— have conceded the seeming test irregularities at their schools. They said they had no advance knowledge that actual or paraphrased test material was being used to coach pupils.

Mrs. Margaret Williams, the acting principal of P.S. 327, said that she would "support" the two reading coodinators who admitted using paraphrased test material as part of their asserted scheme to discredit the citywide tests.

"They are two of my best teachers," Mrs. Williams said in the presence of one of the coordinators. "They reflect the feeling of a majority of teachers in this city that the tests are unfair and should not be used."

All three schools are in Community School District 23, which takes in the largely black and Puerto Rican Ocean Hill and Brownsville sections. Two of the schools—P.S. 137 and P.S. 178—were formerly part of the old Ocean Hill-Brownsville demonstration district.

An investigation into the test irregularities is now being conducted by Deputy District Superintendent David Marcus. This was ordered by Assemblyman Samuel D. Wright, the president of the local school board, at the request of Dr. Harvey B. Scribner, Chancellor of the city's schools.

Mr. Wright said he was "shocked" by the allegations, and he promised a full disclosure of the district's findings. Chancellor Scribner said that he regarded the matter as "very serious" and that he would await Mr. Wright's report.

The standardized tests—given each year to some 600,000 pupils in the second through ninth grades in all city schools—are used to measure pupil achievement. In recent years, the test results have shown that city pupils generally lagged behind national reading standards.

But many teachers and supervisors have long charged that the tests are "culturally biased" against minority-group children and to some extent all urban pupils because of the use of words and situations more familiar to middle-class and rural youngsters.

The tests, known as the Metropolitan Achievement Tests, and published by Harcourt Brace Jovanovich, are widely used by schools throughout the country.

City educators have also complained that the test results are also being used unfairly by parents and others to "rate" the performance of class teachers and school principals.

Over the years there have been general charges that some schools or some teachers or principals improperly coach their pupils for the tests. But these have been weldom supported by specific allegations.

Board of Education officials say that it is permissible, as many schools do, to prepare pupils for the annual tests by drilling them on similar material or even questions taken from previous Metropolitan tests.

There are different examinations for different grade levels but those used in elementary schools have a section on vocabulary to test word knowledge and a section containing several paragraphs, each followed by specific questions, intended to measure comprehension.

The first public allegations of impropriety in connection with the current tests came from Alan Meltzer, a teacher at P.S. 137, at 121 Saratoga Avenue.

He asserted that teachers at the school received in advance sheets of vocabulary words that appeared to be taken from the actual test. Mr. Meltzer, the school's audio-visual coordinator, said he became aware of this situation only last Tuesday and then began inquiring among his colleagues and, in some cases, obtained signed statements from them.

One statement alleged that a second-grade class had actually been shown the reading test last Monday—three days before the pupils actually took it—and that the children were coached on the questions and answers.

Mr. Meltzer's general allegations were supported, in an interview, by another teacher, Ray Landis. Copies of these statements were given yesterday to Mr. Marcus, the Deputy District Superintendent, by Mr. Meltzer.

Within a week, there were two more successive articles on the cheating issue. On 13 April the following editorial appeared in the *Times:*

Truth in Reading

The disclosure that some teachers and supervisors cheated in the administration of the citywide reading tests points up a recurring educational abuse. The bootlegging of test questions, currently at issue, is only a more flagrant version of the long-standing practice of "teaching to the test"—a practice that sacrifices good instruction to a teacher's or administrator's quest for a better professional image.

For generations, teachers in this and other cities have squandered valuable class time and undermined their student's respect for the schools by engaging in sterile coaching for the Regents, and other examinations, using as the textbook commercially produced collections of past tests.

Since the city's so-called merit system for the licensing of teachers and supervisors relies heavily on coaching—cram courses in how to deal with the questions the coach has good reason to believe will be asked—it is hardly surprising to find the same distorted approach applied to tests of children's reading progress.

The losers are the children. If their class and, by extension, their school appears to be doing well, the adults collect professional kudos for a deception that leaves the youngsters without gain. As they try to cope with learning and, later, with the demands made on them outside the school, inflated scores are of small comfort. In the process, a school may even cheat itself out of the benefits of extra funds for reading improvement.

The way to improve deficient tests is to marshall expert and professional arguments for change. Cheating is the wrong road to reform. It undermines the integrity of the learning enterprise, particularly when, as the children cannot fail to conclude, teachers and pupils become partners in deception.

The sentiments in the editorial were commendable. However, the writer did not make it clear that the basic causes of the untruthful practices were (a) lack of media coverage or investigation of previous cheating and (b) inadequate machinery within the school district to monitor test administration. Does the editorial writer know the National Assessment has its tests administered by outsiders and uses sampling to keep costs down and honesty up and that multigoal test systems are an alternative to narrow testing?

On 18 September 1971 the *Times* ran the following piece on the page opposite its editorials. Inevitably, such an article added to the confusion of any person attempting to follow the issues presented by the earlier cheating charges:

The Unfair Tests
by Susan Wilson and Elizabeth Moulton

This year 600,000 children in the New York City public schools were subjected to the Metropolitan Achievement Tests in Reading. And there was much indignation when it became known, shortly thereafter, that some teachers—many of them in ghetto schools—had prepared their pupils by coaching them in advance with the actual test material. At the request of the Board of Education, Chancellor Harvey Scribner immediately promised an investigation of "the conduct of the teachers" involved.

It would be more appropriate to investigate the Metropolitan Achievement Tests.

The tests, prepared by the publishing firm of Harcourt Brace Jovanovich of New York, may be purchased at the option of local school boards throughout the country. They are designed to assess individual performance in reading and to measure children's scores against national norms. Because local school boards lack the wide educational resources to prepare and evaluate their own tests, they turn to major publishing houses which produce such standardized series as the Metropolitan, Stanford, Iowa and California achievement tests.

The tests may be suitable for children raised in Pawling, or Pelham, or in Kansas or New Hampshire, but they are patently unsuitable for children raised in East Harlem. The illustrations and language, poorly drawn and ambiguous in themselves, favor the way of life and the values of white, middle-class, suburban children and discriminate against the black, the foreign-born and the poor in the inner cities.

Consider, for example, two sections of the test given this year to all the city's second-graders. There were 30 drawings and not one black face among them. According to the publishers, changes were made this year to include drawings of people with "minority features," represented he explained, by "kinky hair, large noses and bold mouths." The resulting bow toward the fact of diverse cultures was timidly made with dotted heads and smudged features.

The three-part test was oblivious to city life. The first two sections, designed to test a child's ability to read words and sentences, relied on correct identification of illustrations. But most scenes were set in suburbia: a group of boys holding a meeting in a backyard clubhouse, children wading happily at the seashore. Yet the children in an East Harlem school were asked to associate such illustrations with appropriate words.

One was a picture of a log, and the words offered were "goal, log, leg, make." The Harlem students searched for the word "rug" because the sketch of the log looked to them like rolled-up carpeting. Another showed a telephone pole, and the words were "polite, pole, policeman, stop." They looked in vain for "antenna."

In a lengthy explanation of the test's content development, the publishers declare: "The objective of the test is to measure the extent to which pupils can read words which they already know the meaning of, i.e., words which they have in their listening or speaking vocabulary." Do most second-graders in East Harlem (or Watts or Roxbury) have in their listening and speaking vocabularies such test words as "path," "trail," "lake," "garden," "herd," or "trout"?

Three of the six stories in the third section of the test, devoted to paragraph comprehension, were so wholly oriented to white, middle-class life as to be painful to anyone more sensitive than the test's creators.

Perhaps the most egregious example was this passage: "Once a week we have a very special dinner.Before my mother cooks it, she looks at a book. It tells how to make many good things to eat. Last Sunday, we had a delicious new soup and a chocolate pudding dessert. We all call the Book 'Mother's best friend.' "

Each year in schools all over this city, tension surrounds the preparation for and the administration of the Metropolitan Achievement Tests. All learning seems to stop. The teachers, knowing their children may not perform well on the suburban-oriented tests, try to cram material into their heads. Weak readers, sensing the crisis situation, begin to lose what little confidence they already may possess. The emotional effects of these tests on some children are clearly evident. "I don't want to guess, I want to know—and get it right." One 7-year-old who is made to feel confused and inadequate by these tests can come to distrust any printed material.

The children of New York City—nearly 60 percent of whom are black or Spanish—should not have to take the Metropolitan Achievement Tests in their present form another year. At the very least, the tests must be redesigned to give city children a better chance.

The article suggests that cheating is encouraged to protect the students; but it makes no reference to the desire of administrators and teachers for self-protection from the childrens' parents. Furthermore, there is no discussion about the long-range needs of black children to be able to fit into the world of Pawling or Pelham or about the school's responsibility to help them fulfill this need. I have not seen a single *Times* article presenting an informed, no-test position.

The second case study relates to the general matter of evaluation. First, an article on an experimental school in the *New York Times* of 19 October 1970:

Report Hails Oregon High School's Free-Study Experiment
by William K. Stevens

The cleanlined, futuristic colonnades, courtyards and skylights of Portland's John Adams High School symbolize a fresh view of how teenagers should be educated.

Opened just over a year ago on a site south of the Columbia River, it houses what may well be the country's "most important experiment in secondary education," according to the recently published report of a three-and-a-half-year study of American schools commissioned by the Carnegie Corporation.

Adams High seeks to determine whether ordinary teenagers are willing and able to accept day-to-day responsibility for their own education—planning their own studies sometimes developing their own tailor-made courses and managing their own time.

Thus black senior, Don Bilbrew, is free to embark on a two-year independent study of black history in Portland that requires him to make use of the disciplines of sociology and economics as well as history. At the same time he can, and does, study such subjects as Shakespeare, drama, biology and journalism.

And Diane Crane, a sophomore, can branch out from her state-required biology course and undertake an independent study of genetics.

The Adams experiment is attempting to eliminate what the Carnegie study found to be some of the most damaging features of the typical American high schools: Encouragement of docility and conformity; overregulation of students' lives; and a pallid, uniform curriculum.

The experiment was conceived three years ago by seven young PhD candidates at the Harvard University Graduate School of Education. One of them, Robert Schwartz, 32 years old, is now the principal of the school.

Similar ventures in "free" or "open" education for teenagers are going on elsewhere, but in relatively small, especially constituted environments with selected or volunteer students. Adams, by contrast, is a regular district high school operating within political and economic realities. Its student body of 1,600 is drawn from all social strata, with a heavy contingent from white working class families. A quarter of the students are black.

"If the approach works here," says Mr. Schwartz, "it will work anywhere."

The Adams approach begins with the proposition that the overall climate of a school may have a stronger effect on student learning than the formal curriculum.

"If you require a kid to have a hall pass you're saying you don't trust him," Mr. Schwartz said. "You then undercut the value of any 40-minute lesson in self-direction."

Except for the fact that students must come to school and participate, and that they must obey civil laws, Adams has few rules and regulations.

Legitimate authority at Adams is held to be rooted in experience and knowledge. Since adults are by and large more experienced than children, it is reasoned, they have a kind of "natural" authority that makes itself felt when an adult deals with a youngster on an equal, respectful footing.

Teachers are viewed as helpmates and colleagues, not dictators. "We try not to make decisions for kids," Mr. Schwartz said. "We press the student to confront himself and what he's going to do with his life, and to make responsible choices. We are not permissive."

For many students accustomed to being told what to do, the pressure to choose has been uncomfortable, even painful. Some students have simply refused to act for themselves or to go to class, but Mr.Schwartz said that a large majority adjusted to the new way of doing things.

Students at Adams choose as electives many essentially traditional courses—for example, physics, chemistry, electronics and industrial arts. Often students work independently in such courses, checking with the teacher only when help is needed.

But the pride of Adams's effort at curriculum reform is an interdisciplinary "general education" course set up this way:

Students and faculty are divided into seven "teams," each of which designs its own learning program that will lead students to explore key concepts in the state-required subjects of English, social studies, mathematics and basic science. Typically, a team will do this by focusing on some real-life problem—race relations, for example—that can be attacked through the application of several disciplines.

Thus, a team headed by teacher David Mesirow has begun a unit called "the psychology of self," designed to enable students to become surer about their own identities and their relationship to the rest of the world. The team will focus in sequence on politics, students' rights and the process of change; values, advertising and the media; the experience of poverty; the black experience; alternative life styles; and the urban environment of Portland.

General education meets for half a day every day, but a student may skip the group sessions in favor of independent study if he wishes. Should general education spark several students' interest in some particular subject—say, general philosophy—a six-week "mini-course" is organized.

Each student has two free option periods a day, during which he can do anything he likes, or nothing. Some do nothing.

Students choose whether to be given letter grades or to receive a "credit-non-credit" rating.

Parents' reaction to the experiment has been mixed.

A survey of students indicated that they considered Adams a "humanized" school. "At least you feel like a person here," said one student. But the same survey found that many students felt the intellectual contents of the curriculum should be strengthened.

A year later, the following material on the John Adams school appeared in a professional journal.[9] I do not believe the substance of the material was reported in the *Times:*

The board did reaffirm the report and John Adams will continue as a pioneer school in affording students alternatives and in encouraging them to assume individual responsibility for conduct, rather than merely react to imposed authority.

The superintendent's report on John Adams conceded that a minority of students had failed to respond positively to the climate of freedom and that consequently there existed a need to develop more clear-cut and consistent guidelines for checking student attendance and a clearer code of conduct, as well as alternative programs for students unable to profit from independent study. Need also exists, the report added, for greater sensitivity to parents and other citizens who have sharply different views about the school and for developing effective criteria for judging program outcomes as they affect learning. The last-named goal just might be facilitated by the recently inaugurated Oregon state assessment program which, more than incidentally, may permit comparisons of scores by individual schools.

Present evaluative criteria remain so nebulous and subjective that it is virtually impossible to obtain an accurate overall assessment of the learning that results from any particular program. Consequently, Superintendent Blanchard is forced to make a tentative and imprecise estimate of the first two years of operation at John Adams. His estimate is that "Adams is probably doing no better or worse in achievement than any Portland high school with a student body socioeconomically comparable."

## Conclusion

What happens in education is of interest to the public. Newspapers cover educational developments, and books are written proposing educational reforms. However, most of these presentations are insensitive to the lack of nonintuitive feedback from schools (as well as many other public institutions). Without such sensitivity, the writers cannot get far beyond anecdotes, homilies, and endless discussions of budget issues, although such discussions do not have much to do with student learning.

True, nonintuitive reporting may require a break in traditional writing patterns. The writer may have to discover that he cannot simply trust his direct impressions, and that is a little unsettling. But this does not mean there will be no newsworthy stories about nonintuitive issues: administrators encouraging cheating on exams; principals fighting innovations; charges that increased budgets will or will not help learning; trends toward greater or less learning; or proposals to tie administrator promotions to accountability.

Basically, it may be that more sophisticated media writing about schools is a precondition to school improvement. In other words, the earlier chapters have offered ample evidence of the comparatively static character of school practices. This stagnation is partly due to the low level of public criticism of school operations. For example, the *New York Times* articles and editorials on reading scores were critical of the schools, but missed many of the important issues. I suspect that the *Times* financial page and editorials on economic questions are far more trenchant and sophisticated. But naive analysis and reporting of school issues maintains the status quo or simply stimulates trivial gestures by administrators. Sophisticated public-oriented writing on economics promotes real change. In education, despite the substantial volume of reform-oriented reporting and books, not much important school change happens. Does this not suggest that the current writers and reporters may be chasing the wrong issues?

Footnotes

1. Gerald Grant, "The New Journalism We Need," *Columbia Journalism Review* (Spring 1970): 15.

2. Education Writers Association, *EWA Clipsheet,* 3, no. 1 (June 1971).

3. Education Writers Association, *EWA Clipsheets,* 1, no. 2 (November 1968); 1, no. 3 (January 1969); 1, no. 5 (May 1969); 2, no. 1 (September 1969); 2, no. 2 (December 1969); 3, no. 1 (June 1971).

4. *Philadelphia Inquirer,* 12 September 1968.

5. Harvey K. Jacobson, "Characteristics of Gatekeepers of Education News," mimeographed (Grand Forks, N.D.: Communications Research Center, University of North Dakota, 1970).

6. Rosalind Landes, *Public Education in New York City* (New York: First National Bank, 1969).

7. *New York Times,* 11 November 1969, p. 26.

8. *Philadelphia Inquirer,* 3 March 1968, p. 17. The plan described died.

9. Donald W. Robinson, "Are They Quietly Killing John Adams?" *Phi Delta Kappan,* 53, no. 2 (October 1971): 81.

# 8
# Social Indicators and Accountability: Idea Spillover

> It is essential that all concerned with the development of a system of urban social indicators be prepared in advance to find themselves accused of having betrayed some of those very causes with which they have been most allied.
>
> Daniel P. Moynihan[1]

School output measures are only one of the forms of nonintuitive feedback developing in our postindustrial society. Population statistics, pollution indices, statistics about hunger and malnutrition, and crime rates are other types of noneconomic data receiving increasing public attention. These measures are usually called social indicators: i.e., indicators of the condition of society.

Increased reliance on social indicators are a logical outgrowth of an increasingly complex, large, dynamic, and integrated society. We have a nationwide market, nationwide communications media, expeditious travel, nationwide college systems, and enormous industries. Each of these operations or systems has more and more potential to affect other, apparently remote, events. The people in Oregon watch television and worry about malnutrition of children in the Deep South. The citizens of New Orleans are concerned about Mississippi pollution being generated at St. Louis. New Yorkers ask about DDT on Salinas lettuce. Auto drivers inquire about the nationwide injury rate for seat belt wearers. If the crime rate is rising in Chicago, Chicagoans ask about the rate in Washington, D.C.

Even in our private lives, change has driven us to new data orientations. With the growth of affluence and the decline of calorie-burning manual labor, we have more food to eat and fewer occasions to work it off: obesity has become an increasing health problem. Therefore, as individuals we must replace the earlier automatic controls with measurement, learned rather than innate taste, and conscious choice. We rely on scales and calorie charts, keep count, and make choices. In some ways, this mirrors the social indicators challenge facing society as a whole: the new modes of life may be "nicer," but we must develop new data systems and controls to go along with them.

Social indicators assume that intuitive data is often an unreliable guide. Some systems are so elaborate that no single individual can tell where they are moving; for example, is crime getting worse or better, and what about drug abuse or the infant mortality rate? One individual's impression is a worthless answer to such questions. In many instances, by the time an erroneous policy is intuitively apparent—e.g., when we discover that an airport has been mislocated or an inappropriate housing project built—it may be too late to correct the error. Thus, we need elaborate, scientific, carefully organized, preexisting data collection systems. Generally, these systems rely on survey research techniques, e.g., sampling. Concurrently, we need better means to quantify and describe these phenomena: computers, experiments and research centers to develop new indices, and more sophisticated media to report what the indices mean.

In sum, we can conceive of a sort of race. Large, rationally integrated systems increase our wealth; simultaneously, they create new and often unexpected difficulties. Then we must develop tools to anticipate the dysfunctions, and correct them. Sometimes it seems that problem generation runs way ahead of our problem-solving capabilities.

Unquestionably, social indicator developments will have a spillover effect on school accountability. The methods created and refined—data processing, new indices, sampling techniques—all will have an influence. Even more important, such developments will increase public expectations about school accountability. If we study the actual efficiency of commuter systems, raise questions about pollution indices, discuss sampling techniques to assess crime rates or drug abuse, it is inevitable that we will soon expect increasing output accountability from our schools. In the past, immigration, civil rights, and foreign affairs issues such as Sputnik shaped what happened to schools. In the near future, social indicators for a postindustrial society may have equivalent effect. Let us survey some of these developments to see what they may portend.

## Social Indicators and National Administration

The efforts of the founding fathers to develop a more rational society brought social indicators into play early in our history. The original Constitution required fair congressional apportionment. To transform this requirement into a routine practice, it simultaneously required a decennial census. While many other societies had previously had occasional censuses, the United States was the first one to require a regular census in its basic law. Over time the complexity of census practices and data has grown. Today census data is one of the basic resources of planning. For example, school districts often use such data to assist building plans. Inevitably the issue of what the census should count has arisen in a political context. What shall we seek feedback about? For example, in recent congressional testimony, a former census official said:

> Statistics have been drawn upon in an important way by the civil rights program. Bitter opposition was voiced to the inclusion of a question on years of schooling completed and income in the Census of 1940 by a Southern Congressman, who explicitly stated that the data was sure to be used "to help make the Niggers dissatisfied." . . . His forebodings were well founded.[2]

In the twentieth century, it became increasingly evident that the census approach—despite its great value—could not provide all types of social data needed in a modern society. Many new questions were arising that were not susceptible to simple yes-no answers. For example: Exactly when is a person suffering from malnutrition? How do you measure a crime or auto accident rate? What is an index of drug addiction? What is adequate literacy? How can we tell whether racial integration is increasing or decreasing throughout our society as a whole? All of these issues present delicate conceptual questions. We saw equivalent issues arising in the area of educational measurement. It is not that such measurements cannot be made, but they require research and subtle systems.

The pressures for better social data were inevitably felt at the presidential level. The president is the nation's chief *executive*—and executives need data for administrative purposes. A good example of this federal need—and the uncertain process of its fulfillment—is the crime rate issue.

Crime in the streets has been a critical national political issue for several years. A number of proposals have been made at the federal level that allegedly would alleviate the situation: accelerate the war on poverty, reverse "soft on crime" Supreme Cout decisions, or pass various types of federal anticrime legislation. One of the key items of debate has been the National Crime Rate, compiled by the Federal Bureau of Investigation from local police reports. The crime rate has been termed a "statistical monstrosity." Its shortcomings are numberless.[3]

First, it is an index of reported crimes, and we have only a crude idea about the relationship between actual crimes and reported ones. Undiscovered crimes, such as successful embezzling or dope peddling, can never be reported. Often, discovered crimes are not reported: the victim may decide it is not worth the trouble, or he may fear the police himself. On the other hand, it is suggested that the rate of reported crimes in the South has risen, as blacks developed more confidence in fair law enforcement; the confidence stimulated them to report crimes committed against them that they had not reported in the past. Also, if the police make a strong effort at crime detection, the crime rate may rise. Conversely, if law enforcement becomes lax, the rate may fall.

Next, the reported rate of "serious crimes" counts as similar many quite different crimes. For example, different states have different definitions of a felony. Usually, the definition is partly tied to the cost of the stolen item. Given the past twenty to thirty years of inflation, more crimes are becoming felonies as the prices of stolen items rise past the felony point. Also, the index counts all felonies as equal. But suppose the number of murders drops by 2,000, which represents a 50 percent drop in murders. Then suppose the number of car thefts increases by 2,000 which represents a 15 percent rise in car thefts. We are told the crime rate is the same. This is correct, but important and probably constructive changes are masked by this bland statement.

The basic data are collected by local police stations and finally analyzed by the FBI, both of which may have strong institutional reasons for shaping the pattern of the data. There are innumerable instances of changed local police policies affecting the apparent crime rate. For example, if a new chief demands more accurate reporting, his officers will write up everything significant that comes into the station house. Inevitably the rates will rise, which is bad for the precinct's reputation. Then when a citizen comes in he will be discouraged from filing a complaint. At the FBI level, the most evident bias is the fact that these obviously inadequate statistics have been put out for years without any serious effort to correct or even point out their notorious shortcomings. Year after year, local data collections tend to tighten up, inflation causes certain types of crime to appear to increase, and so on. Most of these shortcomings tend to inflate the data.

We really have no firm idea whether the national crime rate has been increasing over the past twenty to forty years.[4] Homicide is the crime most likely to be consistently reported and least affected by inflation, local systems of definition, etc. The number of homicides has not greatly increased in proportion to the population over these years. We can probably all sense how the interests of the FBI are advanced by the picture of an increasingly lawless nation, even though it is not generally responsible for enforcement. It can excite concern and increase its budget without accepting any responsibility.

As a result of these continuing criticisms of the crime data, and the intense public concern about law enforcement, some statistical improvements are being made. We are moving toward more user-oriented crime statistics, i.e., data that tries to tell us the chance that certain crimes may be committed against us, rather than vague and anxiety-generating national statistics. We are also developing survey research techniques to ask sample groups of citizens about the crimes committed against them, rather than leaving the matter up to police reporting. Such surveys, if conducted periodically by a reasonably impartial agency, will tell us something. But it will be hard to compare this survey data with the rough measures used in the past; in other words, after years of inconclusive controversy, we are only now finally beginning to establish a useful crime index baseline.

As a result of pressures of this character, a succession of twentieth-century presidents have routinely looked for social indicator help. They have usually relied on ad hoc committees. In 1929 President Hoover appointed a number of social scientists to the Research Committee on Social Trends and asked them "to see where the stresses are occurring."[5] Inevitably they discovered that much of the basic data was lacking, and their report had numerous gaps. In addition, since they had to do much of their work de novo, their report was not delivered until 1933 *after* their appointer had left office. President Eisenhower requested a committee of prominent citizens (assisted by a staff including social scientists) to prepare a report on national goals. The report was issued at the time of President Kennedy's election.[6] President Johnson, partly as a result of urgings from the academic community, directed the Department of Health, Education and Welfare to produce a social report. The report was completed and ready for issuance in 1969 on the last day of the president's administration.[7] In 1969 President Nixon, presumably at the urging of Daniel P. Moynihan, then a White House assistant, committed himself to the periodic issuance of such a report by a special White House staff. The first report appeared in 1970.[8] Moynihan has left, and no further reports are now contemplated. All of the reports are of some use, although they are admittedly thin. They all find a need for much further development. But none of them has yet resulted in the establishment of a permanent, highly visible, and decently budgeted agency committed to regular reporting and the necessary research.

The probable explanations for these inconclusive patterns of presidential concern are:

a. The task of setting up a long-range institution is just not of enough interest to the president: he is under too many day-to-day pressures, and its benefits are too remote.

b. If a real institution were set up, it might get too independent of presidential control, so it is better to have an agency report in the next administration or to keep it right under the White House thumb, where it gets lost in the immediate priorities.

c. Incoming presidents are rarely interested in reports prepared by ad hoc committees appointed by the previous president.

In sum, we might say that the president inevitably arrives in office with a set of preexisting priorities. A newly established independent social indicator agency could disturb those priorities; its counting would either eliminate old issues, or generate new ones. Either effect is sometimes politically disruptive. But since the issue of what to count is so important, let us expand on it to some degree.

## What to Count and How to Decide

We understand that numbers can be a way of describing or summarizing a phenomenon we cannot effectively perceive intuitively. However, the development of statistical means to do the job is not always simple; we are now trying to create more precise measures of the degree and impact of crime in America, and it's going to take time and money for research. In other words, we cannot immediately begin counting large numbers of complex phenomena: the planning and research would exhaust our limited pool of talent. So there are restrictions on how much nonintuitive feedback we can afford to collect: choices must be made. These choices can be of critical importance. Wilbur Cohen, a former secretary of the Department of Health, Education and Welfare, observed that: "The man who decides to collect or not to collect statistics on Indian education, or medicare or medicaid or nutrition or hunger is the person who is fundamentally determining the character of the issue or the controversy later on. If you do not have data or if you do have the data, it basically changes the configuration of the issue."[9]

But even when the decision to collect certain data is made, the "technical issues" of measurement can have important practical implications: crime statistics have been collected over time, but the means of measurement employed inevitably made the numbers increase and did not tell us about the impact of crime on typical American citizens. Therefore, the systems of crime numbers give us a misleading picture.

Theoretically we might decide that choices between what to count and debates about whether appropriate criteria are selected are just too unsettling. Like the presidents seem to do, we might decide to forget the whole business and manage things without too much conern for data. But in any enterprise day-to-day decisions must be made: e.g., size and allocation of budgets; programs to be kept, dropped, or enlarged; and who gets hired or promoted. A thoughtful evaluation of the early federal antipoverty programs made this point about the significance of intuitive program criteria: "Where there are few obvious criteria of performance, an institution must turn to indirect symbols of achievement, especially those which earn public acclaim . . . . An institution can become so preoccupied with marginal activities which enhance its prestige that it neglects the less visible work which makes up its true purpose."[10]

Thus, without nonintuitive measures that describe actual progress toward important purposes, institutions may bog down in marginal activities. Indeed, it is even possible to adopt nonintuitive measures that still facilitate this harmful process, such as making attendance, rather than learning, a measure of school efficiency. This indicator would cause us to strive to keep students in attendance even when they have actively begun to resent schooling; past such a point, attendance might stimulate unlearning. But it does seem that nonintuitive measures at least open up more possibilities for focusing on true purposes. They also raise the question, What are the true purposes of large systems? For example, a national social indicators program would inevitably stimulate questions about the major goals of modern American society.

Certainly the goal questions posed by our postindustrial society are unique and they deserve unique consideration.

For instance, throughout most Western history, want and deprivation have helped to provide one convenient answer to the question of national goals: more goods to far more people. In addition, throughout most American history, the challenges of settling a continent and integrating an immigrant population have naturally focused our national energies. So economic growth, national expansion, and assimilation have provided convenient definitions of our social purposes. But these traditional goals are losing their validity. The degree of poverty has greatly diminished: ours is the most prosperous large society in history. It seems as if "manifest destiny" has overreached its practical limits in Vietnam. The proportion of unassimilated immigrants—even if we include blacks in this class—is diminishing. The issue of goals and focus is thus becoming more pertinent. Indicators may be a natural tool for structuring a discussion of this issue. Indeed, the unit that produced President Nixon's social indicators report (and was then disbanded) was called the National Goals Research Staff.

Decisions about social indicators clearly have a multitude of implications: they can determine what the major social issues are, how they will be received by the public, and even what kinds of remedies will be proposed. So any public institution charged with deciding what indicators to develop and what data to collect will become the center of value controversies. It may be asked, Why is the agency counting the quality of sexual life of typical citizens, the extent of religious affiliation, or the intensity of patriotism? Or it may be argued that the measures of the phenomena are inappropriate. Or the complaint may be that failure to count a particular phenomenon is a serious misjudgment. Why not count the number of homosexual "marriages," how citizens spend their leisure time or the proportion of blacks who disavow Black Power? But these disputes, if they are pursued within a legislative or public framework, will inevitably lead to the collection of more information, a larger understanding of the underlying issues, and greater potential for resolution. However, without a public indicators institution, many of the underlying issues will still exist, and reveal themselves in sporadic disruptions. Such disruptions will lend themselves to intuitive misinterpretations. For example, consider our essential ignorance about the social factors related to drug abuse, a current "sporadic disruption." This ignorance is due to our earlier failure to develop a social indicator approach to drug use. Despite this ignorance, legislators and administrators are still driven to develop and apply answers, which may well make the situation worse. Lack of data and collecting institutions has not kept the crisis out of sight; it has simply limited our understanding of an issue we must still deal with. Therefore, new data collection will help us to see and handle the new issues appearing about us.

## The Economic Example

The issue of institutionalizing policy-shaping and counting has been faced before by the federal government. The President's Council of Economic Advisors, which was set up by congressional legislation, plays a major role in focusing economic debate. The example set by the council and the legislation that established it have helped shape the move to develop a national social indicators agency. The council's history can help to show how social indicators might achieve further importance in national policy-setting.

From the 1920s onward, economists have been continuously refining our ability to collect and analyze nationwide economic data. The process was facilitated by the relative need of business for such information and the widespread desire to use the data to analyze the pressing problem of the Great Depression. As a result of analyzing these data, e.g., the gross national product and balance of payments, economists began to derive new explanations for business cycles.

In 1935, when Keynes published his influential work, *The General Theory of Employment, Interest and Money,* it relied heavily on the analysis of such data. Over the succeeding ten years, there was a series of academic, Keynesian debates on the issue of full employment. One outcome of these debates and the public fear of a postwar depression was the Employment Act of 1946.[11] The act was designed to establish new national policies and institutions to facilitate full employment. One of its significant innovations was the establishment of the President's Council of Economic Advisors. Under the act, the president and the council were required to issue annual reports on the economic status of the nation. Such reports would necessarily rely heavily on nationwide economic data. Bertram Gross, who helped draft the act, observed that:

> When the final version of the Employment Act of 1946 was being drafted in the Senate-House Conference Committee, the Act's provisions for the President's Annual Economic Report were a "sleeper." Most of the observers paid exclusive attention to the disputes over symbols such as "full" versus maximum employment. Indeed, many of the participants in the legislative debate seemed to think of government influence over the economy exclusively in terms of spending and controls. Few people realized the subtle power of highly credible quantitative information on which public attention is focused through presidential messages and joint committee hearings.
>
> Since then, it has become clear that the public reporting provisions were of strategic significance .... This wealth of factual information on economic trends and potentials provides major premises for private and public decision-making, even by those who may disagree with the specific presidential proposals.[12]

As Gross suggests, the impact of the reporting provision was not immediate. But over time, the influence of the reports by the president and the council grew. The reports were among the important forces that brought about the first deliberate, large-scale promotion of an unbalanced budget via use of a tax cut (in 1964) to increase employment. As federal policies go, the measure was a resounding success. It was a major factor in reducing the adult male unemployment rate from 5.7 percent in 1961 to 2.6 percent in 1965.[13] Of course, Keynesian economics and the Employment Act have not extinguished all problems of economic policy. Still, they have obviously changed the pattern and level of national economic debate, and major depressions, which occurred periodically throughout our past and which Marxists saw as dooming capitalism, are apparently extinguished.

The relatively successful experience with the Employment Act has had two effects on the social indicators movement:

1. By helping to diminish economic want in the United States, it freed public energies to focus on the noneconomic values of life. This refocusing has caused some people to ask whether we can counteract some of current economic-philistinism by "putting numbers" on some other public concerns.

2. The success of the Employment Act as a specific form of legislation has suggested that the act should become a model for an equivalent social indicators bill. Legislation is being proposed to achieve this end.

## Social Indicators Legislation

The principal proposed social indicators legislation is the Full Opportunity and National Goals and Priorities Act.[15] Senator Walter F. Mondale has been its major sponsor, though many other senators have also supported the bill. It was first introduced in the Senate in 1967 and has received a succession of hearings since. In 1970 it passed the Senate in the Ninety-first Congress by a vote of 31 to 24 but was not acted on by the House. It was subsequently reintroduced in the Ninety-second Congress. There is no value in considering many of the details of an unsettled piece of legislation. However, some of the testimony and commentaries in academic journals are generally applicable.

Naturally, the bill is widely supported among the academic community. Daniel Moynihan's comments are typically intense but state the issue nicely. This testimony was delivered shortly after the 1967 riots in Newark:

> It seems to me, sir, that your proposal is absolutely indispensable. Let's be perfectly frank. A couple of months ago Senator Mondale's bill was thought to be an interesting idea, which a bunch of academics talked some good senators into. Hearings would be held and perhaps a book produced. Thereafter, we could each send each other copies of our testimony and exchange prints and it would be very fine. Well, that has changed. The idea is no longer a quaint and interesting physiocratic notion of the kind academics come up with in the hope of getting hired or having a place to send their grad students after they get their degree.

We are dealing with the stability of the American Republic. We could tear this country apart and you know it, sir. The point is not that the United States is going to collapse, not that it is going to cease to exist, but that we could spoil it.[16]

Joseph A. Califano, a former assistant to President Johnson, offered the following views: "The disturbing truth is that the basis of recommendations by an American cabinet officer on whether to begin, eliminate or expand vast social programs more nearly resembles the intuitive judgment of a benevolent tribal chief in remote Africa than the elaborate sophisticated data with which the Secretary of Defense supports a major new weapons system."[17]

In the various hearings, representatives of the incumbent administrations (Nixon and Johnson) appeared. Their testimony followed a common theme. It could be paraphrased as: "This bill is a nice idea. We are working on this problem ourselves. From 1959 to 1969, annual federal outlays for social statistics have increased from $18 million to $75 million. We have authorized our own social indicators report. At this moment, we think the uncertain state of indicators research doesn't justify the passage of this bill. It would be premature to set up a persisting, formal institution to work on this, since we don't know enough about it."

It is significant that Moynihan, then a college professor, testified in favor the bill when the Johnson administration was in but did not testify at all when he was on the Nixon staff. Likewise, Califano, then in private law practice, testified strongly for the bill during the Nixon administration but did not testify at all when he was in the Johnson administration. Neither man said anything inconsistent with his conduct or words elsewhere, but each judiciously ignored the committee while he was in office. This pattern of conduct is typical of office holders and suggests the pressures for nondisclosure that are generated by the responsibilities of office.

Inevitably, the implications of social indicators for education were raised at the hearings. Mancur Olson, who helped prepare the Johnson administration indicator report, testified: "Each year the Office of Education and the Department of Health, Education and Welfare put out a document called *The Digest of Education Statistics.* You tell how many books there are in school libraries, but in most years this document has not one single page—not one single page—on what kids learn. What else are we concerned about?"[18]

In the testimony, the question of individual privacy was raised. One pollster, Louis Harris, confronted this issue:

> The question of privacy of the individual should not be a very serious problem for the agency involved. As has been pointed out, through the use of survey research, samples are the most efficient way to operate, so this means the likelihood of building dossiers on individuals is slight. To obviate this, one can construct computer models, in which the cells are the so-called live elements rather than the individuals whose responses make up the cells. The cells are nourished by different individual people who come from the same group to make up that common cell. Frankly, I think many of the critics of the collection of data are not familiar with the modern techniques of computerized analysis; the researcher could not care less about the private affairs of the individual. What does matter is the pattern of many individuals and what this means for social policy."[19]

In the earlier Employment Act, Congress also established a joint committee to conduct annual hearings on the economic reports. These hearings focused legislative and public attention on the issues in the reports and increased the level of congressional sophistication about the issues. The Full Opportunity bill is also concerned with this issue of how congressional capability and sensitivity for social indicator data should be increased; without such capability, there would be no congressional resources to promote legislation that might respond to the implications of the data. Senator Mondale's first version of the bill provided for a new joint committee on the annual social report, that might be equivalent to the type provided under the Employment Act. The current version of the bill excludes the joint committee provision, and provides for a congressional office of goals and priorities analysis. Obviously, the final form of this provision is fluid, but the concept of increased congressional concern with social indicators is implicit in both approaches.

## Social Indicators: Where They're Going

Undoubtedly, national reliance on social indicators will continue to increase, but how fast and under what sponsorship? That is far more uncertain. It has taken Mondale's bill four years to obtain a majority in one session of the Senate, but that is no predictor of the rate of future progress. Consider the lineup of supporters and opposition: evidently a good number of legislators favor the bill; the incumbent administration's attitude is usually cool; academics are strong supporters but wield moderate influence; from my view of the media, their support is only mild, though such data forms a key component of many important stories, and it is safe to say the public is largely disinterested.

If the bill is passed, and the agency given some money, it can provide a strong, long-run boost to the social indicator movement. I refer to money because as Albert Biederman said, "Talk is cheap; statistics are expensive."[20] But we must recognize that the important payoffs from the enterprise may take a while, just as the impact of the Employment Act was not strongly felt for ten to fifteen years. Indeed, one of the agency's problems will be the excessive expectations of some of its sponsors. For example, in a recent article, Senator Mondale said: "The real conditions of explosive neighborhoods in Watts, Detroit, Newark, and elsewhere were known—*and their implications understood*—by a variety of social scientists who not only possess such publicly-held knowledge but published it as well."[21] (Emphasis added.)

In effect, the senator's contention is that some social scientists forecast the riots. In one sense, he is correct. That is, out of the twenty thousand to forty thousand social scientists in America, a few of them probably correctly forecast specific riots, at specific locations. However, unquestionably most social scientists did not forecast riots. Indeed, I am sure that some of them forecast that riots would not happen, and some of them probably incorrectly forecast particular riots. The senator could safely say that some social science forecasts are right and others wrong, but we are not very good at separating the right and wrong forecasts until after the event. At this moment, the riot-forecasting powers of social science are at about the level of weather forecasting 500 years ago. This does not mean that such forecasting capabilities might not grow considerably, and in much less than 500 years. But such improvement will be considerably handicapped if we are under pressure to produce dramatic, precise forecasts too quickly.

Still, let us look five to fifteen years ahead, and assume we have a substantial federal social indicators operation. What might it mean for national and local policy? Undoubtedly there will be more, not fewer, debates about the accuracy and implications of numbers. Usually numbers do not provide final answers, and when data becomes more important, more questions are asked about its accuracy and it becomes even more accurate. There should be less inclination to propose quick, radical changes in programs and policies as we see that generating measurable program and policy effects means that things must run for a while. Society should exhibit a growing disposition to move more incrementally and to examine more carefully the implications of social policies. More social indicators questions should be raised at other levels of society, such as, What is the quality of life in our suburbs, and how can we measure it? What is the routine door-to-door time for commutation? What is the crime victimization rate in our city or neighborhood? Perhaps as a result of these trends we may discover that technology has the resources to advance, as well as to threaten, a healthy and better-integrated community life.

## Footnotes

1. Daniel P. Moynihan, "Urban Conditions: General," *Annals* 371 (May 1967): 160.

2. U.S., Congress, Senate, Committee on Government Operations, Subcommittee on Government Research, *Hearings on S. 843, Full Opportunity and Social Accounting Act, Parts 1, 2, and 3,* 90th Cong., 1st sess., 26 June 19, 20, 26, and 28 July 1967, p. 439.

3. Albert D. Biederman, "Social Indicators and Goals," in *Social Indicators,* ed., Raymond A. Bauer (Cambridge: MIT Press, 1966), p. 68.

4. High Davis Graham & Ted Robert Gurr, eds., *Violence in America* (New York: Bantam Books, 1969).

5. President's Research Committee on Social Trends, *Recent Social Trends* (New York: McGraw-Hill, 1933).

6. President's Commission on National Goals, *Goals for Americans* (Englewood Cliffs., N.J.: Prentice-Hall, 1960).

7. U.S. Department of Health, Education and Welfare, *Towards a Social Report* (Washington, D.C.: Government Printing Office, 1969).

8. National Goals Research Staff, *Growth: Quantity with Quality* (Washington, D.C.: Government Printing Office, 1970).

9. U.S., Congress, Senate, Committee on Labor and Public Welfare, Special Subcommittee on Evaluation and Planning of Social Programs, *Full Opportunity Act, Hearings on S. 5,* 91st Cong. 1st & 2d sess., 1969 & 1970.

10. Peter Morris & Martin Rein, *Dilemmas of Social Reform*

(New York: Atherton Press, 1967), p. 46.

11. Stephen K. Bailey, *Congress Makes a Law* (New York: Columbia University Press, 1950).

12. Bertram M. Gross & Michael Springer, "A New Orientation in American Government," *Annals* 371 (May 1967): 7.

13. Ruben E. Slesinger, *National Economic Policy* (Princeton: D. Van Nostrand, 1968), p. 84.

14. *New York Times,* 23 March 1971, p. 62m.

15. Senator Walter F. Mondale, "The Institutionalized Presidency," *Law and Contemporary Problems* (Summer 1970).

16. *Hearings on S. 843,* p. 346.

17. *Hearings on S. 5,* p. 204.

18. Ibid., p. 117.

19. *Hearings on S. 843,* p. 197.

20. Ibid., p. 219.

21. Mondale, op. cit.

# 9

# Numbers versus Sentiment

> I will maintain that American society makes extraordinary demands on its members—that they adapt to chronic social change, that they achieve a sense of personal wholeness between childhood and adulthood, that they locate positive values in an intellectual climate which constantly undermines such values. Together these areas of stress make adulthood demanding in ways which we have only begun to appreciate.
>
> Kenneth Kenniston[1]

In our initial discussion of the accountability feedback cycle, we saw that the public was seen as the crucial recipient of accountability data. Of course, the public's values and attitudes toward schools would be a vital factor in deciding what happened to that data or, indeed, in deciding whether such public-oriented feedback systems should be developed. Although we can understand why some school administrators might be hostile to accountability, we might simply assume that the public would like to have more and better information about the schools; we might take public concern for granted. But such an assumption would be simplistic.

For instance, the concept that such data should be collected is not new. Mann collected it in the first half of the nineteenth century. A major reason for founding the U.S. Office of Education in 1867 was to collect such data. At the turn of the century, Rice promoted systems that were very similar to National Assessment. Indeed, the essential ideas of accountability and output measurements seem quite simple. Almost any layman can comprehend the basic outlines. There are important technical issues, but most of these need not bother the layman; he does not know exactly how the cost-of-living index is calculated either, but this does not stop him making rational use of its data. In other words, it really is strange that accountability has not progressed further than it has. Should we simply assume that despite its apparent merits, school resistance has stalled all the past efforts in this direction?

On the contrary, I suggest that the key historic bar to accountability is not the predictable, and understandable hostility of some administrators—but the unexpected, and deep, hostility of many laymen.

## Laymen Oppose Accountability

This contention is not based on a planned sampling. Over the past three years, however, I have had about a hundred conversations about accountability and schools, with all types of citizens, none of whom were school employees. A considerable proportion of these citizens were opposed to the use of output measures for school accountability. This response most typically came from persons concerned with school affairs, such as PTA officers, school board members, former teachers, employees of federal and state education agencies, and faculty members in schools of education. Many were citizens with humane concerns whose assistance one might solicit in a reform effort, especially since their interests often turned to education matters. Obviously, their positions on accountability can have considerable influence on public policy. For instance, media analyses of school issues are often derived from reporter contacts with such persons, as well as school employees, and are aimed at audiences largely composed of such persons. If this class is hostile to accountability, it can affect the character of media reporting. While a precise estimate of the frequency of their resistance cannot be made here, it is expressed often and is quite intense.

Of course, many persons everywhere simply are not interested in numbers as descriptive tools. But we should not contend that the general public is opposed to numbers. At all levels of society we find people focusing on number issues: stock market prices, cost-of-living indices, baseball standings, poker odds, unemployment rates, school tax rates, miles per gallon, comparative prices, and wages. While there are inevitable differences in human statistical abilities, the events around us clearly demonstrate that there is widespread public interest and talent in the use of numbers. Therefore, if we find persons hostile to output measures in school policy-shaping, this coolness is not necessarily attributed to resistance to numbers, per se. Resistance to accountability controls in education is more a matter of motivation—a lack of desire to use numbers—than a lack of aptitude or a basic public discomfort with numbers.

There is another possible explanation for this lack of sympathy with the concept of school accountability: the critics believe that the idea is a bad one, or they do not fully understand it. Both these factors had important effects on the opinions of the opponents in my informal poll mentioned above. But there is a larger question. Are there common perspectives that identify persons who reach this set of conclusions rather than another? Why do they find something incomprehensible or wrong that other equally intelligent listeners accepted? Is there a theme to the opposition? I think there is. Many of the noneducator opponents of accountability approaches have common values that shape their attitudes.

Of course, the same concept of a common set of values also applies, to a degree, to the proponents of accountability. For example, the two most output-oriented school board members I have met are a banker and an engineer. However, I believe there still remains one distinction between the two accountability factions: while some members of both groups are quite capable of changing their minds as new information arises, the more confirmed public opponents of accountability apparently rest their opinions on the most deeply set values; when the discussion becomes probing, an extraordinary intensity of beliefs is encountered.

The first level of this resistance presumably arises from the common antipathy to change. It must be evident that schools are not run by measures that are especially relevant to student learning; that many of the practices and values within the systems are alien to an accountability approach; and that the adoption of such an approach might provoke extraordinary changes. The objectors I have been discussing are not members of the system, but have often found themselves in the role of sympathetic critics. They are not simple allies of the educational status quo, but they have accepted many perspectives embedded in it. These attitudes include the propositions that one does not evaluate the conduct of professionals but trusts them; that real learning cannot be measured; that assessment of schools will put inordinate pressure on students; and that pupils can be taught for the test.

One might ask why they often strongly persist in these viewpoints, when new information can persuade them they are wrong; furthermore, the application of measures is not a threat to their status. Such a question implies that power interests lie at the base of most stubbornly held opinions. It ignores the reality that many other factors motivate men. The objectors have evolved a way of looking at schools. They perceive that an output approach will promote radical change in this perspective, and new opinions can be painful. As Epictetus said, "It is not actions, but opinions concerning actions, which concern men." This principle was more fully stated by Berelson and Steiner, in their extensive work, *Human Behavior.* Citing numerous experiments, they concluded that man:

> Adjusts his social perception to fit not only the objective facts, but also what suits his wishes and needs; he will remember what fits his needs and expectations or what he thinks others will want to hear . . . . In the mass media he tends to hear and see and he will misinterpret rather than face up to an opposing set of facts or point of view. In the strain toward conscience it is often reality that pays the price . . . . For the truth is, apparently, that no matter how successful man becomes in dealing with his problems, he still finds it hard to live in the real world undiluted: to see what it really is, to hear what others really think and to face the conflicts and threats really present, or, for that matter, the human feelings . . . .[2]

## What Schools Mean to Many Americans

But this lay resistance to accountability rests on more than the natural disinclination to change opinions, or learn new things. In the past fifty to seventy-five years our society has changed its opinions in many particulars; while the tempo of opinion change is often slow (even in the face of "facts"), the lagging change tempo over accountability implies there are other causes for this persisting resistance. To understand these causes, we should once again look to history. We Americans have had a long affair with our schools, and our attitudes have not been flighty and inconsistent.

In the seventeenth-century, not too long after the first settlements appeared in New England and Virginia, the colonists were troubled with the problem of maintaining cultural continuity in a pioneer society. What could they, born in England, do to ensure that their American-raised generations would continue to perpetuate the English values they held dear and had tried to transplant to the colonies? In the established English society they had left, this cultural transition was satisfied by diverse institutions: the church, apprenticeship, the extended family, and the village or community. These long-established forces instructed the young in the values and patterns of adult life. The institutions thus enabled the society to continue and simultaneously assisted the young to ease fruitfully into adult society. Technically, these institutions served the purpose of socialization.[3]

In the colonies these Old World institutions were under unique stress. The high death rate of the adults due to disease and starvation, the mobility of families in a transient pioneer environment, the decline of apprenticeship due to the labor shortage, and diffusion of the population throughout the frontier—all made it harder to assume that youngsters would be able to learn to be integrated adults. In an effort to counter these trends, the colonists gave special emphasis to the concept of widespread formal education. For instance, in 1633, one colonial writer observed, "We in this country, being far removed from the more cultivated parts of the world, had need to use the utmost care and diligence to keep up learning and all helps to education among us, lest degeneracy, barbarism, ignorance and irreligion do by degrees break in upon us."[4]

Within thirty years after the first settlements, the Massachusetts and Connecticut colonies passed laws requiring townships of over fifty households to maintain a teaching institution, in order to ensure that "learning may not be buried in the grave of our fathers." The Virginia colony (with less success) attempted to follow this pattern. The schools were supported by either the town government or the families of the students, depending on the determination of the town government.

Two hundred years later, this early tradition undoubtedly influenced the approaches of Mann and his other New England allies. Once again, in the early nineteenth century, cultural continuity was in doubt, and the social order was apparently threatened, not by the young as a class but by immigrants from an alien culture and the great enlargement of the suffrage. How could the controlling class ensure their successors would be equipped to govern? School was the prescription; not just to ensure literacy, but to give all citizens a common body of culture and social understanding. But the issue of cultural transmission remained a problem for all Americans throughout the nineteenth and much of the twentieth century. Popular education became the widespread answer to waves of immigration; settlers in the remote forest and prairies far from established institutions; and families leaving their relatives and roots in the eastern states, perhaps never to return home.

Today we still apply this principle. As blacks became enfranchised, the unanimous Supreme Court ruled for school desegregation, and the blacks understood that an open education meant a more open society.

Thus, the school as a community builder is a powerful and fruitful American tradition. The tradition suggests that our schools were as much designed to transmit a sense of belonging and community as to pass on specific, cognitive skills. Hence the name and tradition of the *common school.* The concepts of patriotism, rich and poor together, and land of opportunity were all part of this tradition.

Today, I contend, our schools still have many of these meanings for Americans, perhaps expressed as, "Adults may have their faults and prejudices, but perhaps we can create a better society with and through the young." In this sense, schools have become one of our secular churches: a tool for binding and remaking our society. To support this proposition, let me quote from an in-depth study of a modern suburban community. The study described the community's school attitude as follows:

> The community of Crestwood Heights is, literally, built around its schools. It is the massive centrality of the schools that makes the most immediate physical impact on any outside observer coming into the Heights. The churches, impressive as they are, remain marginal to the area spatially, since almost all are on the outskirts of Crestwood Heights proper, and perhaps morally. It is not by accident that Crestwood Heights has grown up around a school. This development has the same social logic as had the cathedral-center communities of medieval Europe, or the chapel-governed towns of New England. There could be no better indication than this central focus in the school that a great cultural shift has occurred towards a society most of whose dominant concerns are now secular.[5]

As a result of this pattern, persons who give special weight to communal values in our secular society are especially supportive and sympathetic to schools. Some of these persons are educators, hence the higher proportion of affiliative values found among teachers in attitudinal tests. But most of the communalizers are not professionally in education. They are better-educated upper-middle-class adults, often community-oriented women, who have a special concern with school issues. Generally, they also can afford the time. They get the bond issues passed, become school board members or get the right members elected, fight off Birchers and black separatists, head the PTA's, etc. Because of their organizational skills, relative knowledge and interest, they are key school representatives to the larger community, and vice versa.

It is true that persons of this type are not only worried about school issues. Their children, and later they themselves, supplied the white allies for the civil rights conflicts, demonstrated against the Vietnam War, etc. However, school is one of their points of focus. It is literally close to home, and it is a continuing issue. Since it involves the welfare of children of all classes, it is a far less divisive issue than zoning; tax rates; or grubby, spoils-oriented, electoral politics. It thus offers these concerned citizens a holistic sense of communal altruism, while at the same time they are assisting their own children. These words are not said in criticism; these are the same motives that stirred Mann, Rice, and the desegregationists. This would be a poorer country without such citizens. However, it does demonstrate that these lay people have strong communal aspirations. Conversely, these citizens are likely to be especially hostile to trends that they see as divisive or anticommunal.

## What Numbers Mean to the Same Americans

Accountability essentially rests on description; we must be able accurately to describe a phenomenon before we can tell whether or not it has been done. Numbers are the essential descriptive tool of accountability. If we wished, we might substitute other descriptions, such as a letter system—A, B, C, D, etc.—or different colors of progressive intensity—yellow, orange, red, etc. But such efforts would only generate less precise and more confusing substitutes for numbers. In the end, the graded substitute would still be treated pretty much the same as numbers anyway. So accountability inevitably means numbers, and there is a special characteristic of numbers that is critical.

Some of the elements of this characteristic were first articulated by the mathematician John Von Neumann.[6] One could say there are three divergent ways of considering an event, person, or substance:

1. By concluding that it is essentially similar to all other events, persons, or substances (e.g., all votes cast in secret ballot are equivalent to each other, all men are similarly mortal, or all children are lovable)

2. By determining whether it is in or out of one relevant, specific category (e.g., big or little, young or old, soft or hard, or intelligent or stupid)

3. By measuring it, and perceiving it as a graded value, i.e., by placing it on a spectrum (e.g., weight, 147 pounds; age, 31 years; or with a hardness scale, 17).

Let us consider some of the implications of each of these three approaches. The first method, which assumes everything is the same, is the most expeditious means of description and analysis. In the short run, it greatly simplifies many of the problems of life. We need not bother about how to weigh individual ballots, worry which men are immortal, etc. However, the widespread application of the principle of sameness would mean the end of human life. All men do not have equal intelligence, ability, or honesty; all goods are not of the same value; all needs do not have equal weight. Thus, the sameness approach leaves us unable to describe or analyze many phenomena. It is used in special environments, where unique conventions have grown up to protect it and where it serves particular social ends. It is applied in churches, voting, and many "head count" situations: demonstrations, parades, etc.

The second method—we might call it the in-or-out approach—is one step toward gradation. It is a sort of concession to the human need for description. Thus, we have citizens and noncitizens, church members and nonmembers, etc. The in-or-out approach is an accelerated mode of description, since description depends on one act of assessment; the event is either in the category or not.

The third method, gradation, permits the transmission of more information, since it can communicate many more shades of meaning. However, it has certain technical shortcomings. For example, it is redundant. That is, if the event happens to have a measurement of many units, e.g., 100 pounds, then we must make a separate assessment for each unit we count: Does it have one pound? Yes. Does it have two pounds? Yes, and so on. Thus, it is a cumulative system. However, redundancy is also used by the human nervous system in transmitting recognition messages to the brain. For instance, we say an object we touch is hard, because we receive a number of successive signals through our nerves that total a certain degree of hardness. We do not have one signal for hard and another for soft but a number of signals that give us a degree of hardness. This cumulative recognition system complicates the body's perception process. Furthermore, it creates greater complications when the principle is applied in other perception situations.

The three descriptive systems I have sketched represent a continuum of progressive complexity and communication power. But the gradation system, with its cumulative approach, differs from the first two in an especially important way. Any system may err; if it relies on *sameness,* there may be more than the one category it recognizes; if it is *in-or-out,* we may place the item in the wrong category; or if it is *gradated,* there can be an error in any count in the cumulation. However, a mistake in any count in a gradated system will simply mean the item should have a slightly greater or lesser numerical value, while any sameness or categorical mistake is a 100 percent error. Therefore, cumulative recognition systems are less pronc to large-scale error—if the right categories are established. This insurance against gross error is one of the important reasons why numbers are such a valuable language. It is not that they are precise: indeed, they are almost always slightly off, but they are usually proximate.

While Vaon Neumann's presentation is a potent statement on behalf of gradated assessment, it also makes the psychological case *against* gradated descriptions and *for* bipolar or all-encompassing categories. Who likes the idea of living in a multicategory world, where there are always outsiders as well as insiders, and you may be in an outside category yourself. Or, if we cannot have just one category, why must we have a graded world, of indeterminate gray values, where there are only degrees of good or bad and where we are persistently denied the gratification of being fully satisfied or completely angry. An entire psychological doctrine has focused on just the issues raised by these questions. The doctrine deals with the principle of cognitive consistency.[7] *Cognitive consistency* refers to the universal human drive to perceive events and materials in simple consistent patterns: to govern our conduct and values by a few common rules and avoid the strain of awkward, tension-promoting choices or decisions.

Numerous experiments have demonstrated how the tendency to sustain consistency has affected the perceptions and conclusions of subjects. The counterpart of cognitive consistency is *cognitive dissonance,* which refers to a state of conceptual or perceptual disharmony. The ability to accept a substantial degree of dissonance is termed *tolerance for ambiguity.* Tolerance for ambiguity suggests the resilience required to perceive and adapt to inconclusive data and premises: to operate in areas of uncertainty.

All humans possess some of both characteristics: a desire for cognitive consistency and a certain tolerance of ambiguity. The former is necessary to make life manageable: we cannot exist in perpetual uncertainty and conflict. The latter is needed because the events and values of this world do not always satisfy simple patterns. If we excessively pursue consistency, we ignore reality and expire; if we excessively pursue "reality," life becomes sterile and desolate.

Our need for cognitive consistency is partly satisfied by the institutions and values that sustain society. Religion, patriotism, the customs of our city, neighborhood, friends, and family all support patterns of consistency. They either offer consistent explanations of the events around us, channel these events into consistent forms, or prohibit or restrain inconsistent events. Thus we are protected from an excess of ambiguity or cognitive dissonance. But the growing dissonance in our postindustrial society is a notorious phenomenon. For instance, the widespread polarization apparent in the United States—the seeing of events in "we-they" or "good-bad" terms—is one aspect of the striving for consistency. It is an effort to escape from the complex and subtle judgments demanded by reality.[8]

However, a we-they polarization is a poor psychological substitute for a holistic community. For obvious reasons, this dissonance and diminishment of community is especially painful for persons associated with schools. Therefore, such persons are hostile to dissonance-promoting devices, such as numbers, that increase distinctions, further disclose the complexity of reality, and thus generate greater dissonance. This hostility may be evinced either by (a) striving for a polarized and, thus, categorical view of the world, or (b) seeking to promote a large, diffuse, humanistic, same-oriented, world vision, that extinguishes all distinctions among people.

## Practical Implications

This hostility, based on psychological and philosophical needs, is reflected in numerous practical instances. For example, it significantly affects the character of reform-oriented books written for the general public about schools. This is understandable. The authors of such books are typically not professional educators who have been concerned with managing public schools, but academics interested in school issues or persons who have served for a brief period as teachers and left to push for reform. They include writers such as Fantini, Kohl, Kozol, Henlein, Herndon, Leonard, Holt, Friedenberg, Dennison, and Borton. Their nonprofessionalism is part of the source of the considerable influence of these books. It gives their authors perspectives and skills that may not work in bureaucratic structures but make them good communicators to nonbureaucratic laymen.

I classify these authors as the romantic critics. Their general theme is antinumber and hostile to gradation. They seek to promote either polarization or a noncategorical world, and they are very influential in inhibiting accountability perspectives, partly because their perspectives preclude incremental approaches, and partly because they direct public attention toward antistatistical alternatives.

If we examine some of the examples of the romantic critics, we can get a better sense of their underlying premises. For instance, Joseph Featherstone, a contemporary American writer about the English infant school movement, observes that "England remains, like America, a caste-ridden capitalist society."[9]

Of course, *caste* is synonymous with *category,* and *capitalism* implies a focus on numbers and divisions. But Featherstone's angry statement is both incorrect and meaningless, because: (1) the United States is notoriously far less caste-ridden than the comparatively static English society, and (2) the ideologically loaded word *capitalist* has meaning only in Chamber of Commerce booklets and Soviet news releases. But Mr. Featherstone may be advancing a faith, not a reform. Clearly, his approach is alien to the spirit of gradation.

As another instance, consider some remarks by Charles S. Isaacs, a young teacher participating in the 1968 Ocean Hill-Brownsville school decentralization experiment in New York City. The experiment was aimed at promoting *community* schools. Mr. Isaacs was not a professional educator but a person sympathetic to the experiment. In an article in the Sunday magazine section of the *New York Times,* he voiced the following objections to output evaluation and accountability:

> An even more fundamental obstacle is built into the very nature of the project. Our experiment will be evaluated in terms of the conventional criteria: reading scores, discipline, a standardized achievement test, etc., some of which measure what they are intended for *middle-class children.* We have a problem when these criteria fail to measure the extent to which a child has been educated, when they simply test rote memorization, stifling of initiative and training through standardized examinations. Unleashed creativity or a critical outlook, for example, would probably lower a child's score on these exams rather than raise them.
>
> If these conventional criteria measure the wrong things, their effect is harmful to our students, yet they will determine to a great extent whether or not we will be free to develop our own yardstick. In effect, we must miseducate the children before we will be allowed to educate them.[10]

The words in the article associated with opposition to output measures are: *community schools, unleashed creativity, free to develop,* and *initiative.* The words associated with output measures are: *rote, standardization, discipline, stifling, conventional,* and *miseducation.* It may be that Mr. Isaacs' strident tones are evidence more of the psychic needs that particular school policies fulfill for him, than of the pros and cons of whether children are learning to read. After all, creativity first requires the creator to be supplied with information to manipulate. In any case, Mr. Isaacs does not need to worry about his literacy; he is already a published writer. However, given the pattern of reading scores of children from poor black families, the parents of his students may have good cause to be worried.

Ironically, Mr. Isaacs' tirade is not too different from the fulminations of progressive educators (principally upper-middle-class school reformers) against testing in the 1920s. They, too, were disinterested in evaluation and not really sensitive to the problems of lower-income groups.

As a matter of fact, the concern of the school humanists that tests will take over the schools may reflect their own paper-oriented, academic values more than the true temper of our society. A cross-sectional sample survey of all Americans showed that they have what I think is a very healthy sense of proportion about the value of objective tests. Most of them were not against limited reliance on such tests; however, they listed test scores as ninth in order of priorities for determining a person's intelligence.[11] First on the list was work performance. This data suggests that the danger of the "tyranny of testing" is a chimera generated in the minds of school supporters. I suspect that school supporters actually think tests are more important—and fear their implications more—than the relatively less educated American cross-section. Ironically, research about the long-range prediction power of tests tends to support the cross-section's point of view; that is, tests are pretty good as school predictors (for whatever importance school has), but they have only limited value in predicting "life-success," presumably because school does not actually have that much to do with life.[12] In sum, the supporters have generated a double bind for themselves: schools are extraordinarily important; therefore, we dare not look at them analytically. The more typical public attitude is: schools are useful but not sacred; therefore, let us look at test data because though it may not tell us everything, it may tell us something.

This discussion may seem especially critical of school supporters, and I must point out that these supporters have made invaluable contributions to school policies. Without community builders and persons with emotive values, we would live in a bleak world. Unfortunately, the American sense of community has been taking a beating recently. It is understandable that some persons of sensibility have become supersensitive to anticommunal and rationalistic themes such as accountability. Still, if we maintain that improving schools is one step toward regenerating community, we may need to explore ways simultaneously to maintain community and develop accountability measures.

Incidentally, this discussion suggests one forgotten perspective that should be recognized by the humane reformers. Despite the traditional communal elements of schools, they have evolved into the largest, most thoroughly integrated bureaucracy in the United States. As a practical matter, you can usually feel closer to your hairdresser or gas station attendant than your child's teacher. The teacher's responses are tied to the patterns of a closely meshed system with 40 million pupils, 2.5 million employees, and a $40 billion budget. As I pointed out earlier, almost all important decisions about school operations are made within state and national networks that are often controlled by educational professionals; the amount of true local autonomy in the school system is probably less than in the armed services. However, the existence of this meshing is not recognized by most laymen.

Thus, we are told that school board members are against a national testing system, which would commit schools to follow a national pattern. But this is a nonissue! We already have such a system in operation: the college boards and the other national college entrance tests. Since almost half of the students hope to go college, these tests already determine what is taught for most students. The issue is not whether we should let our schools become centralized and bureaucratic; since they are already centralized and bureaucratic, the issue is how to make them less centralized and more humane and efficient. One step would be to study the "inhumanity" that now may exist; this is accountability.

As we have seen, output measures, coupled with sampling techniques, have potential for evaluating the learning of humane values. For example, careful accountability systems may tell us much about the causes and nature of student unrest and how to do something about it. And the explanations for the unrest are not self-evident; so far research has suggested that student dissidents are not really very dissatisfied with teaching and school administration, newspaper headlines to the contrary.[13] So, if we want to help the students, we have got to find out more about what is really going on. Thus, if school reformers perceive that output measures can stimulate schools to promote the values to which they now give only lip service, they may abandon some of their hostility to gradation.

These speculations about cognitive consistency, accountability, and evaluation explain some of the conflicts one senses between blacks and whites concerned with school reform. Sometimes blacks have evinced hostility toward output tools, which were often used to classify or degrade their children and thus to diminish a sense of identity or community. Today, some black spokesmen are interested in output measures for accountability; Kenneth Clark, for example, has proposed that output measures be used to determine whether schools are doing their job.[14] On the other hand, many well-educated whites, who identify with the problems of black students (such as Mr. Isaacs) are still antioutput. Apparently, they are hostile to the divisive, rationalizing aspects of output measures; to them, school reform means promoting community, rather than just giving blacks a chance to "make it." To add to the confusion, many blacks appear to be concerned with making it in an economic sense and want their children to attain literacy. A special irony affects this complex pattern: the whites concerned in such affairs often are better educated than the blacks; their education often gives them the technical skills to deal with statistical issues, but their emotional perspectives often make them predisposed against using those skills.

The prodata black position described above may be subject to erosion as a generation of black school administrators emerges. We can imagine that the prospect of output accountability may make them as uncomfortable as their white predecessors, and they may tend to adopt some of the antidata bias of their predecessors. However, such attitudes are only an exercise of their instinct for self-protection. A Kenneth Clark is not responsible for running any school and can comfortably propound the principle of accountability. This is why "ivory towers" are established: to encourage people to propose ideas they do not have to implement.

## Prospects for Synthesis

In view of these consistency themes, what are the prospects for accountability for schools? Must the present deep hostility of many school supporters to such measures continue? Are there no prospects for a reconciliation? There is an important American historical tradition, outside of education, that might be seen as helpful. It is rooted in the Declaration of Independence and the Constitution.

While the declaration does not pronounce enforceable laws, it has affected the values of our society. We do not always heed its mandates, but when our divergence from it is pointed out, pressures are generated for returning to our "basic creeds."

The declaration is a statement of large, noble, unifying, and hard-to-define principles. It states uncategorically, "All men are created equal." We might question the meaning of *equal,* for example, but despite their indefinite elements, there is a chord in all of us that responds to such statements. We sense that our fellows, too, are committed to these principles—precisely because they are vague—and warmly respond to the concept of bonding beliefs. It is a good feeling.

The Constitution is a carefully designed system, pervaded with diverse role definitions for the mundane business of running a nation. It was the product of extended negotiations and analytical discussions. It outlines decision-making principles so that citizens and their representatives can know how disagreements will be settled. It is statistically oriented. It prescribes terms of office, numbers of votes required, a census every ten years to allocate congressional seats, how a veto is to be overridden, who votes on what, the votes required for constitutional amendment, etc. The Constitution assumes that varying roles and conflicts will persist even in a wholesome community and offers plans for defining the roles, articulating the conflicts, and resolving them. While it also includes high principles, it is a more precise document than the declaration.

Many of the men who adopted the declaration helped to draft the Constitution. They saw nothing inconsistent in being concerned with both ennobling principles and precise statements of policy. They recognized that both elements are components of an effective institution. The broad statements supply emotive bonds and inspire the society toward exalted goals. For instance, I saw Dick Gregory make excellent use of the declaration's text in defending black militancy before a southern audience, and that was one of the reasons it was written. However, a large society governed only by the declaration would disintegrate into frustrating rhetoric and, perhaps, under the eventual pressure of necessity, into "clarifying" totalitarianism. The declaration does not have the precision to say what we want, how we are going to get it, or how we will select or judge our leaders. The declaration—without the Constitution—ignores internal conflicts. It is an invitation for adept groups to manipulate its principles to advance their interests. And that may be what sometimes happens in schools. The statements are wholesome and the ideas often noble, but the results are obscure.

The Manichean values that underlie the desire for polarization or holistic sentiments appear to be a potent and growing force in the United States. Their effect on accountability may only be a minor aspect of their impact on our times. Psychoanalyst John L. Schimel proposed that a driving interest in categorical, absolute values might be compared to a desire to structure events in a gamelike pattern. This generates a simple, satisfying world with villains and heroes: forces for good and forces for evil. He concluded that:

> In an analysis of games and game playing, a crucial phase occurs when the prospect of giving up games arise. "What will I do instead?" is not an infrequent puzzled question. Indeed, some who have given up game playing have initially reported that life has become dull and without flavor for them. It is true enough that the arts of peace are more subtle, sensitive, and I believe, less tangible, an emotional sense than the strategies of war. They require more insight, delicacy and consideration of the other person's role as an individual. A poem is less substantial than a punch, more elusive, and beyond the reach of many.[15]

Dr. Schimel does not tell us in what direction our semipolarized society may move, or how school output developments will go; but his analysis suggests the profound philosophical values that underlie these apparently political conflicts.

## Footnotes

1. Kenneth Kenniston, *The Uncommitted* (New York: Harcourt, Brace & World, 1960), p. 205.
2. Bernard Berelson & Gary Steiner, *Human Behavior* (New York: Harcourt Brace, 1964), p. 664.
3. Bernard Bailyn, *Education in the Forming of American Society* (Chapel Hill: University of North Carolina Press, 1960); Lawrence A. Cremin, *American Education, The Colonial Experience* (New York: Harper & Row, 1970).
4. Cremin, op. cit., p. 177.
5. John R. Seeley, R. Alexander Sim & Elizabeth W. Loosley, *Crestwood Heights* (New York: John Wiley & Sons, 1963), p. 224.
6. John Von Neumann, "The General Logical Theory of Automata," in *Modern Systems Research for the Behavioral Scientist,* ed. Walter Buckley (Chicago: Aldine Publishing Co., 1968), pp. 97-107.
7. For useful discussions on cognitive consistency, see Robert P. Abelson et al., eds., *Theories of Cognitive Consistency: A Sourcebook* (Chicago: Rand McNally, 1968); Roger Brown, *Social Psychology* (New York: Free Press, 1965).

8. Of course, there are divergent perspectives on these developments. Some studies on the current social tensions include: Kenneth Kenniston, *The Uncommitted* (New York: Harcourt, Brace & World, 1960); Eric Hoffer, *The Ordeal of Change* (New York: Harper & Row, 1952); Richard Hofstadter, *The Paranoid Style in American Politics* (New York: Alfred A. Knopf, 1966); Warren G. Bennis & Philip E. Slater, *Temporary Society* (New York: Harper & Row, 1968); Kurt Baier & Nicholas Rescher, eds., *Values and the Future* (New York: Free Press, 1969). In the latter, Rescher observed that "The systematic study of the formation of intellectual and social fashions would be yet another important task for the development of an adequate predictive organon for future-oriented studies." (p. 108) This chapter is a small effort in this direction.

9. Joseph Featherstone, "The British and Us," *New Republic* 165, no. 11 (September 11, 1971): 20-25.

10. Charles S. Isaacs, "A Junior High Teacher Tells It Like He Sees It," *New York Times Sunday Magazine,* 24 November 1968, p. 28.

11. Orville G. Brim, Jr., John Newlinger & David Glass, *Experiences and Attitudes of American Adults Concerning Standardized Intelligence Testing* (New York: Russell Sage Foundation, 1965), p. 122.

12. Otis D. Duncan, *Socioeconomic Background and Occupational Achievement* (Ann Arbor: University of Michigan Press, 1968).

13. Robert Somers, "Mainsprings of the Rebellion," in *The Berkeley Student Revolt: Facts and Interpretations* (Garden City: Doubleday & Co., Anchor Books, 1965).

14. *New York Times,* 13 July 1970, p. 23, Col. 1. The plan, proposed by Clark for the Washington, D.C. public schools, includes a provision that teachers be paid according to their ability to raise the reading achievement of their pupils.

15. John L. Schimel, "Love and Games," *Contemporary Psychoanalysis* 1, no. 2 (Spring 1965): 109.

# 10

# Money and Accounting as Measurement Systems: What Happens in Business

> Given the nature of the French planning process, in order to be "qualified," the trade union representative would have to have access to information and knowledge possessed only by businessmen . . . . Thus, in the planning situation, the businessman has a quasimonopoly on certain kinds of "qualifications" that give business the initiative.
>
> Stephen S. Cohen [1]

We see that greater public attention to school accountability will increase the controversies arising from interpretation and application of the measures. Inevitably, innumerable "technical" disputes will arise. These may include such issues as who should do the measuring, how he should be paid, who should decide whom to hire for the job, what he should count, whether his report should be public, how the report should be analyzed and discussed, and so on. Of course, one can sense that the particular resolutions that develop from these technical debates will largely determine the impact and significance of accountability. If we could better forecast the direction of these debates, we might move them in healthy directions. One forecasting tool may be the study of historical analogies. I suggest that the history of the development of money and accounting as measurement systems for business can provide us with such an analogy.

Business has traditionally been *the* environment where comparative numerical measures, e.g., profits and sales, have been central to policy-setting. Some observers have felt that school changes toward businesslike patterns, including greater emphasis on accountability perspectives, would be very desirable; others have said that such a "dehumanization" of education is exactly why they oppose accountability. In either case, a dispassionate look at the historical role of accountability in business, where it has undergone extensive evolution, may generate greater understanding about its implications for schools.

Since the objectives of business is to produce profits, the essential outputs of business are profits and profit-related indicators. Businesses that produce many goods might fail; those that made a profit on miniscule production could be a success. How has this focus on profit accountability affected the character of business, and what are its implications for nonbusiness enterprises? Our study will selectively survey several thousand years of history to identify the most useful concepts and themes for our purposes.

## Money: The Root of It All

The development of the concept of money as a tool for measuring output was a major step toward the complex accounting systems in use today. Unquestionably, the concept was the product of invention and unconscious evolution. The theme of invention underlies Mirabeau's proposition that money—"the language of self-interest"—is one of the greatest inventions of the human mind.[2] The proposition has two important implications: (1) It recognizes the importance of the role of money in human affairs, and (2) it perceives that money is a communication device: a language, or vocabulary for transmitting information and concepts.

The notion of money as a vocabulary should be expanded: our vocabularies determine what we can conveniently communicate and, thus, the ideas or thoughts we can receive from others or communicate to them. The Stone Age Eskimos of northern Canada have over twenty-five words to describe different types of snow. Therefore, they can engage in careful analytic conversations about snow and plan their life in the snowy wastes more efficiently. The Eskimos might die out within a year if, all at once, they were permitted to use only one word to describe snow. Their vocabulary has evolved from the needs of their culture and made their culture possible. (School accountability measures may promote restructuring of school operations; conversely, the nonexistence of these measures may also produce certain structuring effects on the existing culture of school administration.)

But what about the vocabulary of money? We should first recognize that, like all vocabularies or symbols, money has inherent shortcomings. The dollar value of some objects may tell us much, or little, about the character of the object. It may even seriously mislead us. But compared to other means of defining the general public regard for some objects, there is no doubt that prices "summarize a great store of information about consumer preferences, physical and cost efficiency, and so on."[3]

The concept of money as a language suggests a number of perceptions about its dynamic characteristics; some of these have clear implications for education. For instance, Harold Innis, an intellectual ancestor of McLuhan, attempted in *Empire and Communications*[4] to explore the relationship between (a) languages and other media of communication and (b) the division of power in different societies. He suggested that different media favor different divisions of power. Thus, a language with a complex alphabet or other involved writing techniques may favor the control of power by a clerical-religious elite such as trained scribes. Only such literate classes have the necessary skills for effective communication: only they can interpret the written laws, read the sacred books, and manage the accounts. Innis also proposed that tensions might exist between scribe groups, which retain their status by written language, and persons whose powers rested on oral language or other symbol transmission systems. In essence, he saw diverse configurations of language use as generating or structuring patterns of conflict within or between societies. Innis proposed that healthier social systems require a tension or balance between language modes. Prolonged reliance on one mode or another is inherently undesirable, since each mode has some potential for generating unhealthy imbalances. Such broad concepts are not susceptible to incisive proof. However, they can create useful sensitivities.

For instance, we might ask ourselves what class or social interest was favored by the development of the "new" language of money, and whose status was diminished by the development. Similarly, we might consider the current "language" of school operations: credentialed teachers, degrees, number of graduates, pupil-teacher ratios, fixed salary scales, tax rates. Does this language favor some class, group, or value system by the framework it implies? For instance, essentially, does it not describe rather than evaluate school operations? In other words, the current language about schools reflects and implicitly approves the status quo. On the other hand, new groups, concepts, and interests are assisted by the use of accountability language. Indeed, the word *accountability* may in itself be insurrectionary, because it implies a new pattern of responsibilities between school administrators and citizens. Can we not characterize the tensions that arise over the attempts to apply output measurement to schools as conflicts over which language to apply to describe an institution?

To suggest answers to some of these questions, it seems that (a) many education researchers—psychologists, statisticians, economists—and some undefined members of the public may find their influence strengthened by the larger adoption of accountability systems by schools; and (b) teachers; some current administrators, whose status is founded on the existing body of education knowledge; and certain groups within schools of education may all find that the new language diminishes their influence. Today, laymen are reluctant to argue about what is the best technique to teach reading, or what kind of field trips or salary systems are best. Discussions on such topics seem to flounder in conceptual bogs. On the other hand, in an output-focused discussion, laymen may feel more comfortable in criticizing a professional (regardless of justification) for not equaling the performance of some other system or school. Even if the premise of the laymen's output criticism is incorrect, the belief that one is *right* or sensible is an important source of self-confidence. Thus, as long as laymen believe that courses in schools of education give administrators and teachers unique information about education, the laymen's self-confidence and power to criticize is diminished; conversely, if laymen believe that they can use accountability measures as a standard, their power will grow. Therefore, the introduction of the language of accountability may result in a shifting of power in school management.

There are other analogies arising from the theme of money as a language. Language is an evolutionary product. It is never perfected and its symbols can become obsolete. The capability of growth or mutation is perhaps the most important characteristic of a language.

People may shape a new or alien language to serve their unique needs; it need not stay foreign. Both rational and emotional forces affect its development. The impact of language depends on the skill of the user and the perception of the listener; use is a two-way process. All these themes portend a complex evolutionary development for output measures in schools.

## Business Without Money

Another way to study the implications of money and accounting history for school accountability is to study a business environment without money. In other words, a business that operates without money may give us new insights about the significance of money as a concept. Maybe business without money can be equated to schools without learning measures. For practical purposes, Soviet business in the immediate past operated in a nonmoney environment. Let us see what happened.

In postrevolutionary Russia, business management was evaluated by its success in producing certain quotas of goods, rather than in achieving a particular rate of profit. The Soviets adopted such output-of-goods goals partly because of (a) the instability of money as a measure in the chaotic postrevolutionary society and (b) their ideological hostility toward money, the capitalist tool par excellence. Theoretically, Soviet industries were also supposed to maintain certain rates of profit. However, the overwhelming effect of the planning-incentive structure was to stimulate managers to achieve or overachieve their product goals: "profits" were secondary. Various devices could be developed by managers to juggle the books or otherwise play down a poor profit rate, but the production was carefully defined and monitored. Underproduction was inexcusable, and overproduction was well rewarded.[5]

As a result of this structure, production was the focus of all management efforts. Every device was used to meet the quota. Since managers realized that success would win them promotion or transfer, they were not concerned with the maintenance of the plant to which they were assigned; if production could be increased by postponing or ignoring maintenance, they did so. Since the number of goods rather than profits from their sale was the test, they downgraded quality. If machinery to increase production could be obtained through some deal, they bought it regardless of cost. If accountants from the central accounting office were assigned to keep an eye on costs, they won cooperation by giving the accountants a cut of the quota fulfillment bonus. Since *goods produced* were defined as goods on the production line, they maintained large quantities of half-manufactured goods on the line; when the definition changed to mean only goods shipped, they quickly shipped poorly finished or incompleted goods. When quotas were being set by central planning, they used every device to keep their quotas low.

When we consider the Soviet experience, we see that they have not rejected accountability measures per se but have attempted to devise an alternative output measure to money. Their efforts to devise such an alternative proceeded at a rapid pace due to their drive for industrial development. In effect, the Soviet experience offers an example of the *accelerated* application of output data as a tool for control. The Soviet planners tried to invent and rigorously apply a new accountability system in less than a generation. Their effort was a success in the sense that it met some of the needs of the times. Now, however, they are moving away from production as the only output measure, and toward using profit and money as additional standards. They have recognized that money and modern accounting techniques have more potential as summative standards. They have also seen that money can measure more diverse achievements than can be measured by production output. Depreciation rates can be determined for unused equipment; values can be set for materials in inventory, and interest can be calculated for loans. While these factors were theoretically applied in the earlier production economy, the overriding focus on production encouraged manipulation of the fiscal indices. The evolution toward a more genuinely money-oriented economy has actually meant movement toward more diversified and subtle standards of success.

Several principles for education accountability measures can be derived from the Soviet experience:

a. The creation of useful accountability measures is an evolutionary process; it involves large elements of trial and error.

b. A diversity of measures is important: since any one measure may tend toward corruption or may simply represent a mistake, insurance is needed.

c. Persons whose performance is rigorously measured by one output measure may undesirably warp the operation of their enterprise to attain the goal or corrupt those who may detect their evasions.

d. Inspection, discussion, and publicity at all stages are vital aspects of preventing dysfunctions in accountability systems. In fact, one of the openest aspects in the whole Soviet society—the grievance and complaint reporting patterns of the government press—became an important tool for monitoring the application of production quotas; the frank complaints of consumers, workers, and inquisitive reporters were often given a wide play and helped keep the system moderately honest.

## Accounting: First Steps

The development of money as a vocabulary of value is the foundation of the concept of financial accountability. The ancient Egyptians and other Middle Eastern people used numbers to control financial or commercial operations. Interestingly, the democratic state of Athens offers an early example of public financial accountability: the financial records of Athenian public officers from the fifth century B.C. have been found engraved in stones exposed in public places; the records disclosed the major incomes and expenses for the government of Athens during the administrations of certain officers.[6]

The language of money is one of the developments that laid the foundation for the modern business systems of Western society. A number of other societies have used money, but most of them have not gone much further toward a complex commercial system. Our capitalist industrial system is founded on the medium of money, but it uses that medium in unique ways.

These unique ways first appeared when money lenders and merchants in northern Renaissance Italy evolved a level of accounting concepts far superior to those practiced elsewhere. An important step in this evolution was the gradual replacement, over 300 years (between the twelfth and fifteenth centuries) of Roman numbers by "vulgar" Arabic numbers. It was impractical to use the awkward Roman numbers to maintain coherently the emerging double entry bookkeeping records. Thus, the development of double entry bookkeeping went hand in hand with the extinction of the Latin number system. The change was sharply criticized by humanistic scholars.

As accounting concepts sharpened in the early fourteenth century, Genoa enacted a statute prescribing the account forms to be followed by banks. By the early fifteenth century, the Medici required the managers of their branch banks to submit annual balance sheets to the senior partners. The improved communications fostered by the new practices permitted decentralization and larger enterprise. As a later English treatise on bookkeeping observed, "men are obliged to join in Partnership, which so often blows up with great discord, if they have not a true form to satisfy the Concern what has become of their Stock."[7]

The larger operations involved more partners and more capital. Gradually, the family basis of business diminished, as the basis of confidence within the firm shifted from blood ties to accurate, common information about business operations. Enterprises became more productive and more impersonal. Many of these accounting practices were described in a treatise on double entry bookkeeping written by the Italian scholar Luca Pacoli in 1494.[8] Pacoli's *Suma* may be the most significant book on measurement ever written. It went through six Italian editions in the next forty years, and was pirated by German, French, Dutch, and English writers in the same period. For several hundred years, the methods described by Pacoli were the standards of good accounting practice.

The word *accounting* is derived from *count,* and means a system of keeping count. Accounting includes accounts kept for internal or external purposes and encompasses bookkeeping—i.e., the making of entries—and auditing. The concepts of auditing evolved as the practices of accounting became refined. Questions logically arose about the accuracy of the accounts and "accounting to whom." The audit was born. The word *audit* derived from the word *auditore,* to hear. It signified that the account books were reviewed by one or more disinterested parties at a public meeting or hearing in the presence of all concerned persons. Any party objecting to the accuracy of entries had a right to speak out. If the auditors were satisfied at the conclusion of the audit, they would attest to the accuracy of the accounts.

For instance, in 1695 the burg or village of Sterling, Scotland, had an ordinance which provided that:

neither provosts nor bailes should be auditors of the accounts [of the burg], but that, in addition to the ordinary number of auditors chosen by the town council, two merchants should be chosen by guildry and two tradesmen by the incorporate trades; that the auditors should have the exclusive power to approve or reject the accounts as they see cause; that the burgesses should be entitled to inspect the accounts and state objections during the auditing; that the members of council should, at their electing, be sworn to observe these rules at all times coming.[9]

Auditing also played an important role in the management of English manorial estates, where the lord of the manor used outside auditors to inspect the books kept by his managers. Over time, the public hearing element diminished, and the books were simply examined by the auditors. However, certain basic principles still obtained. The auditor was independent of the persons who maintained the books on a day-to-day basis. At the end of the audit, he had to vouch for the accuracy of the entries. The auditor had to deliver a final written report to the bookkeepers and to the owners of the goods or money involved.

The principles of auditing came into play in business ventures such as partnerships, where inactive partners had entrusted others with the management of their money. Still, the concept of the auditor as an outside party was not refined in business but in more political contexts, such as the affairs of cities, burgs, and manors. Only in such cases, in preindustrial societies, was there typically a substantial enough delegation of money control to require a third party's assistance to settle the accounts.

The forms of accounting and auditing evolved continuously. Meanwhile, improvements in transportation, communication, and eventually industry and science, brought about forces that made accounting—particularly double entry bookkeeping—of great pertinence to the development of capitalism. Schumpeter's lyric proposition on the interrelation between capitalism and the concept of double entry bookkeeping is perhaps appropriate:

it exalts the creation of the monetary unit—not itself a creation of capitalism—into a unit of account. That is to say, capitalist practice turns the unit of money into a tool of rational cost-profit calculations, of which the towering monument is double entry bookkeeping. Without going into this, we will notice that, primarily a product of the evolution of economic rationality, the cost-plus calculus in turn reacts upon that rationality; by crystallizing and defining numerically, it powerfully propels the logic of enterprise. And thus defined and quantified for the economic sector, this type of logic or attitude or method then starts upon its conqueror's career, subjugating—rationalizing—man's tools and philosophies, his medical practice, his picture of the cosmos, his outlook of life, everything in fact including his concepts of beauty and justice and spiritual ambitions.[10]

The growth of financial combinations as tools for pooling capital received a serious setback in the early eighteenth century, with the South Sea Bubble scandal in England. The scandal was partly due to excessive abuses—including faulty record keeping—committed by joint stock companies or corporations. In response to these abuses, Parliament passed the highly restrictive South Sea Bubble Act in 1719. This act severely limited corporate growth.

Despite these restrictions, the need for accountants grew with the progress of the Industrial Revolution in England. Between 1811 and 1847 the number of accountants listed in the directories of London grew from 24 to 186, while the population just doubled.

In 1844 and 1845 Parliament passed the first of a series of Companies acts to assist financial combinations and developing industries. To avoid another South Sea Bubble scandal, Parliament reached back to the tradition of the manorial audit; the Companies Act required annual examination, disclosure, and certification of corporation records and information by independent auditors. Under the legislation, "the shareholders stood in the place of the lord of the manor, the directors represented the bailiffs as stewards of the estate, and the auditors, under statute, still retained his place as the personal representative of the lord appointed to inspect the record of stewardship."[11]

At first the auditors were stockholders; after a time, accountants acted as representatives of the stockholders. The number of practicing accountants in London grew still larger: from 186 in 1847 to 840 in 1883. Concurrently, accountants began to see themselves as a unique profession, and they created their own professional organization.

With the recognition of the role of the auditor in the Companies Act, two intertwining themes appeared in accounting. These themes have important implications for education accountability. The first was the desire of managers to maintain control over their business by keeping fiscal information secret. Such secrecy protected the managers vis-a-vis their competitors and their own shareholders. Of course, the former motive was the one proclaimed in public. The second theme centered about the internal use of accounting data by managers as a tool to permit greater efficiency. As we will see later, these two themes sometimes tended to merge.

The secrecy theme was the subject of recurring tension. From the first moments under the Companies Act, questions arose about the adequacy of the disclosure of data to stockholders and auditors. The act's theoretical framework was sound; however, there was ample room for evasion of its real intent by determined managers. The auditors actual authority was poorly defined by the act. They were given short notice of the annual meeting, and left with little time to review complex books. Actually, the act was only the first step in a progression of English Companies acts continuously refining the disclosure obligation of corporations to their shareholders. Throughout this legislation, the recurrent theme has been, how can effective disclosure be compelled? Simultaneously, the constant plea of management has been that "excessive" disclosure will put the company at a competitive disadvantage and hurt shareholders.

## Accounting in America

The controversies over corporate disclosure in England had important repercussions in the United States, where the corporate form was concurrently enjoying tremendous success. American reformers, especially in the early twentieth century, offered numerous proposals for restricting corporate abuses, particularly the mulcting of stockholders. Perhaps the most articulate of these reformers was the lawyer Louis Brandeis. His book, *Other People's Money and How the Bankers Use It,* is a brilliant model of lucid, analytic, data-oriented advocacy.[12] The text first ran as a series in *Harpers Magazine,* then was published in book form. Brandeis took as his major theme the proposition that "Publicity is justly commended as a remedy for social and industrial diseases. Sunlight is said to be the best disinfectant; electric light the best policeman." Throughout the book, Brandeis made frequent reference to the British disclosure requirements. Using information developed in his role as a public advocate (a sort of early Ralph Nader) and by the 1912-1913 Pujo Investigating Committee of the House of Representatives, Brandeis skillfully dissected and exposed many of the unscrupulous and sometimes unlawful practices followed by investment banking firms. The fact that Brandeis, a vigorous business critic, proposed disclosure, rather than regulation or restriction, had an important long-range impact on public policy.

The crusades of Brandeis achieved full fruition fifteen years later in 1929. The stock market crash and Franklin Roosevelt's later election set the stage for full-scale federal intervention in stock market practices. After the investigation, some reformers proposed restrictions on what stocks should be permitted to be sold. The administration largely opted for the disclosure approach originally urged by Brandeis. Roosevelt's message accompanying the proposed Securities Act of 1933 said: "There is, however, an obligation upon us to insist that every issue of new securities to be sold in interstate commerce shall be accompanied by full publicity and information, and that no essential important element attending the issue should be concealed from the public."[13]

The act, and almost all important succeeding legislation affecting corporation/stockholder relations, adopted a disclosure theme. The government did not attempt to take away from every citizen his inalienable right to make a fool of himself; it simply attempted to prevent others from making a fool of him.[14]

Like the auditing requirements framed in the first Companies Act, the Securities Act did not end all disclosure controversies. It was simply an important step in an evolutionary process. However, the act did establish the principle that informing the stockholder took priority over the claim of "business secrets": the stock frauds of the 1920s had undercut that plea.

This historical survey of auditing suggests the complex patterns that have brought about the establishment of the principle of public disclosure in accounting. Concepts were needed to give us information to disclose. Commercial and industrial systems were needed to produce the goods and profits measured by the data. New professions were needed to apply and continually refine the concepts and to propose useful change strategies. Reformers, congressional hearings and publicity were needed to stimulate public indignation. Political systems took these diverse materials, and shaped and reshaped them into viable forms. These events took place over a long period of time, although developments have proceeded at an accelerating tempo. These interactions have obvious parallels for school accountability measures. However, it is important to recognize that in the field of business the underlying issues of how and what information to communicate to stockholders are still somewhat unsettled.

## Accounting to Whom?

For the moment, let us leave the theme of external disclosure to stockholders and return to the bypassed issue of accounting as an internal control tool. We will see that the internal/external lines have closer relationships than we might imagine. At earlier times—until perhaps the mid-nineteenth century—businessmen had seen accounting as a policing device: a tool to prevent embezzlement, to keep track of money due the enterprise, to record debts, to reassure stockholders or partners, etc. These activities were necessary but did not contribute to profit. They were maintenance affairs.

However, as enterprises grew in size and complexity, the problem of feedback gained importance. Intuitive managers became less adept at predicting the effect of corporate decisions on profits, sales, costs, or overhead. In order to "steer" these enlarging "ships," more subtle measuring instruments were needed. Accounting as a means of communicating information to management about the state of the business, came to be crucial as an internal feedback device. For example, over time auditors became less concerned about the accuracy of individual entries in the books and more interested in the formats and theories underlying the books. What entry categories most informatively portrayed the nature of the business operations? What represented the real costs and profits of the enterprise? Once these items were defined, what indicators could quickly inform the management of the firm of developing trends, to permit efficient "steering"? As in the case of school survey research, expeditious, inexpensive sampling procedures were substituted for lengthy, cumbersome studies.

Perhaps one of the most perceptive writers on the concept of accounting as feedback is Raymond Chambers. His aptly titled book, *Accounting, Evaluation and Economic Behavior,* is an intensive survey of the implications of accounting as a communications system. Chambers directed his study at the questions of communicating what to whom for what purpose. He contends that answering these questions is a precondition to assessing the conceptual precision of accounting information. His essential point is that accountants have been severely handicapped by the early appearance of accounting as a tool for *internal* management rather than *external* communications to stockholders and the public. The internal emphasis has inhibited the generation of more productive accounting concepts for either internal or external use, since the exclusively internal perspective of the concept designers has restricted their insights. Chambers' criticisms are inferentially supported by (a) many recognized shortcomings in current accounting practice and (b) historical patterns suggesting that the important conceptual advances in accounting have evolved from debates provoked by its application in a public context. In other words, internal data and measurement systems tend to develop dysfunctions over time that can only be corrected by subjecting their products to public disclosure and debate.

However, these imperfections do not support arguments for the abandonment of accounting. We are analyzing a communication system: a tool for transmitting concepts, ideas, and values. *The first characteristic of any such system is imperfection.* Perhaps the strongest defense for current accounting despite its imperfections is that the imperfections become more tolerable if we consider any other large areas of our society where the numerical control systems are not even as good as the admittedly imperfect systems in accounting. Is divorce the best measure of the state of the family? Is the average number of years of schooling a good test of the state of public knowledge? What makes the growth of the GNP the appropriate test of national well-being? Accounting imperfections reflect the diversity and complexity of human values; the fact is that the only substitute for imperfect communication may be either death or even more imperfect communication.

The inevitability of imperfect communications does not foreclose improvement. Indeed, Chambers and the other critics are proposing conceptual improvements they believe desirable and perhaps attainable. But there are more important forces for improvement than the prods of intellectual critics. These forces are suggested by the interplay between external public accountability (essentially via auditing) and improved internal controls. At one time, as we suggested, these were seen as discrete problems. The fact is that they are inextricably intertwined. The more important refinements in accounting sprang from the need to develop records that would satisfy the need to inform new partners and others in an outside status rather than merely the traditional owner-manager. The owner-manager tended to be satisfied with intuitive data, but this handicapped the development of more analytic and communicative accounting systems. Chambers argues that the key fact is that the accountant's communications responsibility is at least three-sided: involving the manager, the stockholder-outsider, and the public. The narrow internal communication tradition has not been a fruitful framework for concept design or communication improvement.

There is empirical evidence to support Chambers' proposition. At the turn of the twentieth century, the accounting disclosure practices of American firms advanced beyond those of their British counterparts. The advance was not compelled by any mandate in the law. It was primarily the product of different corporation-stockholder relations patterns that arose in the two nations. Admittedly, the disclosure practices in the United States were inadequate by current American standards, but American disclosure was still in advance of British practice at that time. That "gap" has been maintained, since the tempo of changes in statutory provisions have kept American accounting practices more open than those in Britain. During those same years, American management developed and applied more effective internal accounting controls than were used in Britain. For instance, the discipline of cost accounting received an important boost in England during World War I when an Englishman who had become a partner in a New York accounting firm returned to England to establish a cost accounting unit in the munitions industry; he was knighted for his work. Thirty-five years later, a British productivity team visiting the United States concluded that among the prime tools possessed by American businessmen were accounting systems that produced comprehensive future-oriented data.[15] Thus, it is reasonable to hypothesize that further refinement in accounting depends on the degree to which data and information is produced for public use.

From the foregoing, we can see that the refinement of accounting as a language demonstrates an important correlation between disclosure and public debates over data, on the one hand, and the improvement of the art in the interest of all users, on the other.

From other material in this book, we have also seen indications that the public controversies surrounding school accountability data may have a stimulating effect on the improvement of research theory and practice. The example offered by open financial accounting underlines the importance of this interaction.

## The Effects of Business Data

If we accept the principle that the disclosure of accounting data, although imperfect, communicates information of importance, the question arises: what effects have such disclosures had? As we have suggested above, one effect has been to stimulate forces pushing the refinement of data. The first data disclosed is never complete, or completely adequate. But what have the persons and institutions who receive this data done with it? Let us consider four important classes of business data users whose purposes, to some degree, will overlap: (1) stockholders and "the market," (2) business managers, (3) economists, and (4) the larger society. At the same time, we will consider the implications of each of these categories for the field of school accountability measurement.

### The Market

Evolving even a primitive model of the impact of accounting information on present and potential stockholders' conduct is an enormous endeavor. Some authors have attempted to develop researchable concepts, but we are a long way from generating theories and models that may be tested in actual operations.[16] The problem is that markets in Western societies are awash with such information. Almost no pieces of accounting news can be considered "news." Nearly every data-based announcement, report, or analysis is rooted in some previous semipublic development. One informed commentator has said: "I sense that knowledge affecting common stock prices is not perfectly disseminated at any one time, but that it comes more as a steady flow than as intermittent jogs, such as reporting dates of accounting data."[17]

In fact, a major effect of an efficient market is to actually prevent or anticipate the occurrence of dramatically new or unpredicted information. Under these circumstances, it is difficult to estimate the impact of any one piece of information. These are, however, interesting clues about how information is disseminated by corporations.

Major businesses consider it important to keep their stockholders informed. The National Industrial Conference Board's survey of ninety-four important publicly held firms, disclosed that they spend about fifty-five cents per shareholder in preparing and publishing their annual report. In contrast, widely distributed school district annual reports probably cost from five to ten cents per copy (except for the Columbis, Ohio, and Oakland, California, reports[18]). The survey also revealed who sought information and their diverse means of collection:

> The firms studied spent more time and effort communicating with financial professionals [investment and commercial bankers, brokerage firm partners, pension and mutual fund managers, security analysts, and business reporters specializing in financial news and analysis] than they do with stockholders . . . because of the influence they can bring to bear on the company's market performance and acceptance of a stock.[19]

For example, twenty-five of the ninety-four firms said their officers and staff participated in 100 or more interviews a year with such professionals.

The quote portrays the market as a multilayered information-disseminating and action-influencing network. In the network persons with lesser involvement tacitly delegate some of their collecting and analyzing chores to specialists and react to their conduct or suggestions. This picture is consonant with many other studies of the circulation of public and political information, which disclose concentric circles of more informed citizens who are also more influential. The information and influence of the informed are not usually related to secrecy (though this is the case at some levels) but simply to interest, information-collecting skills, time available, and experience. The quote also highlights the importance of face-to-face contacts, even where the discussions encompass quantitative information.

Against this backdrop, the formal report to stockholders is a document seen in the light of other information the stockholder has received via stock quotations, the recommendations of his broker, the opinions of his friends, etc. Ironically, much more significant information might be transmitted if the report were not sent; in other words, since most companies issue a report, failure to do so would be an action of high information significance.

These considerations give us further insights into school affairs. I recall one activist parent interviewed in New York City. She observed that the publication of scores showing low pupil achievement in her local school had not told her circle of activists anything new; when perhaps only one child on a block in their neighborhood went to college, they did not need more evidence about school output. However, she conceded that the data may have given legitimacy to the parents' complaints in the eyes of less informed persons. Presumably, most formal data essentially serves such a legitimizing purpose. The informed person is rarely surprised by data; after the Coleman Report came out, many experts said, "We might have predicted its conclusion in the first place." Still, without the legitimizing and focusing effect of publication, the impact of the professional analyst's judgment is moderated, and in the long run his sources of information dry up.

Other school implications arise from these patterns. Possibly even the most "objective" data will be more useful if interpreted by an independent professional who has also *interviewed* the school personnel concerned and is prepared to offer analytic interpretations. However, the outside professional will be useful only if he is seen as an agent, not of the school system, but of the consumers. We can anticipate the appearance of such professionals in some form. In the stockmarket, these experts are supported by the commissions brokerage houses earn from the sale of stocks or by the subscriptions paid for newsletters. These payment systems put pressure on the experts to offer good advice; otherwise, their customers will go elsewhere. Presumably, some equivalent form of compensation must arise for educational accountants and account interpreters.

Finally, it is evident that wide variations of stockholder sophistication about accountability exist. Perhaps we may also see such varying patterns of public sophistication evolve about school accountability. Surely, there will always be some uninformed and comparatively disinterested parents or stockholders. But it is also necessary for there to be some parents and citizens who read and talk about data and understand something about it. These citizens may include legislators, school board members, and officers or employees of parents' groups. This increased sophistication would be the product of new communication efforts.

### Business Managers

What has a dollar- and profit-oriented environment done for managers? And what might accountability mean for school administrators? A response to this question must include consideration of the psychological level. The studies of many behavioral psychologists have reiterated the importance of feedback as a stimulant to achievement and, just as importantly, to job satisfaction. David McClelland has done the most extensive work in this area. His work has demonstrated that doing, creating, achieving personalities perform best in environments where they are routinely informed about the success or failure of their efforts. McClelland compared the pattern of a feedback-oriented business environment to an environment without accountability data:

> The doctor knows whether his patients get well or not, the lawyer whether or not he wins his case. However, a teacher, a clergyman, or a civil servant may have only the general kind of feedback as to how well he has accomplished what he sets out to do. In all such cases, a man must often be satisfied with the conviction that he acted as he should have acted according to the norms generally approved at the time. But he cannot have the definite concrete feedback that the businessman often has in the form of quantified knowledge of profitability, percentage of control of the market, rate of growth, etc. From a psychological point of view, it does not automatically follow that all kinds of people like to have concrete knowledge of results of their choices of action. Such knowledge is a source of anxiety because it cuts both ways: it provides not only proof of success but also inescapable evidence of failure. Consequently, some people ought to prefer functioning in an occupation in which a person can rest assured that he is doing a good job if he follows established traditions closely—to want more definite feedback is to run a greater risk of being wrong. Contrast a businessman and a priest, for example. A businessman can operate according to the best established policy, efficient production procedures, etc.—and still fail. Despite doing everything "correctly," his produce may not sell or may not bring in sufficient return to keep his business going. His success is determined by "results" not by following established practices. A priest, on the other hand, knows only that he is being a better priest if he obeys more rigorously the rules of his profession, or more scrupulously follows its prescribed rituals. He cannot "fail" in the same concrete sense that the businessman can.[20]

As we might expect, businessmen regard numerical goals as a

major measure of their own business success. In a recent survey of over 300 business chief executives, their first measure of management success was "growth, evidenced by share of the market, assets, sales, but most significantly, profits—profits expressed as return on investment, earnings per share and indirectly, by price-earnings ratios."[21]

We will see later that this flat statement may require some qualification. However, it is accurate to say that even the qualifiers agree with the need for growth as a precondition to the application of the qualifications they proffer.

Questions naturally arise about the character of the environment in which these goal-oriented businessmen work and the kind of man it fosters. Is their world one we might wish to have enlarged? There may not be a simple answer to this question, but it is safe to say there are many oversimplifications about the businessman and his world. A number of authors have produced academic and semipopular writings portraying the business world as a sterile, conformity-ridden environment. There is no doubt that these themes exist in parts of such an enormous system. Conformity may also tend to concentrate on certain levels. But the critics may be failing to segregate the innate conformity that exists within many human beings—wherever they work—from the conformity that is unique to businessmen. For instance, we are told that "teachers, like many other marginal men, are overeager to conform."[22] How do we weigh this against the conformity of the junior executives portrayed in *The Organization Man?*

Moreover, other themes of research on business present a different picture. One study pointed out that goal-oriented performance records favorably affected the work satisfaction of a group of professionals because they made the work more "collegial."[23] "The freedom from close supervision and from rigid operating rules that the records made possible enhanced work satisfaction." The prerecord environment was described as "pseudo-democratic." Allegedly, the professionals in the past had been participating in the management of the enterprise. However, before the introduction of performance criteria, the necessity of focusing on doing things the "right way"—rather than on achieving—inevitably restricted their freedom of decision. In effect, they were told they were professionals but were treated like children. Other experiments on the effect of feedback on output and work satisfaction have produced similar results.

Michael Crozier offered important parallel insights drawn from a series of studies of bureaucratic environments, where output measures did not apply:

> The bureaucratic world is an arbitrary world. People are protected, but at the price of being partially cut off from reality. They have security and are protected from the sanction of facts; but they have no way of taking the measure of their own endeavor. This engenders secondary kinds of anxiety and explains the paramount importance of human relations within a bureaucratic system. What people gain through security, they lose in realism. They must rely on human relations sanctions instead of the usual achievement sanctions. Theirs is a world of petty bickering and endless battles of the war of position. People escape the lower middle class status panic; instead, they develop the skimpy outlook of the petty power struggles of a tight social system.[24]

There is a larger, almost philosophical issue that overrides these experimental observations. As McClelland said, some personalities prefer structured environments, where following procedures is the test of effectiveness, rather than actual success. If we wish to be polemical, we may call the procedure-oriented persons "priests" or "marginal men," and the others "achievers" or "slave-drivers." In any case, no revised pattern of organization is going to remake all employees in one mold. Each organization, regardless of its structure, will retain within itself some mixture of priests and achievers, though the proportions will be affected by the values of the system. The issue is, what proportion of each type is optimal for the organization? For instance, education has had, and needed, stimulators, such as Horace Mann, John Dewey, Admiral Rickover, and Frances Keppel, as well as its priests. Business has surely had priests as well as John Paul Getty, Howard Hughes, and Thomas J. Watson. Many business observers have been critical of the achievers, but the educational observers have just as often been dissatisfied with the priests.

For example, consider the implications of line promotion practices in education. These patterns emphasize procedure orientation. They mean that school superintendents have usually started at the teacher level and worked up. In essence, almost all superintendents have (a) taken a number of education courses in college, which cuts out all college students who do not like education courses (and a great number of them have such a dislike), (b) been a teacher, which cuts out all persons whose temperament is not adapted to working closely with the young in a school setting, (c) worked in a school environment for a long time, (d) avoided disagreement with procedure-oriented superiors, and (e) attained a higher degree in education. In sum, we can sense that many of these operating qualifications tend to sort out aggressive people with high drives for achievement and innovation. As one commentator said, "The widespread practice of promotion on a line has had a deadly effect on all school operations including business management of district affairs. The account clerk, or bookkeeper, or business teacher . . . is not likely to emerge at the age of sixty as the ideal innovator."[25]

### The Economists

Economists were the first social scientists to direct their attention to business. In fact, their discipline came into being for the purpose of analyzing dollars and other output measures. The measures provided a way of aggregating the operation of business and commerce. Monetary systems were thus more amenable to focused analysis than other social systems. Economists used the data to (a) reproduce large-scale, tabular output studies; (b) establish conceptual frameworks for the design of theoretical models of human economic conduct; and (c) design quantitative models for the study of public institutions and policies and the operation of large firms.

These activities have produced theories and research that have had numerous practical and ideological impacts on public policy. They have justified the passage and revision of laws, the planning of business policies, the management of foreign affairs, and even to some degree the conduct of violent revolutions and international wars. Indeed, it is probably safe to say that economics has been the most influential discipline in the modern world. Economists have not only shaped policy intellectually; distinguished economists have served as prime ministers of France, Germany, England, and Italy, as well as secretary-general of the United Nations.[26]

It is also noteworthy that many prominent economists have expected their theoretical treatments to become subjects of public controversy and have invited such controversies. Marx was president of the First International; for a time Keynes was a senior British bureaucrat and wrote both popular and technical works; contemporary Americans John Kenneth Galbraith, Walter Hansen, and Milton Friedman have all sought the public ear. These airings of diverse views have not all been neat and pretty. However, in the long run they have greatly stimulated the refinement of the science of economics. Thus, economics, far from being a remote, technical, abstract science, has also been actively identified with politics, power, and public controversy.

Many of these concept-producing efforts of economics have had spillover effects on education research. For instance, the aggregation of output may be compared to the national education evaluation efforts such as the Coleman Report and National Assessment. Firm-size models are being exploited in districtwide accountability projects and in efforts to apply programming-planning-budgeting systems to school districts.

We should also consider the relation between financial data and economic planning. Modern economics has been able to use the aggregate approach underlying output measures to design many tools for economic planning policy. These tools have ranged from complex, macroeconomic models of national output, which permit simulation of the effect of various proposed changes in policy, to fairly primitive rules of thumb. Sometimes the policy benefit of the tools has come more from generating a focus for debate—such as the commitment to raise the GNP or employment rate by so many percentage points—than from the design of refined policies.[27] Still, regardless of the techniques, economic planning has become a powerful tool for enabling societies (via their governments) to affect economics policy. Such planning has become so universally accepted that it has been removed from ideology. No modern government disavows its responsibility to participate in setting national economic priorities.

While there is a large body of literature on education planning, however, the lack of output data has limited its potential. This lack is especially felt in "advanced"societies. In such societies, literacy is largely taken for granted, and school completion is thus a poor indicator of educational productivity; the typical products of education in such societies are more advanced skills than literacy. One cannot assume that such sophisticated skills are automatically produced simply by extending schooling. One might even contend that schooling diminishes some important skills. However, most educational plans allow for the production of only certain numbers of graduates. But the plans can pay only slight attention to whether the graduates are well taught, since we are not now able to identify the quality aspect of education.

Under these circumstances, educational planning focuses on peripheral statistics: dollars spent, classrooms built, certified teachers, students graduated, etc. There can be public participation in determining these numbers, but the participation essentially centers on a very primitive measure of knowledge, i.e., dollars. Even a debate about how much to spend on automobile production is also a debate about how many cars we want. But we can only guess that school "dollar fights " have to do with better learning. What would be the effect on pupil learning of giving a teacher a pay raise or cut, putting in a swimming pool, or changing pupil-teacher ratios? The answer is "It's anyone's guess." In such a vacuum, the planning process has large elements of sham; public participation excites demagoguery, rather than debate. Thus, without accountability data, educational planning will remain a sterile and disillusioning process; with it, we may have more fruitful, democratic, and productive change.

There is another area of economics-education interaction we must consider. Education is viewed by economists as part of the service component of our gross national product. Service activities maintain equipment and provide citizens and institutions with information and advice. They are differentiated from the producing component, which manufactures or grows goods or staples. As our material prosperity has grown, our citizens have spent more of the nation's income on services such as health, education, recreation, travel, maintenance of goods, research, communication, and information storage.

This trend is attributable to two factors: (1) The service sector has not increased its productivity as fast as the production sector, and (2) it is possible that our postindustrial economy actually needs more services than earlier economies.[28] Whatever the combination of reasons—the lack of precise data prohibits us from deriving more exact answers—the extraordinary growth of the service sector poses serious questions. For example, Peter Drucker observed that *if* the trend in education continues, by the year 2000 half the population will spend half the day in school and then be dismissed to spend the rest of the day teaching the other half of the population. In other words, it is essential that more data about service industry output (including education) be developed, so that we can better perceive productivity trends and stimulate research to increase service productivity. The National Assessment is an instance of a move in this direction.

In closing our consideration of economics, one can say that output accountability has made the discipline possible, and the discipline has evolved concepts that have enabled it (and business and commerce) to be of immense service to society. There is no discipline peculiarly identified with education, in the sense that economics is identified with business. Hence, we have educational psychology, educational history, educational sociology, etc. Psychology is perhaps the most educationally focused discipline, and it is fairly output oriented, though it often gets its data from experiments rather than actual school operations. Perhaps the lack of a definable goal focus within schools has discouraged the development of a unique school discipline; perhaps the lack of data has also forced researchers who might be concerned with education to direct their efforts to other fields and support their prescriptions for actual school situations by deductions. In any event, one might forecast that (a) the collection of large amounts of school output data could accelerate the development of a new or enlarged discipline of school research, which might increase our knowledge of how schools can help children to learn; and (b) the adoption of more focused goals might generate different, more perceptive, and perhaps more fruitful theories of education.

### The Larger Society

The accounting-dollar forces we have analyzed have undoubtedly attained their highest refinement within the complex of nations we describe as Western society. Even where these societies have adopted socialistic policies for some particular enterprise or portion of the economy, the preceding accounting-dollars-profit framework has still been part of the picture. In managing the socialized enterprise, the citizens have had the recollection of the dollar-output framework as a tool of assessment. In effect, they have asked these government-managed industries for a full balance sheet. Also, the citizens concurrently have before them the model of privately owned enterprises operating within a competitive market and subject to stock market forces. This inevitably means pressures for the disclosure of data about growth, profits, earning per share, etc. These

Western nations are the most productive in the world; their citizens enjoy high material levels of productivity; and they have high levels of communication and the largest degree of political democracy.

It would be naive to describe these benefits as the simple product of a system of measurement, yet it would be foolish to deny that a system of measurement might have an important part in producing such effects. After all, the system has produced a major discipline (economics), attracted and kept a special class of activists in business, and provided a structure for focusing investments in the enterprises with the largest output measures. Despite all the benefits that we may attribute to the measurement system, it also seems that the importance of its role in determining business policy may be diminishing. If this is correct, what are the implications of this issue for school output developments?

Certainly, some contemporary analysts have contended that the profit motive has diminished as the goal of the large-scale Western business enterprise. The contemporary oligopolist has increasingly moved toward the recognition of a multigoal environment, perhaps even an environment in which process, rather than achievement, might be the goal. The development arises from the excessive success of the profit structure. Successful oligopolistic businesses routinely finance most of their expansion with undistributed profits. Their shareholders have been "trained" to expect that only a fraction of the annual profits will be distributed as dividends and that the undistributed profits will be retained to finance business expansion. Shareholders accept this because the expansion of the business will mean an increase in the share value in the long run. This means decisions about business expansion need not be put to the direct test of the stock market, i.e., offering new shares to finance the change; the managers can simply spend their retained earnings on the change. This pattern gives management great apparent discretion, since:

a. The shareholders have only minute influence on the operations of the corporation, due to the diffuse nature of their holdings, their ineffectual communications about corporate policy, and the fact that the company is satisfying the crucial test, i.e., paying dividends.

b. There is no reason to solicit the support of new stock purchasers.

Perhaps the first writers to recognize the potential within this pattern were Berle and Means in 1932, in their influential work, *The Modern Corporation and Private Property.* They concluded that:

> It is conceivable . . . indeed, it seems essential if the corporate system is to survive . . . that the "control" of the great corporations should develop into a purely neutral technocracy, balancing a variety of claims by various groups on the community and assigning to each a portion of the income stream on the basis of public policy rather than private cupidity.[29]

In sum, the freedom from public and stockholder control, which the management had won due to the success of the system, required the establishment of new forms of control and new ways of setting priorities. These forms would supplement the traditional criteria of profit, growth, etc.

Later studies all suggest these new controls have tended to evolve.[30] In 1959 Berle wrote:

> Self perpetuating boards of publicly held corporations are primarily concerned with their public position . . . that is, with the opinion of them formed by the business community and later by the general community . . . . The real legitimacy of power-holding, at base, depends on its acceptance by the consensus.[31]

Berle concluded that the oligopolies managed themselves as if there were an imperfect, rough, but effective formal machinery making them accountable to their stockholders and the larger society for their economic and social goals. In other words, business had moved from (a) the multigoal perspective implicit in precapitalist societies, through (b) the profit-oriented perspective of traditional society, to (c) the multigoal oligopoly of the *New Industrial Society.*

The authors of these propositions admitted that the problem of identifying and assessing the nonoutput goals of business is complex and uncertain. However, their analyses discussed above offer an instructive thesis-antithesis-synthesis construct.

None of the authors contends the matter is settled. Still, they suggest we have done better than might have been expected, and they are striving for better tools and concepts to improve our control of these new forces. The social indicators movement (see chap. 8), another macro-oriented form of output measure, may be one tool they choose to apply. The indicators may give us means for assessing and managing the noneconomic effects of businesses.

From this outline, it seems that business is moving toward the adoption of unclear, multigoal structures akin to those found in education. Conversely, it appears that traditional business perspectives are becoming more attractive to some persons concerned with education. However, such patterns are not as paradoxical as they appear. Business has used fairly tight goal structures to achieve a high degree of productivity and has apparently now found that other goals have been slighted in the process or that they can now afford to pursue diffuse goals. Perhaps schools, in their efforts to achieve a profusion of uncertain goals, have neglected to develop techniques to achieve essential minimum goals. Thus, both large systems might be simultaneously revising their former goal structures in different ways to meet the demands of their different levels of development.

## Footnotes

1. Stephen S. Cohen, *Modern Capitalist Planning: The French Model* (Cambridge: Harvard University Press, 1969), p. 325.

2. Harold Innis, *The Bias of Communication* (Toronto: University of Toronto Press, 1951), p. 8.

3. Harold Wilensky, *Organizational Intelligence* (New York: Basic Books, 1967), p. 113.

4. Harold Innis, *Empire and Communications* (Oxford: Clarendon Press, 1950).

5. The description of the Soviet experience is derived from David Granick, *Soviet Metal Fabricating and Economic Development* (University of Wisconsin Press, 1967); P. J. D. Wiles, *The Political Economy of Communism* (Cambridge: Harvard University Press, 1962); and Joseph S. Berliner, *Factory and Manager in the USSR* (Cambridge: Harvard University Press, 1957). Berliner is especially helpful.

6. The description of accounting history is derived principally from A. C. Littleton & B. S. Yamey, eds., *Studies in the History of Accounting* (Homewood, Ill.: Richard D. Irwin, 1956); A. C. Littleton, *Accounting Evolution to 1900* (New York: Russel & Russell, 1933); Richard A. Brown, *A History of Accounting and Accountants* (Edinburgh: T. C. & E. E. Jack, 1905).

7. Brown, op. cit., p. 156.

8. R. Emmett Taylor, *No Royal Road* (Chapel Hill: University of North Carolina Press, 1942). The biography of Pacoli.

9. Brown, op. cit., p. 89.

10. Joseph A. Schumpeter, *Capitalism, Socialism and Democracy*, 3d ed. (New York: Harper & Bros., 1950), p. 123.

11. Littleton, op. cit., p. 290.

12. Louis Brandeis, *Other People's Money and How the Bankers Use It* (New York: Fredrick A. Stokes, 1913), p. 92.

13. Louis Loss, *Securities Regulation* (Boston: Little, Brown, 1961), p. 127.

14. Ibid., p. 126.

15. Nicholas A. Stacey, *English Accountancy* (London: Gee & Co., 1954), pp. 98, 207.

16. William J. Burns, "Accounting Information and Decision-making: Some Behavioral Hypotheses," *The Accounting Review* 42, no. 3 (July 1968): 468-480.

17. George J. Benston, "Published Corporate Accounting Data and Stock Prices," in *Empirical Research in Accounting, Selected Studies, 1967* (Chicago: Journal of Accounting Research), p. 17.

18. See, e.g., Howard O. Merriman, *The Columbus School Profile* (Columbus, Ohio: Columbus School District, 1970); Division of Planning, Research and Evaluation, Oakland Public Schools, *Achievement Test Results, 1970-71* (Oakland, Calif.: Oakland Public Schools, 1971).

19. National Industrial Conference Board, *Investor Relations*, Studies in Business Policy, no. 124 (New York: the board, n.d.) p. 26.

20. David C. McClelland, *The Achieving Society* (Princeton: D. Van Nostrand Co., 1961), p. 231.

21. National Industrial Conference Board, *The Chief Executive and His Job* (New York: the board, 1969), p. 9.

22. Andrew Halpin, *Theory and Research in Administration* (New York: Macmillan Co.,1966), p. 246.

23. Peter M. Blau & W. Richard Scott, *Formal Organizations* (San Francisco: Chandler Publishing Co., 1967), p. 178.

24. Michel Crozier, *Bureaucratic Phenomenon* (Chicago: University of Chicago Press, 1964), p. 208.

25. H. Thomas James, *Education and the New Cult of Efficiency* (Pittsburgh: University of Pittsburgh Press, 1969), p. 56.

26. Daniel R. Fusfeld, *The Age of the Economist* (New York: William Morrow & Co., 1968), p. viii.

27. Cohen, op. cit.

28. Victor Fuchs, *The Service Economy* (New York: National Bureau of Economic Research, 1968).

29. Adolph A. Berle, Jr. & Gardiner C. Means, *The Modern Corporation and Private Property* (New York: Harcourt Brace, 1932), p. 312.

30. See, for example, Adolph A. Berke, Jr., *Power Without Property* (New York: Harcourt, Brace, 1959); John Kenneth Galbraith, *The New Industrial State* (Boston: Houghton Mifflin, 1967); Richard M. Cyret & James G. March, *A Behavioral Theory of the Firm* (Englewood Cliffs, N.J.: Prentice-Hall, 1963).

31. Berle & Means, op. cit., p. 110.

# 11

# Analysis and Forecast

> To make a government work requires no great prudence. Settle the seat of power; teach obedience; and the work is done. To give freedom is still more easy. It is not necessary to guide; it only requires to let go of the reins. But to form *a free government,* that is, to temper together those opposite elements of liberty and restraint in one consistent work, requires much thought, deep reflection, a sagacious, powerful, and combining mind.
>
> Edmund Burke

In chapter 1 I presented a model of school accountability in operation and said the book would be devoted to the analysis of the operation of that model. For the reader's convenience, the same model is presented once again.

In the preceding text, we have considered each component of the model: (a) the state of the art of output research; (b) the implications of its findings; (c) the attitude of the polity, school professionals, and education researchers and disseminators about these matters; and (d) the current proposed and existing applications of accountability. To give perspective to our analysis, we have also considered subjects that might serve as precedents for accountability developments: (a) some instances in American history of public intervention in school policy-shaping; (b) recent trends in the application of social indicators; and (c) a survey of the history of public accounting, with a consideration of its implications for school accountability.

The presentation has made it apparent that the intervening forces may play a critical role in the evolution of school accountabili-

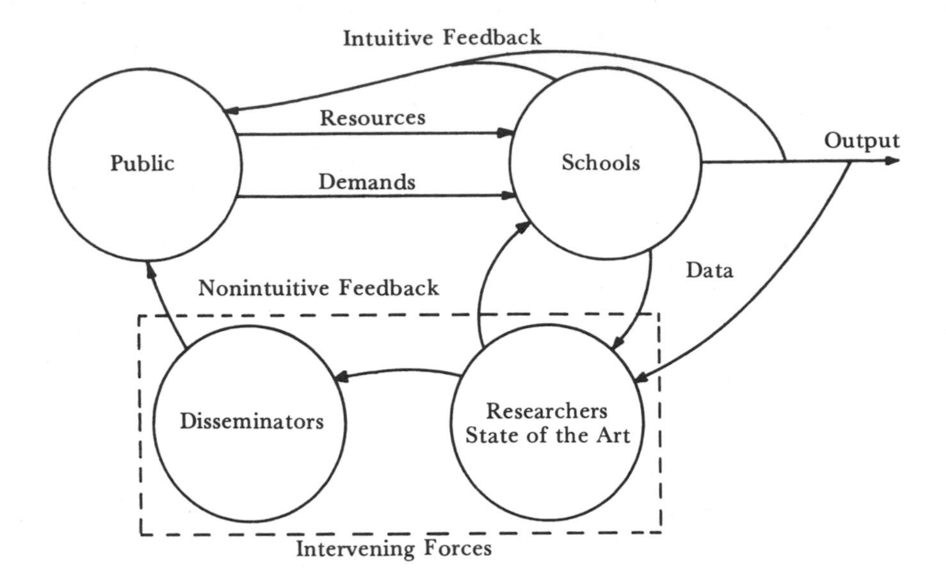


ty. That role may not be greater than that of schools and the polity; however, the typical analysis of issues such as accountability gives overwhelming emphasis to public and school professional attitudes, thus undervaluing the intervening forces. Therefore, focusing on the often underrated intervening forces may give us a unique degree of insight. In this analysis let us first consider the current role and future prospects of these forces.

## Education Researchers as Intervening Forces

At this moment, education does not have a substantial class of researchers performing as an intervening force to assist accountability. There are a number (perhaps five thousand) of education researchers. Unquestionably, many of them do have a sense of professional identity. However, a large proportion of traditional education research is not done on school output data or on routine school operations, but in experimental settings. Even the research done in schools is not typically focused on the comparative learning efficiency of operating schools. Also, the researchers' conclusions are usually produced in a format that is of interest principally to other researchers and, sometimes, "decision-makers," i.e., school administrators. There is no significant tradition of researcher communication with the public, or "stockholders." Nor is there any apparent interest among researchers in devising statistical systems that will usefully communicate with the public in the same way the cost-of-living index, a development from economic research, communicates economic information to the public. All these factors limit the amount and quality of nonintuitive feedback produced.

School hostility to accountability is another basic handicap to the development of a public-oriented research profession. Evaluators must usually "win" the cooperation of the schools they hope to evaluate to get the necessary data. Such victories are often costly to the evaluator's independence.[1] It may be a while before any district invites Moynihan or Coleman to evaluate its outputs. But while there is not yet a *substantial* class of public-oriented evaluators, there are some persons who see themselves in this light, and there are more of them today than there were ten or perhaps even five years ago. For example, the American Education Research Association, the principal professional organization of education researchers, is sponsoring a Network for Better Education, to increase communication between education researchers and lay organizations seeking to improve schools.[2] An organization like the network might facilitate such greater researcher-polity. The fuller implications of researcher-polity interaction, and of the network, are explicated in Appendix B, "Education Researchers—A Profession in Search of a Constituency."

The matter of researchers and school change brings another insight to mind: the role of other professions in past and present school change. Professionals were clearly involved in the past: Mann was a lawyer, Rickover an engineer, and Jerrold Zacharias (who helped spark the post-Sputnik reforms) a physical scientist. Kenneth Clark, whose research was cited in the Supreme Court's desegregation decision, is a social psychologist. Moynihan probably regards himself as an intellectual jack-of-all-trades. The professions of these men did not focus on education. Still, these effective professionals were often able to transfer their skills and perspectives to education problems. However, it may be that the development of a policy-oriented profession focusing on educational accountability is a prerequisite to further education change; the questions may be too complicated for progress to depend largely on the engagement of able men from other fields who come in to troubleshoot.

## State of the Art as an Intervening Force

If researchers with the appropriate perspectives do exist, is there something worth saying to policy-makers and the public? Or are the technical problems of applying output measures to policy issues so far from solution that publicity and debate would only create obfuscation, false hope, and unmanageable pressures for answers? For instance, to consider school reform in another era, the progressive education reformers of the first half of the twentieth century may have found their agitation far in advance of their knowledge. They felt that contemporary schools were dysfunctional, but they lacked methods for deriving concrete, operational alternatives.[3] Given time and resources, they might have developed such alternatives. But they were driven to propose alternative school principles that were necessarily vague. This rendered them particularly liable to co-optation: everyone claimed to be following their doctrine, whatever it was.

Accountability and output measurement are surely not perfected arts; as methods they are barely at puberty. Can they prescribe any policies with precision? Actually, they can prescribe quite a few.

The output data collected suggest that the ways schools are now run—the teacher-training process, seniority systems, salary scales, most classroom practices, the types of buildings used, staffing patterns, tests administered, promotion criteria for staff, hiring practices, and almost everything else you can think of—are largely based on an established wisdom. There is no proof that these policies greatly assist learning. There are interesting analyses suggesting that many of them should be radically changed and that some of them are counterproductive. There are bits of respectable research suggesting that some of these present practices may make some sense. But any intelligent citizen who proposes an important, systematic revision in school practices that makes intuitive sense may be right. All conceptual options are open. As Peter Drucker observed, "We still know very little about learning and teaching. But we do know that what 'everybody knows' about learning and teaching is largely wrong. And this may well be a greater and more important advance than any of the new science and new technology of which we are so conscious today."[4]

Here are some examples of what this might mean. Suppose we

compared the learning rate of children who went to school only alternate days, with those of children following the traditional schedule. Assume the alternate day curriculum was specially revised. I doubt that we would dare predict the results with much certainty.

Suppose we compared the effectiveness of traditionally trained teachers with groups trained in radically different modes or simply with randomly selected college graduates? Or suppose we restructured schools so that most teaching was done by children tutoring other children, with teachers simply acting as trainers of the teaching students? Would anyone say with any certainty that some forms of incentive compensation for administrators—coupled with more delegation and other structural changes—could not have constructive effects? How do we know it is not best to try to recruit our best college graduates into teaching, waive all education course requirements, and assume that they will stay for only a few years: which would, in effect, deliberately make teaching a transient career for the cream of our society? What about the diverse proposals for contracting out education or giving parents more choices among schools via vouchers? Again, as we improve our techniques of measurement, could we not subsidize employers to train high school age employees in cognitive skills while they are working in apprentice jobs? The subsidies will cover the employer's cost, the tests will make sure the skills are learned, and the job environment may lend special relevance to the training. None of these proposals is necessarily impractical financially.

Scattered theoretical objections can be raised to the instances offered, but we do not know enough to dispose of these proposals conclusively. With some developmental work, they may be as good as or better than our current systems. Furthermore, we can undoubtedly come up with even more interesting proposals if we loosen up a bit and are not concerned with acceptability to schools.

But beyond the individual proposals, the output research has demonstrated our need and ability to engage in incremental educational development: going into change one step at a time; using theories, intuitions, and hunches to start us off on a small scale; and collecting data and changing our techniques as we proceed. Eventually, such developmental processes may permit us to engage in larger scale efforts than we can now imagine, because we will have done our homework, relying on data rather than dogma and faddism.

In sum, the current state of the art of accountability justifies much more radical educational development and experimentation than is now taking place. It also offers the means for conducting and assessing such chances. Such potential fully justifies focusing greater public attention on the implications of output measures. Indeed, one might wonder what has kept the issue buried so long. As we noted earlier, perhaps the major block is the coolness of romantic education reformers and critics to quantitative approaches.

## Publicists as Intervening Forces

The intervening forces included disseminators, such as publicists and the media. These terms need operational definition. They include employees of various media, but they also include persons who write or speak out about output measures and schools in a thoughtful, effective, popular style, with the aim of reaching a public audience. There are precedents for such efforts. Mann was such a publicist, as was Rickover. Kenneth Clark, in *Dark Ghetto,* is too. There are a number of education writers today whom we might call publicists: John Holt, Edgar Z. Friedenberg, Jonathan Kozol, Paul Goodman, and so on. It is evident that many of these publicists are hostile to output measures. In many instances they display the antinumber values discussed earlier. On the other hand, a group of prominent publicists focusing on outputs has not yet appeared. True, Moynihan is oriented in this direction. Hence, his impact on the President's Message on Education Reform, which included the statement that "When educators, school boards and government officials alike admit that we have a great deal to learn about the way we teach, we will begin the climb up the staircase toward genuine reform."[5] Coleman wrote a nontechnical article for *The Public Interest* discussing some of the implications of his report.[6] However, these efforts account for a fraction of the popular education reform literature. But we can still give consideration to the principles that affect the appearance of publicists, whether they are mediamen or articulate researchers.

Probably there is a relationship between the appearance of such persons and the preexistency of an interested public. Rice might not have chosen to produce his spelling expose unless he had felt that many citizens were concerned with school affairs. Perhaps there is no existing interest in output measurement. However, this relation between a topic and the public may be mutual: skillful publicists with the right issue may crystallize amorphous public opinion. By making the citizens of Massachusetts aware of the importance of common schools, Mann created an environment where his future writings had an enlarging audience.

Today, parents constitute a public that is interested in school output data, but the character of their interest is constricted. The data sporadically become a trigger to stimulate citizen hostility to some school practice. In other circumstances, it is used by mobile upper-class and middle-class citizens as one criterion to determine the school area where they will choose to live.[7] But these publics have not seen the data as a useful tool for more extensive change. In general, the media have not promoted such insights either. Still, the earlier discussions suggest there is more news value in output measures than the media realize.

## The Proposition and Its Implications

I have proposed that, if accountability increased and more information about school performance reached the public, the relationship between schools and the polity would undergo great tension. Does this proposition hold? Yes. The data have been a source of controversy in the past, and there is no likelihood that it will be less upsetting in the future.

The larger issue is the hypothetical increase in accountability. It is not certain that more data will be available. It is true that (a) the methodology is continuously evolving, (b) the National Assessment is committed to collecting and publishing results, and (c) numerous other accountability operations are planned or underway. Still, educators have displayed enormous determination to keep data uncollected or out of sight. A significant class of data-oriented reformers has not yet appeared. The implications of accountability developments apparently are not recognized by the media. Certain classes of lay educational reformers seem attracted by antidata values. Thus, it is problematic whether the data, if collected, will be offered to the public in comprehensible form in the foreseeable future, say, over the next ten years. Or, if such popularization should occur, it may require the intervention of institutions or groups of persons not currently prominent on the scene.

For the moment, let us adopt a heuristic approach and continue our analysis on the assumption that school accountability occurs to a much enlarged degree. This is the most useful assumption, for it permits us to consider a number of provocative and productive questions.

If accountability was in large-scale operation, one might forecast the following changes affecting education:

1. New relationships between schools and the public.
2. Accelerating use of output measures.
3. New controversies over teaching priorities.
4. New professions or the transformation of existing professions.
5. New tensions between teachers and administrators.
6. New responsibilities for school boards.
7. New styles for school administrators.
8. More productive education research and development and more research and development.
9. More diversified types of schools and school programs.
10. More funds spent on school data collection.
11. Better learning for more children.

Let us now consider each of these forecasts in some detail.

### Radical Change in the Relationship between School Systems and Communities.

Today all schoolmen give lip service to accountability. No one dares be against it, whatever it means. However, there exists no understanding of how accounts are to be rendered. Perhaps because of this uncertainty, many perceptive members of the community see education as a collection of obscure rituals, managed by persons whom they do not completely trust. Despite this vague distrust, few community members are comfortable about sharply criticizing the educational process, because they feel they lack adequate credentials or vocabularies to make effective criticism. Such inhibitions create additional strains between the public and educators. The public does not believe that educators have proved themselves in fair and open debate—as have businessmen, politicians, or scientists—but that they have changed the debate rules to freeze out opposition.

Output measures represent accountability tools that can be

merged with this latent discontent and may equip laymen to break through the defenses that school administrators have erected. Very possibly, administrators already perceive this likelihood and, partly for this reason, vigorously oppose such measures. As the sociologist Max Weber observed, the public's control of public institutions may depend on the "transparency" of the connection between the institutions and the events they effect. If output measures give transparency to the murky issue of whether schools are teaching well, the public will win new power over the management of schools.

A clue to the potent implications of output controls can be found in *Technology and Change* by Donald Schon.[8] In the diagram below, he suggests the change potential of different innovations: exactly how much difference a particular innovation might make. The nearer an innovation is to the center of his "risk circle," the more provocative its potential. He views the imposition or variance

Figure 4. Innovation, Uncertainty and Risk

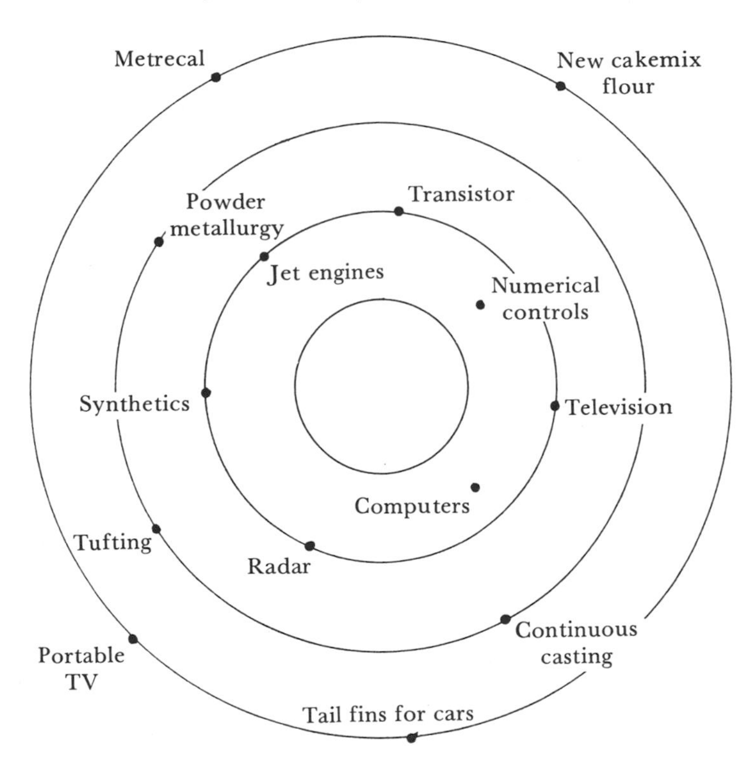

of numerical controls as one of the most significant of all possible innovations. It goes to the essence of an enterprise. Of course, change per se is neither automatically good or bad; but Schon's analysis does alert us to the powerful impact that accountability may have.

Radical changes in power relations usually do not occur smoothly. Often change involves creating new institutions or reshaping old ones. Today, the major national organ for citizen-school involvement is the National Congress of Parents and Teachers, the PTA. The word *teacher* in the name is significant. The association's premise is that there is a persisting and pervasive continuity of interest between parents and school administrators and teachers. Therefore, in its deliberations, the association's policy is affected by the voice of schoolmen. This is especially true where issues of "professional competence" arise. The schoolmen's presence must inevitably cramp all efforts to discuss touchy questions frankly, and thus colors the shape of school-public relations. There is an interesting analogy in labor relations.

Antiunion employers have long recognized that workers in any large plant will inevitably associate to exchange experiences and consider their interests. Employers perceived that it was unrealistic to stifle such efforts; they would just continue underground. The employers organized, or encouraged the organization of, "company unions" in which supervisors played an active role or which were subtly dominated by employer sympathizers. Such associations distracted worker efforts from more effective forms of independent organizations, by appearing to fill a vacuum and permitting employees to associate without incurring the employer's ill will.

The employers discovered that a small number of foremen or company sympathizers could restrain employee militancy within a large company union. With the employer's considerable power over the employee's job status, the presence of any employer representative during interemployee discussions could be profoundly inhibiting. In the PTA context, it is not irrelevant that each parent in a local chapter has his child in the custody of a teacher and/or administrator; under such circumstances, the parents may hesitate to discuss school shortcomings, because they are afraid that they will anger the educators who are present and that the teachers' resentment may be taken out on their defenseless children. Of course, both the foreman and the teacher may choose not to retaliate but simply to ignore the remark. In both cases, however, the essential helplessness of the worker or child (how can retaliation ever be clearly proven or prevented in the factory or classroom?) is a powerful inhibitor.

In 1935, the Wagner Act was passed to encourage union organization.[9] One of its important provisions outlawed such company-dominated unions. The extinction of these groups encouraged the creation of genuinely representative unions. Interestingly enough, under the stimulus of the CIO organizing efforts of the 1930s, some of the company unions shook off their traditions of employer domination and became "legitimate operations."

Of course, in the modern union meeting, workers often speak hostilely about the boss and understand that the words may get back to him, perhaps even via the publicly distributed union newspaper. However, the modern union that workers have created has powerful and effective restraints against employer retaliation: contracts, arbitration agreements, shop stewards, etc. Parents and students have no such effective protection against school retaliation, because powerful parents organizations are nonexistent. Thus, at the current primitive stage of parent organization, the intrusion of educators is extremely inhibiting.

If an accountability movement appeared, the PTA would be radically reshaped by activist parents (probably teachers would be excluded), or new and more militant organizations would be formed. Perhaps the reshaping and the creation of new organizations would occur concurrently, as it did in the civil rights movement. The ferment introduced by these changes and the new responsibilities parent groups would have to assume for counseling parents about output evaluation would generate an increase in parent group membership and change the characteristics of the members, leaders, and staff. The periodicals and pamphlets issued by the organization would also change in content. Presumably, there would also be dues increases, as more services and more valuable services were rendered to parents.

### Accelerating Use of Output Measures

Incidents involving the application of output measures have been appearing more and more frequently. There were about sixty years between the writing test of Horace Mann and the spelling test of Joseph Rice and sixty more between Rice and Project Talent. Only six years elapsed between Project Talent and the Coleman

Report and only four between Coleman and the National Assessment. During the same four or five years, Title I evaluation appeared, along with the poor people's demands, the United Bronx Parents, the Pennsylvania State evaluation, the New York and California efforts, President Nixon's Message on Educational Reform, contracting and voucher arrangements, and a number of other items that are not covered here. It seems likely that this rate of diffusion may accelerate even more.

The concept of the S curve is pertinent. Analysts of patterns of innovation or social change have observed that diffusion or adoption of almost all innovations is usually characterized initially by a slow rate of diffusion among a limited number of persons or institutions. After a substantial period of time, akin to incubation, if the innovation is to be widely adopted, it will suddenly be widely applied by a number of users over a short period of time. After the great bulk of potential users have been converted, the remainder of this class will be picked up over a lengthier period of time. The rate of adoption of an innovation by potential users typically can be plotted by an S curve:[10]

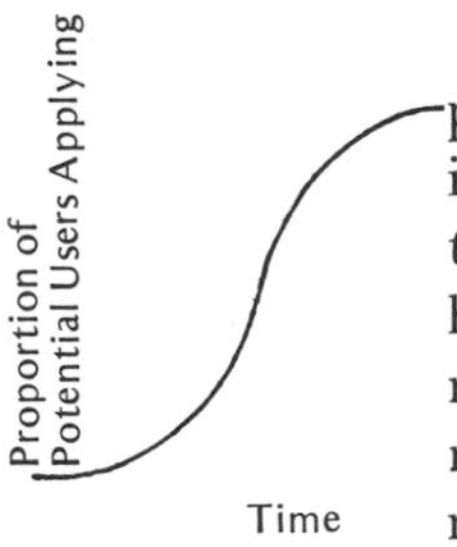

Proportion of Potential Users Applying

Time

There are inevitable complications to such projections. There are no firm rules for distinguishing a "spurt and eventual abort" from an innovation at the "takeoff point." Just becuase nothing has happened to an idea or development does not mean that it must succeed. Still, the curve does make the point that a quiescent possibility need not continue to develop at the same pace and that when things begin to move they can often accelerate extraordinarily, like black activism after Montgomery. The incubation period for school output measures may be ending.

### New Controversies about Learning and Maturation Priorities

Are children learning spelling or how to read? Should they get sex education? Do students need more science? What is the extent and character of drug abuse in our school district? Are our high school graduates prepared to enter the world of work, or are they only fitted to go on sitting in classrooms in college? With a voting age of eighteen, do they know how to move into politics productively?

Such disputes are traditional in our society and a natural by-product of public institutions in a democracy. But in the past they really focused on what was supposed to be taught rather than on what was learned. Output measures may give greater focus to such debates or stimulate more of them. In the past it has sometimes seemed that the debates were pervaded with excessive suspicion and tension. However, this may be inevitable when no one knows what schools actually produce. For example, after Sputnik, a "Johnny Can't Read" debate occurred against a backdrop of lengthening and increasing school attendance and apparently rising literacy. But without any concrete, popularly acceptable data to prove the increased level of reading, the essentially sterile controversy flourished. Thus, more debates with more accountability data, will not necessarily mean greater polarization.

The National Assessment has already provided us with some experience in citizen goal articulation via output measures. The assessment used mixed committees of citizens and schoolmen to decide what school goals were to be measured.[11] This required that they determine the goals of schools. Once the goals were set, the instruments to measure goal attainment were designed by psychometricians. Ralph Tyler observed that, although these committees included citizens from all parts of the country and of different political persuasions, they were able to achieve substantial agreement about what they thought schools should be doing. All this does not mean that the assessment goal-setting process was an ideal model. Tyler further said that after the lay-professional committees determined professional goals to be measured an exclusive educator committee considered whether the questions gave priority to the matters usually taught by schools; if they did not, the questions were not asked. This process really discouraged widespread public consideration about whether these topics *should* be taught, since censoring of the questions buried the issue within committee records. However, this professional review process probably did help the assessment attain some degree of educator acceptance.

As accountability gives more focus to debates about school priorities, increased transparency may inspire new parties to join the discussion. Such an enlargement may be for the good; society could gain a great deal from realistic, wide-ranging informed disputes about what outputs education should produce.

However, if such debates do arise, the output structures ideally should allow for interregional and intrastate and intradistrict variations in school goals. This might mean that almost proximate school districts—e.g., New York City and Scarsdale; Washington, D.C. and Montgomery County, Maryland; or San Francisco and Palo Alto—might have varying output priorities. Perhaps we would even allow for divergencies between Harlem and some upper-income area in Manhattan.

Such explicit goal variations would be a considerable improvement over the allegedly decentralized schools we have today. At present, while the schools are subject to almost no form of local accountability, they actually have many policies set by their students' need to obtain adequate scores on the national college entrance exams. This shapes the curriculum and many other local school practices. In this essentially homogeneous country with nationwide mobility, there are inevitably going to be vital pressures for common nationwide school patterns. But if we explicitly recognize these pressures and consciously attempt to devise alternatives that still satisfy certain national minimums, we may win more room for constructive local variations. These variations may be more possible if we can explicitly see what the variations aim at (via accountability tools) and how the schools are still satisfying essential national norms. For instance, if all or part of a district believes that creativity or black consciousness is a vital educational goal, but it still wants its children to go to national colleges, it may be able to attain both ends, if it can assure parents that (a) their children are still satisfying national test norms and (b) the unique district goal is being attained to some measurable degree. Without accountability data, however, these debates sink into frustrating, paranoid morasses.

But diversity in some goal elements does not preclude national responsibilities. Certainly, there can be a vital role for federally financed research and development and a variety of effective measures to choose between. Perhaps we can have a catalogue of goals and measures. In addition, we may see federal or state legislation to facilitate the development of local accountability systems. The legislation might offer grants to school districts to pay the costs of developing and operating such systems, on the condition that the data is made public and that public representatives are involved in developing the goals or priorities measured. Such citizen involvement would heighten citizen understanding of the accountability process and generate pressures for the disclosure of the data. Legislation of this nature would not involve an aggressive intrusion of the federal or state government into local affairs. Each district would be free to accept or reject the money and devise its own accountability system. The law would compel disclosure to citizens of only the data collected with the federal or state funds. The grants would lessen the fiscal pain of designing the system and diminish the ability of local schoolmen to fight off accountability by "poor mouthing."

Incidentally, in the state of Massachusetts, it has been proposed that additional state aid grants to local school districts be conditioned on the establishment of local accountability systems. The state superintendent of education would police any complaints arising from the operation of the local system. The essential idea was that additional state grants should not be made unless there was a shoring of local district movement toward accountability.

### Creation of New Professions or the Transformation of Existing Ones

Persons with technical competence in output measurement will be in great demand, especially if they have the skills to translate the language of their craft into concepts useful to policy-makers and laymen. Their synoptic presentation and interpretation of complex data may result in new and more informative measures. Researchers will have a considerable opportunity to advance the technical state of their art, because the ensuing debates will raise questions about the correct interpretation of technical issues.

Marx, Keynes, Galbraith, Robert Heilbroner, Arthur Schlesinger, Gunnar Myrdal, Kenneth Clark, and Walter Hansen stand out as social scientists who combined professional competence with a flair for public communication. Their prescriptions were not always correct. But their eloquence focused public attention on important issues and helped set research priorities for their professional peers. Such debates stimulated their professions to greater heights of creation. The "educational accountants" may have their insights interpreted and applied by another new class of information brokers: semipolitical figures, organizational spokesmen, or parent activists who will use the data to advance their public status or office, just as different civil rights activists now use different research data to support different ideologies or strategies. Of course, public acceptance of one strategy over another can mean the preference of one organization and class of leaders over another. This is not a criticism of the information-brokerage process. The mechanism increases the quality of public decision-making. The problems arise when research, theory, and professional articulateness lag behind evolving policy issues, as seems to be the case in education.

### New Tensions between Teachers and Administrators

It appears that an implicit alliance is being created between teachers' unions and school administrators in some school systems. Each group has a potent interest in combining against the public interest. The teachers supply administrators with political muscle to resist threatening school changes. The administrators supply the teachers with tacit support in their contract negotiations. At present, the public has only one primitive weapon against this alliance: it can reject teacher salary raises. However, the raises often have some justification. The real question may not be whether to give raises or revise work rules, but what raises or rules will increase productivity or recognize current productivity. Unfortunately, such changes are not necessarily those promoted by the union. This is the sort of thing that management must push on its own. But if school administrators want to comply supinely with the teacher demands, it is next to impossible for the community to run the details of bargaining negotiations. Currently, the community's only tool is the meat-axe. However, accountability pressures on the administration may correct this imbalance. If administrators are required to deliver real results, they may act as other managements do and use contract negotiations as tools to trade the advancement of their and the public's interest for concessions to their employees.

Pay increases could be traded for new personnel practices that administrators believe will produce better learning. One cannot say for sure what such changes might be, because administrators have rarely had to think about such matters in the past. The changes might relate to conducting school at different hours, requiring teachers to participate in new kinds of training, granting promotions and raises on new criteria, asking teachers to work in different types of classroom settings, etc. These subtle requirements can never be effectively compelled by direct public pressure. But they can be brought about if administrators are held accountable for results. In sum, accountability may discourage the tendency toward a large-scale alliance between teachers and administrators, and bring about the return of appropriate healthy tensions.

### Revival and Restructuring of the Local School Board

It is ironic that a discussion of school policy can get this far and only pay modest attention to existing organs for community control of school policy. But this silence reflects the judgment of many commentators on the current role of the school board. In general, the commentators have concluded that most boards exist principally to serve as buffers, shielding the policies adopted by the administrative staff from community judgment. Somehow, current boards have not been able to translate current public concern into constructive school change. They are not always committed to the administration, but they seem to become eternally involved in "fire-fighting" and "bits-and-pieces" criticism. There is simply no pattern of firm, policy-oriented criticism of administrative dysfunctions.

Perhaps a major cause of this pattern is the lack of conceptual tools for evaluating existing policies. Administrators have evolved a lengthy list of requisites to successful learning: certified, trained teachers; appropriate materials; certain class sizes; types of buildings; and so on. One commentator observed to me that the ideal pupil/teacher ratio is always 10 percent less than what a district has at present. Inevitably, there are shortages of these requisites. Boards spend most of their policy-making time trying to figure how to get more of these "essentials," juggling the limited supply that exists, and being told that performance will not be satisfactory until some unattainable resource level is achieved.

Suppose a board spent its time (a) deciding what student performance levels schools should be achieving in what subjects, (b) determining whether an adequate accountability system was being maintained, (c) devising rewards for superior performance by administrators, (d) attempting to detect the bugs that might arise as a result of a new system, (e) concerning itself with only the largest issues of budgeting, and (f) reporting to the community the results of the accountability program. In making these arrangements, the board would have to have the direct help of competent, independent consultants or accountability experts, just as corporate boards of directors feel free to use consultants and management advisors to give them perspective on corporate operations.

Such a school board would have an important impact on school policy. It might be even seen as the focal point of proposals for school change. Indeed, it is also possible that the persons who volunteer for such a board might differ from many current board members, who are often sincere and well-meaning citizens, but who seem ill-equipped to offer effective alternatives to the proposals of administrators. Speaking from personal experience, I wonder whether able persons now refuse to serve precisely because social scientists have not devised the conceptual tools to restructure an unsatisfactory status quo. I was once active on a committee recruiting school board candidates for a large urban district. One extremely able and responsible woman I tried to recruit said, "I will not touch that can of worms. I have a reputation for effectiveness to protect." Was she so wrong?

In this connection, the unsuccessful efforts of the New York City Board of Education to recruit a prominent noneducator as chancellor (the equivalent of superintendent) are interesting. According to the press, for almost a year before hiring a professional educator, they unsuccessfully approached Wilbur Cohen, former secretary of the Department of Health, Education and Welfare, Ramsey Clark, former United States attorney general, and a number of persons of like status. It is likely that their recruiting failure was partly due to a recognition by their first-preference targets that we do not yet have the accountability tools to permit a powerful superintendent actually to take command.

### New Breeds of Schoolmen and Teachers

Countless commentators have bemoaned the profusion of "unauthentic personalities" and "marginal men" peopling school administration.[12] At the same time, we have not been conscious of the forces that have brought about these patterns. One former assistant principal put it to me nicely: "I felt my career essentially depended on seeing that the annual high school dance went smoothly and without disorder." He left education partly because of such trivia.

Fair, plain, and relevant structures for evaluating the most critical part of administrative performance—improving student learning—do not exist. Thus, promotions at all levels depend on essentially nebulous or peripheral criteria. Once such criteria are applied, they inevitably corrode even the vision and conduct of teachers. Such corrosion is the natural by-product when a supervisor's advancement is based on whether his teachers help him manage a "smoothly run" school, whatever that has to do with education.

At the same time, achievement oriented personalities—doers, self-starters, innovators—are "very much interested in knowing how well they are doing. They like to work at a task which gives them *feedback.*" (Emphasis added.)[13] But the system prevents the development of accurate feedback. Today, the school "is a despotism in a state of perilous equilibrium," steeped in "irrelevant competition that discourages the strong."[14] Accountability changes that redefine performance in rational, recognizable criteria might (a) help revise the attitudes and conduct of current schoolmen, (b) change the types of personnel that are retained by schools today (plenty of the "right types" may come in now, but they rarely stay), (c) help recruit new types of persons into school work, and (d) increase the salaries paid to school administrators as public confidence in their performance and understanding of their responsibilities grows (today, the best paid school administrators receive about fifteen times more than the lowest paid school employee; in comparable businesses, the spread is about twenty-five times).

### An Increase in the Amount and Productivity of Educational Research and Development

Currently, educational research is a comparatively marginal activity: .5 percent of all annual American education expenditures go into research and development; in industry, the equivalent figure is 3 percent; in health, 5 percent; and in defense, 10 percent.[15]

If we assume that there is some relationship between the size of the research effort and the results, productivity prospects for education research are encouraging; there may be many good things left to be discovered. But the paucity of education research expenditures leads us to another observation: that paucity can be seen as the product of the efforts of educators to escape accountability. In other words, education research expenditures are low because educators have not committed themselves to increase school productivity, or at least they have not been striving to measure such increases. Without such striving, there has been no pressure for large-scale or effective research. If output is not measured, why strive to increase it? There is no motivation to lobby for appropriations for research.[16] Whenever dollars are allegedly appropriated for education research, they are often not used for research but spent as operating funds.

Consider the contrast with the military. Every general or admiral apparently believes that the safety of society (and the future of his career and the size of his unit) depends on his researchers inventing a new threat or counterthreat annually. It is not clear that all these inventions are desirable. However, it is evident that the general's motivation has greatly increased the development rate of weaponry. At the same time, the interservice budgetary and political debates that focus on these developments and apply the data available tend to introduce elements of realistic evaluation into the process. Perhaps schoolmen would develop the same desire for improvement if accountability were introduced. Recognition can be awarded for success, just as officers and their service units are rated on the quality of the weapons they develop.

The claim can still be fairly made that much existing educational research is unsatisfactory. But this conclusion misreads the essentials of research process. Effective research requires interaction between operators and researchers. The operators must feel pressure to improve performance, increase profit, or simply keep the company in business. The researcher must have adequate resources, a respected status, the cooperation of the operator, and the feeling that operators are seriously interested in improving output. These conditions do not exist in education: "no public school has ever been put out of business due to poor teaching."[17] Thus, much current education research assumes the nature of a holding or justifying operation; all educators ritualistically admit they need research, but nothing requires the effort be taken seriously. Researchers, too, sense they are not really wanted; this affects the direction of their work and the caliber of men who go into educational research. Accountability may improve these attitudes and values.

The output measures can also produce invaluable research data, but the schools have often been unwilling to cooperate in developing the necessary public data banks. When such data are routinely collected and publicized as part of the accountability process, researchers will be better able to (a) analyze the data, (b) find more productive school programs, (c) find out why they are successful, and (d) design and try out new programs that capitalize on the ideas of successful schoolmen.

### Greater Variety in School Programs and Operations

The shallowness of the current conventional wisdom may compel its proponents to hold desperately to a narrow mythology: things must be done in a particular way just because we cannot be sure that this is the right way. Ritualistic rigidity is the defensive tactic of ignorance. The tightness has reflected itself in diverse legislation, setting comparatively inflexible requirements for teacher certification, principals' promotions, class size, salary patterns, etc., and in similar civil service provisions. These measures severely restrict important school innovation. But accountability may make the public conscious that there is no objective evidence to support these restrictions and that learning will continue if they are removed. Indeed, there are indications that programs that break these bounds may increase productivity. In other words, public focus on results—rather than direct attack on the prescribed rituals—can so undermine the rituals that we may finally provoke variations. An immense number of exciting possibilities—for example, greater reliance on various contracting arrangements—may appear as we become less concerned with whether the ritual is followed and more concerned with whether children are learning.

### Increasing Expenditures for Data Collection and Analysis

Growing efficiency often inspires still more requests for data. This is consonant with the patterns followed in our more productive businesses. At one time in industry, the idea was to maintain and enlarge the investment in production workers—the men on the line—money for paper was a superfluous luxury. But as productive forces increased, the coordination of production became the major challenge. Coordination and greater efficiency is partly the effect of intelligent paper work and data collection. This need for coordination is one of the causes of the continuing expansion of the knowledge industry.[18] It is our growing number of clerks, communicators, and counters that have helped to make our society the most productive in history.

Conversely, in schools we often hear the plea that funds should be devoted to "classroom expenses": essentially, higher salaries for teachers and more teachers. At the same time, we do not know what makes a teacher effective. We do not know whether some types of teachers work better with some children or how to identify these different types. We do not know what mixes of teachers, other specialists, and paraprofessionals are optimal in what circumstances. We do not know if children are learning better as a result of additional expenditures or, if they are learning better, the causes of success. Until we improve our diagnostic, analytic, planning, and incentive structures, we have no tools for increasing or upgrading manpower. None of these issues will be resolved without more data. Essentially, our low investment in data collection and analysis is another current aspect of the efforts to resist genuine planning and accountability to the community, since such efforts require more and better data.

### Better Learning for More Children

If these developments occur, as projected, it is self-evident that the quality and quantity of all student learning will increase.

## Footnotes

1. For details about school hostility to evaluators, see "Symposium on Evaluating Educational Programs," *Urban Review* 3, no. 1 (February 1969): 1-21.

2. In June 1970 the Advisory Council of the American Education Research Association passed a resolution that committed the association to increasing communication between education researchers and change-oriented members of the public. *Educational Researcher* 21 (September 1970).

3. "For all the claim [of Dewey's laboratory school] to be a laboratory, papers emanating from the staff suggest that the inspiring of emulation took precedence over inquiry." Lee J. Cronback & Patrick Suppes, eds., *Research for Tomorrow's Schools* (New York: Macmillan Co., 1969), p. 50.

4. Ralph Melaragno & Gerald Newmark, "The Tutorial Community Concept," in James W. Guthrie & Edward Wynne, *New Models for American Education* (Englewood Cliffs, N.J.: Prentice-Hall, 1971).

5. Richard M. Nixon, "Education Reform," *Weekly Compilation of Presidential Documents* 6, no. 10 (March 3, 1970): 312.

6. James S. Coleman, "Toward Open Schools," *The Public Interest,* no. 9 (Fall 1967): 20-27.

7. The *New York Times* began publishing the New York City per school median reading scores annually in 1966. *New York Times,* 25 December 1966, IV, p. 5. A *Times* education reporter told me that throughout the year they receive phone calls from persons who want to know the date of the last issue of the paper with this data. The callers say they have school age children, they are planning to move, and they want to know the reading performance of the schools so they can determine where they want to move. Real estate brokers have told me equivalent anecdotes about potential home buyers.

8. Donald A. Schon, *Technology and Change* (New York: Delacorte Press, 1967), p. 39.

9. 29 USC § 158(a)(2).

10. Daniel Bell, "The Measurement of Knowledge and Technology," *Indicators of Social Change,* eds. Eleanor Bernet Sheldon & William E. Moore (New York: Russell Sage Foundation, 1968); Everett Rogers, *The Diffusion of Innovations* (New York: Free Press, 1962), p. 29. Two careful works.

11. See the discussion of the role of laymen in helping curriculum priorities for the National Assessment, Tyler, "History and Sociology," in Guthrie & Wynne, op. cit.

12. Halpin, *Theory and Research in Administration* (New York: Macmillan Co., 1966), pp. 212, 246.

13. David McClelland, "Why Men and Nations Seek Success," in *Readings in School and Society,* ed. Patricia C. Sexton (Englewood Cliffs, N.J.: Prentice-Hall, 1967), p. 157.

14. Waller, *The Sociology of Teaching* (New York: Russell & Russell, 1961), pp. 10, 453.

15. The figures for research in education, health and defense are cited in Richard M. Nixon, op. cit., p. 310. The figures for agriculture and industry are from Lecht, *Goals, Priorities and Dollars* (New York: Free Press, 1966), pp. 290ff., 222.

16. For amplification about the disinclination of most education interest groups to lobby in support of education research funds,

see Norman J. Boyan, "The Political Realities of Educational R & D," *Journal of Research and Development in Education* 2, no. 4 (Summer 1969): 3-18

17. Halpin, op. cit., p. 200.

18. For background on the knowledge industry, see Fritz Machlup, *The Production and Distribution of Knowledge in the United States* (Princeton, N.J.: Princeton University Press, 1952).

# 12
# Checklist of Steps to Assist Accountability

If any readers conclude that they want to assist the movement toward school accountability, they may find the following checklist of interest. The list is subdivided into different categories of persons and groups, e.g., administrators, parents, and parents' organizations. The suggested steps are stated in summary form, since they spring from discussions elsewhere in the text.

## School Administrators

____Try to have funds put aside in the budget to cover accountability costs.

____Arrange for the release of scores of all objective tests currently given by the school or school system. Attempt to accompany the releases with clear explanatory material. Where the data is deficient, frankly discuss its shortcomings.

____Conduct discussions with educational researchers about how your school(s) can develop improved accountability systems. Assume that such systems will apply sampling processes and measure multiple goals. Invite school board members and parents to participate in the discussions.

____Move toward using output data as one of the promotion and salary criteria applied to subadministrators, such as principals.

____Support plans to give larger authority to individual schools or subdistricts. See that authority is coupled with commitments to accountability goals.

____If contracting or voucher systems are attempted, make sure that the accountability elements are well defined and qualified measurement experts are consulted.

____Arrange for your school board to set aside time for accountability-oriented discussions.

____Develop report cards that are criterion referenced and are also keyed to national test scores. See that the delivery of the cards is accompanied by teacher-parent conferences, even if school must be shut down to create time for such conferences.

School Board Members and School Board Candidates

____Insist that your district develop a multigoal, reliable accountability system. Assume that it will take some money, persistence, determination, and outside help to obtain such a system. Do not give up.

____Locate school districts where such systems are under development, and find out what they are doing.

____Consider whether the school board needs the equivalent of a public accountant for accountability: i.e., an outside expert who is directly selected by the board and evaluates the accountability system for the board.

____Insist that the administration keep output results in mind in making salary and promotion determinations for administrators. Find out exactly how the results are weighed in such instances.

____In hiring new superintendents, engage them in frank discussions about their commitments to accountability. Ask them what they have done to promote such developments in their previous positions. Also ask them to propose quantified goals to measure the effectiveness of their management of your district.

____Offer your superintendent a bonus if he exceeds accountability goals.

____See that the administration releases accountability data on local schools or other administrative units. The release of data should be accompanied by adequate explanatory material.

____Encourage the development of school decentralization, with accountability systems being used to ensure local responsibility.

____Work with community groups and administrators in developing multigoal accountability structures.

____Promote legislation to assist accountability and expanded education research (as long as laymen help establish priorities).

____Produce and distribute publications explaining accountability for laymen.

Parents

____Vote for or support school board members who promote accountability.
____Expect your schools to give you meaningful accountability data, with a multigoal orientation.
____Ask to receive a criterion-oriented report card on your child, which also includes pertinent national or statewide exam scores.
____Ask your parents' organization to push for accountability. Assume that it may mean more money for dues as you receive more worthwhile technical services from the local or areawide unit.
____Be prepared to see more radical school change as accountability stimulates genuine innovation. Insist that such changes be subject to careful, impartial evaluation.
____Expect that more data will cost more money and will be worth it.
____Assume that media reports on schools will consider accountability issues. If they do not, speak up.
____Ask your legislators and other elected officials what they are doing to assist school accountability.
____Explain to your children that tests and report cards are, in part, ways to evaluate teachers and schools as well as children and that adults have responsibilities in the learning process, too.

Media

____If reporters are unsure about accountability and statistical issues, consult with qualified statisticians or educational researchers.
____Be careful about reporting on unevaluated school programs. Would you praise a new drug before qualified, impartial researchers had assessed it?
____Do not be reluctant to ask school administrators and school board members hard questions about statistics: How are you sure the tests are honestly administered? What kinds of additional data are needed for adequate interpretation? How can such data be obtained? Who is responsible for getting it or not getting it? When will the next steps to get the data be taken?

____If necessary, send reporters back to college to learn something about these issues, or hire full- or part-time reporters with statistical and evaluation skills.

## Elected Officials and Candidates for Office

____Try to raise accountability issues in public debates. Support laws requiring state school superintendents to develop multi-goal, sample-based accountability systems. Ask school boards in your district about accountability reports.

____Propose and support legislation and appropriations for statewide or local accountability systems or accountability-oriented research; legislative aid to school districts should be conditioned on establishment of locally directed accountability systems.

____Hire staff members on legislative committees who understand something about school accountability.

____Assume that, as accountability grows, the demands for enlarged educational research appropriations will also grow. See this as an appropriate development. Furthermore, be prepared to remove many current legislative and civil service restrictions on flexible school practices, e.g., teacher credentialling requirements, rigid salary structures, restrictions on voucher and contracting out arrangements.

## Education Researchers

____Try to present the concerns of the profession to public audiences by contacting mediamen, politicians, and parents' spokesmen. Concentrate on writing and talking in clear and accurate prose.

____Seek means of funding or financial support that are free from the influence of school administrators.

____Train undergraduate and graduate students to help communities and groups develop accountability systems.

____Give more attention to the development of measures of effective learning.

____Design and publicize plain and fair means of reporting accountability data.

____Work with groups of researchers and laymen that focus on accountability issues.

____Propose systematic changes in school practices that question more of the existing elements of the system: certified professionals dominating the learning process, apparent limitation of learning to school situations, existing salary and promotion structures.

____Seek the assistance of researchers in other disciplines that are concerned with assisting accountability and feedback structures in other public institutions.

## Parents' Groups

____Seek the help of education researchers on accountability issues.

____Try to maintain a dues level that permits the group to obtain technical assistance. (Teachers union dues run about twenty to thirty dollars a year.)

____Make accountability a major goal of the organization.

## Students

____Understand that students, parents, and educators all share responsibility for the success of the learning process. Expect that systems will be created to determine whether the responsibility is being met.

____Ask why students cannot participate in decisions about accountability design or evaluations of the effectiveness of instruction. Student evaluations should not be definitive, but are one appropriate measure.

____Expect to receive a criterion-oriented report card and to have the teacher explain it to you.

# Appendixes

Several of the subthemes in this book warrant more detailed analysis than was appropriate in a text that required balance and cohesion. The materials in these appendixes expand three of these subthemes by offering: (a) a description of an actual accountability-oriented school district by its director of evaluation and research, (b) a statement by a real school superintendent committing himself to accountability, and (c) a proposal that education researchers give more attention to the political implications of their discipline.

# A
# Case Study of an Accountable School District

Largely as a result of the Title I programs of the Elementary and Secondary Education Act, the public began increasing pressure on the Columbus schools for information about how well students did on achievement tests. Under existing practices, each school in the system administered achievement tests at certain grade levels. Schools were permitted to select any one of three achievement batteries, or combination of subtests. Individual student test results were not released or shown to parents. Concern over (a) how well the schools were doing, (b) the amounts being spent per pupil by school, and (c) balancing school staff and student bodies racially, all generated community pressure. This pressure was exerted on school classroom teachers, building principals, central office administrators and the board of education. The board of education was asked to have a team of experts, not associated with the school system, conduct a study. Civil rights groups and board members could not agree on experts, and finally accepted the offer of President Fawcett to provide the resources of the Ohio State University (located in Columbus) to make the study. The study was chaired by Luvern L. Cunningham, dean of the university's college of education. It was begun in mid-March and completed by June 1968.[1] It is difficult to briefly capture the flavor of a 322-page report. However, accountability, responsibility, and responsiveness are themes which run through the entire report. One might describe the system being studied as a

Howard O. Merriman, Executive Director, Evaluation, Research & Planning, Columbus, Ohio, Public Schools.

"closed" system; the report recommends institutional changes toward an open system.

One chapter of this report was entitled "School System Assessment and Accountability." The summary of this chapter states:

> Most people are interested in how their own youngsters fare in school. They are likewise interested in how well their school system is achieving its mission. Questions about how schools rank in comparison to other schools too are often raised. Such questions are asked honestly and humbly and represent a very modest request. What most people do not realize, however, is that evaluating an institution as complex as a school system is a most difficult assignment. This is true whether it is done internally by the staff or by an outside group.
>
> A comprehensive evaluation of the Columbus schools was not the assignment of the commission. Our attention was focused on problem areas, one of which was the need for continuing assessment of the system. Three recommendations are made in this regard.
>
> An office of evaluation and research was authorized in May 1968 by the board of education. The commission is encouraged to note this development and commends the board and administration on the purposes and objectives chosen for that office. Our first recommendation is that the board support this office generously.
>
> Secondly, we urge that school district policy on the sharing of test results be revised to allow for an annual report on school achievement. Such a report should include such items as follow-up information on graduates, changes in pupil achievement, new types of testing that are being tried, characteristics of the student body being served, and where appropriate, comparisons with other school systems.
>
> Third, we recommend that regional subdistrict school assessment committees be established in 1968-69 as a part of the general recommendations for decentralization which are made later in the report. There is a genuine need in all school systems for improved ways of developing community understanding about schools and school understanding about communities. To repeat, many people want information, they want to understand, they want to take part and, above all, they want to be confident about the quality of education their children are receiving. The regional assessment committees would have leading laymen, teachers, administrators, and students as members. They would meet each month and report at least annually to the board of education and to local building PTA's and other community groups.

What has happened since that report to make the Columbus public schools accountable?

The proposed office for evaluation and research was installed as a department within the division of special services in September

1968. Virtually all of the personnel who had been trained at the Ohio State University Evaluation Center were attracted to the school system, and formed the core of the new department. These persons included professionals, secretaries, and clerical workers (called MAT's—manual analysis technicians). All but the director of the office and the classified office manager were supported by funds for Title I evaluation and state programs. The local districts' direct support for the initial installation was about $25,000 on an annual basis.

However, another recommendation of the report called for passage of an operating levy, to commit the district, itself, to routinely supporting the improvements. This levy passed; the department of evaluation and research was given a "green light" to implement the second phase of its five-year plan. This phase included the recruiting and selection of a permanent professional staff to provide for evaluation (and research) capabilities for the system at large. Simultaneously, the existing (district financed) staff of one was developing the format of the first *Columbus School Profile,* evaluating the existing citizen advisory and assessment committees, meeting and talking with a multitude of community groups, and consulting with system personnel on evaluation problems.

The new department set about staffing-up. It employed the equivalent of fourteen full-time professionals, and three interns, who were half-time students in doctoral programs at Ohio State. Most of these persons had been trained and taught in the classroom, then taken advanced degree work. Staff members ranged from brand new bachelor's degree teachers with undergraduate minors in research to master's degree candidates and Ph.D. candidates. Areas represented, besides educational research are: social work, sociology, nursing, psychology, curriculum development, information science, administration, and political science. Assimilating and molding this group of highly motivated persons into a team has been an exciting challenge—which has not ceased to be a challenge.

Obviously, the new personnel were recruited to meet needs for certain skills and competencies, some of which we could identify easily, such as design and statistics. Others we are still identifying. As we were recruiting, the question we kept discussing was, "What is the role of the department?" The early, simplistic answer was, "We're going to evaluate, so that the school system can be accountable."

Accountability, in the past, was a matter of budgeting, keeping account of expenditures, and avoiding deficit expenditures. However, under the "new accountability" an additional dimension has been added.

No longer are we solely concerned with inputs. There is ample evidence that millions of dollars have been put into education which have had no noticeable impact on education. There is nothing to prevent this from continuing unless we become concerned with output. Accountability, the new accountability, is an accountability to not only the taxpayer, the public, but parents and students as well. This accountability is not only by the board of education, but administrators and classroom teachers. Accountability is not just for input, in dollars, but for output, in terms of units learned, in terms of postschool accomplishments. The facilitating method for this accountability is not a bookkeeping system which only keeps track of dollars, but a system which keeps track of output—and in time, will have to relate input to output.

Accountability is like a double-edged sword. That is, not all of our school outputs are good, nor are they all bad. They are both positive and negative. It's necessary to admit the areas that need improvement, as well as provide information about the successes you're having. The negative reports not only help identify problem areas which generate support for needed change, but enhance the positive reports, make them more credible.

The Columbus schools established the department of evaluation and research as a response to the problem of accountability to the educational community.

It is essential to consider the term *educational community.* An educational community consists of those persons in a community who have an interest in education—parents, teachers, students, administrators, and often, just interested citizens. *Each of these categories represents a set of educational decision-makers.* Parents decide to support and reinforce a school—or not, as the case may be. Teachers make decisions about decisions—they may follow administrative directives or covertly ignore them. Students choose to learn or not to learn, as reflected in their level of motivation. Citizens affirm school goals, programs and progress through their approval of money issues at the polls. Other groups have other means of expressing their satisfactions and dissatisfactions with the schools.

The evaluator is concerned with improving educational opportunities for children and also providing information to members of the educational community so that they might have an awareness and understanding of these educational opportunities.

Many equate accountability with school public relations, or the "trade puffery" familiar in advertising. The information with which the evaluator is concerned is not imaginary, nor should it be "puffery." Anyone examining the situation, using the same instruments, the same criteria and the same analyses, should be able to derive the same results. In short, evaluators must be credible.

The evaluator is a middleman. He does not have an "ideal" set of criteria to use in evaluating all programs. One man's criterion is another's poison! He must evaluate, not to tell an audience what it wants to hear, but to satisfy their need for information. Their need for information varies from audience to audience, dependent upon their value structure, their life style, their economic and educational concerns. Thus, the evaluator has a multivariate problem with multiple criteria.

With this understanding, you can group some of the reasons for the frequent charges of "whitewashing," of irrelevancy, of obfuscation. If the evaluator determines the criteria for an evaluation, he may well be overlooking criteria of importance to some audience. Thus, he must attempt to identify these audiences beforehand, and stimulate them to identify their criteria and goals. If a program were evaluated on only one criterion framework, such an evaluation could well be disregarded by other audiences. It seems to be more prudent to anticipate this multi-criterion problem, and allow for it in evaluation designs and reports.

A further problem is determining the acceptable level of performance or activity. It is possible to establish a level which is satisfactory to only a small group of persons or to a limited number of rules in the educational community. Indeed, desired performance levels may vary within audiences. Rather than reporting information based on a simple criterion level, we must attempt to provide alternatives—reporting all data so that reanalysis can be performed, reporting information resulting from application of several criterion levels, etc.

## Why Have a Department of Evaluation?

I take it as accepted that systematic, scientific evaluation should be performed. It may not be as evident that decision-makers, though they evaluate every day, are not likely to be able or inclined to perform the systematic evaluation which we have been discussing. It is a rare decision-maker who can dispassionately view a program or situation in which he is involved.

The evaluator (and I use the term collectively, whether it be one or thirty) who works only for, or under, one decision-maker has a narrow limited audience. He will probably prepare narrow and limited reports for that audience. However, if the evaluator is established separately, if his identity is not linked too closely to any one audience, he may be more objective, or at least, broader in perspective. Such semi-independent evaluators must relate across many different groups of people, with quite divergent views.

Since "he who holds information has power," the evaluator is both threatening and simultaneously subject to pressure. If he has a degree of autonomy, and demonstrates his "fairness" or "objectivity," he is less threatening and less likely to be pressured. He must be able to obtain information, and also be at an institutional level where he sees "the big picture." He should have access to the decision-making power structure, so he can identify information needed for those decisions.

Now I'd like to make a stab at an experience-based definition of accountability:

> Accountability is the willingness to provide information and develop the capacity thereof, by an agency about whether the commitments of the agency are being met, *and* the responsiveness of that agency to the concerns of the educational community in selecting, pursing, and reviewing its goals and objectives.

I believe that accountability should be a positive action; not a defensive ploy. An agency, no matter how proper, must be perceived to be accountable. It cannot just say, "We're being accountable" unless the community finds the statement credible. The agency must not only say, "We're willing," but must demonstrate its accountability by recognizable action. The next stage may be even more difficult. I hear, over and over again, the comment, "You've given us all this information, beautiful charts, facts and figures, but we want to know, what are you going to do about it?" The second part of the definition included the phrase "responsiveness of that agency to the concerns of the educational community in selecting, pursuing, and reviewing its goals and objectives." This means the agency will tune in the community, and listen to its concerns.

## What Have the Columbus Schools Done to Operationalize Accountability?

First, the system made a commitment to accountability by putting up local school money to support the department.

Second, the system established personnel policies which made it possible to hire competent personnel for nonadministrative roles at competitive salaries.

Third, the system established accountability-type policies. These include:

1. A policy which requires a standardized testing program, comparable across schools and grade levels.

2. A policy which requires a published annual report to the community on student performance on a school-by-school basis. (See the school profile sheet in chapter 5.)

3. A policy which provides parents with access to performance records of their child on the tests administered, and the student himself, as well.

4. A policy which established survey committees, consisting of elected students, community people, parents, and faculty members, at each school, whose function is to serve in an advisory capacity, to facilitate communication between school administration and students, teachers, parents, and citizens. Meetings are open to other students, teachers, and citizens to bring their concerns to the committee.

5. A policy calling for follow-up on the careers of their school graduates. This includes data on school performance and post high school performance, as well as feedback from the graduates themselves.

The seeds of these policies can be found in the basic recommendations of the Ohio State University Advisory Commission. On the whole, the school system could be said to have met these recommendations well. I'd like to mention some of the other areas in which we've been working.

Student unrest resulted in some unfortunate incidents in the spring of 1969 in several of our secondary schools. In one building, many students engaged in a sit-down strike, and were hauled off to jail. This action resulted in reaction; it was clear that a plan to cope with student unrest was needed. As the plan to handle student unrest developed, we saw we should also plan to prevent student unrest. The resulting student relations policy is multifold: The first section deals with things the school must do to respond to student concerns, to assess student attitudes, to provide legitimate channels of communication for students, to insure broad representation of the student body in student government, etc. The second part of the policy is to prevent escalation of student unrest, if the first part of the policy fails. Finally, the policy provides for moderate handling of eruptions which have not been prevented. Note that building administrators, faculties, parents, and students all have responsibilities and rights which are being recognized. Also note the building administrator is accountable for having taken the preventative measures.

Another step in accountability was taken in 1970-71, when the board of education agreed, in professional negotiations with the local teachers union (the Columbus Education Association) to an annual building evaluation, to be conducted by faculties, on a form to be jointly developed by the board and the association. This evaluation was to cover professional environment, staff support, student relations, and cocurricular activities. Our office helped develop the instrument, aided in its administration, and are now developing a systemwide report for the board. The faculties in each school reported their findings to their principal and the association. I'd note, parenthetically, that we made friends with a lot of teachers during that experience, but alienated a lot of building principals.

We are now in the process of reciprocating. The board and the association have agreed to a new system of evaluation of teachers, which we have been asked to develop. This is partially in response to demands from the community that teachers be accountable, and partially in response to the need for information to make decisions about rehiring, terminating, and promoting to tenured status.

In another sphere of evaluation concerns, our system is plagued with overcrowding, a defeated building proposal and an interest in the space-saving economics attributed to the Year Around School. As part of the accountability policy, we are now engaged in a comprehensive study of the Year Around School, on which the board will base their decision.

Accountability extends to all board of education meetings, Committee of the Whole meetings and subcommittee meetings being open to the public and the media. We are all learning how to do business in public.

Much of what has been said relates to total system activities and policies. I'd like to deal for a while with the kind of policies which permit a capability for accountability to exist.

## Policies

First, and perhaps the most important, is the need for the school district to be completely open with the department. The department must know what's going on and what's planned in the district, so they can anticipate information needs. The department must also be credible to *all* its audiences; to all members of the educational community. This demands an openness of reporting, and the right to publish evaluation findings in an unexpurgated form—both good and bad—while at the same time, sensitizing administrators to the findings, so that they can provide a well-thought-out response.

Second, the department must have unlimited access to data in the system, with the understanding that individual, name-labeled data, such as reports on teachers and students, will not be revealed publicly.

Third, the department must be involved in setting its priorities, but these priorities must be congruent to the goals of the system.

Fourth, the department must have continuing budgetary support for systematic evaluation and research. Up to 1 percent of total system budget has been recommended. This level is moving towards the level of R & D budgets in industry. Separate budgets for mandated, funded projects (Title I) may run 5 to 7 percent of the budget. Our office has never gotten to the 1 percent level. We were operating at about a .5 percent level. In addition, the system now has a budget deficit, so we lost the equivalent of 6.5 professionals from our district supported operations. Keep in mind that evaluation costs are also opportunity costs. You may have thousands of dollars over several years by having evaluative information about programs. You may avoid costly program investments with low payoffs, or be able to terminate or modify such programs before they become costly mistakes. Or you may be able to maintain the public's confidence that a course of action being followed is the best of available strategies.

Fifth, the department must have competent personnel. It is important to recruit, train, and retain the personnel necessary to perform the task at hand. I would like to make a case for evaluation or accountability personnel being different from traditional district employees. They're not classroom teachers on special assignment; they're not guidance counselors doing program evaluation; they're not principals who have retired from the battleground. They are competent specialists, rather than generalists. They have probably received some specialized training, or should receive such training, to meet the information providing needs of their position. Universities should be doing more to train evaluation personnel to work in the field. More evaluators are now being trained in the field, on the job, than in our graduate schools. This could easily be a collaborative venture of an educational administration faculty, a research and evaluation faculty, and the public schools near the universities. We must foster collaborative relationships between the universities and public school systems. There are evaluation and developmental tasks which are beyond the means of either institution operating solo. There is a need for on-the-job, field training of grad students through internships. We have used such interns. They receive, in addition to their formal classroom training, on-the-job training—a reality orientation. We receive a source of personnel, a recruiting mechanism, and a major source of ideas. I regret to say that the budget cuts have reduced our internships to zero, with no restoration in sight.

For evaluation to be successful, and for accountability to work effectively, school systems must also consider revising other policies. One of these deals with the utilization of extant data wherever possible. This means generating a standardized data base that can be counted on and called upon, that data can be retrieved from, effortlessly and painlessly.

The evaluator must have access to information in the system of the decision-maker is to utilize the data in making decisions. How often is data ignored if it is not readily available, or available only after the fact? Some data can be used, over and over again, for many different purposes. For example, we have computerized the beginnings of a student file, which includes standardized test information. This data is used for preparing individual pupil profiles of test results, and made available to teachers, counselors, principals, parents—and even the students. We have found ways to present the data so that the old business of releasing a point estimate of a test result is no longer a problem. We use the same master file to summarize information for each classroom and for buildings. We are ready to provide, on an optional basis, an item analysis of standardized test results to classroom teachers, and to curriculum specialists, as well as scoring and returning teacher made tests along with such an analysis.

We use the same data for the *School Profile,* the building-by-building summarization of test results and other factors published and made freely available to the community.

Finally, the same data is utilized in context evaluation for identifying problem areas, used as a basis for proposal writing for Title I projects, and for allocating resources within the school system.

The evaluator is dealing with information which may be negative to the maintenance portion of the system. Therefore, he must have a measure of autonomy from the maintenance parts of the organization—for protection, as well as to maintain credibility for accountability. My colleagues in the system may not always appreciate this, but to have evaluation reports taken as true is an important part of accountability. The day when major sectors of the educational community mistrust our office, I have lost my usefulness and must be replaced by someone who is credible.

## Does a Department of Evaluation Do Everything Related to Information?

Remember my definition of education evaluation: the process of delineating, obtaining, and providing useful information for judging decision alternatives. This definition might lead one to believe that evaluation and the department of evaluation are attempting to deal with, and control, all the information a decision-maker uses. Nothing could be further from the truth. Educational evaluation is, in fact, just one more way of knowing. To be of utility, educational evaluation must provide information which is not available by other means, cannot be obtained at lower cost otherwise, and is useful in the judging of decision alternatives. While evaluators may at times sound like the answer to all our problems, we are not and indeed can do no more than help in the solution of problems toward the improvement of education.

Many evaluation activities are of an ad hoc or special purpose nature. The demand for our direct services in evaluation far exceeds our capacity and will continue to do so. Recognizing this, we have established several developmental task areas, to extend our capacity to serve the information needs of the school system. We are attempting to apply the concept of *leverage,* which is used by financial institutions and holding companies. Our aim is to increase the system's evaluation capacity without a proportionate increase in cost. We have chosen to do this because resources are scarce: funding, personnel, and space are limited. Either one only attacks problems with the highest priority, or uses leverage, or a combination of both.

Our concept of leverage works like this: many evaluations, Title I, State DP, the *School Profile,* etc., require the same or similar data. Much of this data is already being created and collected for some purpose in the system already. We are working on a systematic identification of extant data which our office can utilize. This, of course, is one of the first steps in systems analysis. We have developed a standardized testing program to fit the needs of teachers and counselors and also provide our office with approximately 75 percent of our testing requirements for Title I through this step alone.

Having some direct involvement with program evaluation, such as Title I, provides us with a developing and testing ground for evaluation personnel and techniques. Once tried and modified as necessary, a developed technique can be used by other persons in the school system with the knowledge it will work. Thus, in effect, we provide consultants on evaluation to the whole system. These field team consultants help field personnel such as principals, teachers, curriculum supervisors, etc., with evaluation designs, instrumentation, data reduction, analysis, and reporting. However, the responsibility for conducting these ad hoc evaluations will remain with the school. We hope our field consultants will concurrently be trained persons throughout the system, through an on-the-job training experience, so that, when they are through, they have a greater understanding of, appreciation for, and usage of evaluation. We are trying to work ourselves out of business by training others to "do it themselves."

## Products

Typical products of our department include:

The *Columbus School Profile*
The *Columbus Testing Profile* and its data by-products
The Student Opinion Survey
The Building Evaluation System
The Neighborhood Seminar Reports
The Graduate Follow-Up Study
Voter Intention Surveys
Special Program Evaluation Reports
Mandated Evaluation Reports

## Phenomena

Results of *School Profile* and other activities:

1. The large problems (system-wide) are broken into smaller ones (building level).
2. The credibility of the school system is improving.
3. Decisions are more informed—Neighborhood Seminar recommendations, Survey Committees in secondary schools, Voter Intention Surveys.
4. Higher degrees of data utilization—not just flowing from bottom up, but flowing back to the source of information.
5. Removal of myths and assumptions, for example, the transfer and assignment of teachers.
6. Dealing with substantive questions, not with questions of accountability.

The department of evaluation and research has a tenuous, shifting base of support. We are not winning popularity contests. Theoretically, we should be able to convince everyone that we are there to help them do their job more effectively. Practically speaking, we threaten them. But still, we have attained real achievements: we have to look at the success of the school system over the past two years in beginning to be accountable; we believe we are suffering less from being accountable than we were from being unaccountable.

We have to look at the last school year and the significant improvement in the degree of student unrest.

We have to look at the total educational community and its beginning efforts to work with the school system to improve educational opportunities.

We find, in these things, real hope that accountability will work, the school system will improve and the community will benefit.

## Footnotes

1. Luvern L. Cunningham et al., *A Report to the Columbus Board of Education* (Columbus, Ohio: School of Education, Ohio State University, 1968).

# B

# Oakland's Time Is Now: A Statement to the Staff

It is with a great deal of pleasure that I welcome you back to the 1970-71 year in Oakland's public schools. I've been here but a short time, and my days have been filled. I've been talking and listening to teachers, students, parents, and administrators, to religious leaders and businessmen, and to plain people of the community. What I have heard has moved me profoundly, and filled me with a sense of awe. There is in Oakland a fresh wind stirring, a movement within men and women from all walks of life, a message so unmistakably clear, so tangible that you can almost reach out and touch it with your hands. And that message is this—*Oakland's time is now.* Our season, our opportunity to seize the main chance, our time to write a new chapter in the history of American education.

There have been charges and countercharges here in Oakland, as well there might be. We have had dissent and turmoil, and there has been much about which persons of good will might disagree. Yes, our own school system, as well as those elswhere at every level, have been both the focus and the locus of the social revolution. And I say, this is as it should be. No other institution has promised so much, yet the chasm between our promise and our performance, particularly for the urban poor and minority groups, is there for all to see.

And all this is not behind us. Indeed, in our drive to systematize our approaches to teaching and learning, we cannot, we must not attempt to shut out the world. As Mark Shedd, the superintendent of

---

Marcus A. Foster, Superintendent of Schools, Oakland, California.

Philadelphia schools has said, "It is the passion and power of humanity that we seek to explore and expand when we teach reading and math. And if we divorce school subjects from the guts and hopes of human beings, we can expect students to find them gutless and hopeless."

So what shall we do here in Oakland?

We are going to have to utilize the new techniques of management. We must subject ourselves to a process of identifying both citywide and schoolwide objectives. We have to use the problem-solving approach. Our management has to be done in terms of our goals, our objectives, and our cost effectiveness.

We have to set up a kind of accountability system where each one in the system is saying what he will be responsible for over a given time span. This is almost a trite concept. But unless we hold ourselves accountable all along the line from the superintendent, his staff, the teachers, custodial staff, cafeteria staff—not much really happens. All of us will be goal oriented. We will be holding ourselves accountable.

We are going to need data about student progress, and this brings me to the need for testing. You heard me say in talking to some groups last week that testing is an essential part of teaching. I like to use the analogy of the doctor and the teacher. When you go to the doctor you don't stand in front of him and say, "Here I am, guess what's wrong with me." You subject yourself to a diagnostic procedure. The teacher in dealing with the youngster in the class can't expect to put the statement to the youngster, "Tell me what's wrong with you." We have to begin using certain diagnostic techniques to find out where he is, to assess his present status. And that's testing—diagnostic testing. Even the boy scout wandering in the woods has to know where he's been, where he is, and have some notion of where he's going, or else he's lost. And if a boy scout in the woods needs this kind of information, certainly a teacher who's playing a critical part in the life of a child has to make some assessment of where a child is at a given moment.

Returning to the analogy with the doctor, he begins a course of treatment. After a certain length of time he tests again to see if the patient is improving. You might call that a kind of achievement test to see what progress is being made in getting well. The teacher, after

having made some assessment through diagnostic procedures of what the child's needs might be, applies treatment—her instructional program—and at some point she wants to turn around and say, "Now how well are we doing; has my teaching been effective?" That's testing again. And then in the light of these data the teacher begins to revise her practices if they have not been effective. The same as a doctor. If the treatment is not taking, he doesn't try the same thing, he alters the treatment procedure. After altering the procedure if the patient fails to get well, the doctor's not embarrassed to say, "I want to call in a consultant, someone who has specific knowledge in this area of difficulty." And so the teacher, after she has gone through her instructional program, tested, and found out that her teaching is not getting through, shouldn't hesitate to call in the psychologist, the counselor, the parent, anyone to give additional information, so the treatment program can be revised. *Yes, there will be testing.* We can't argue that there has been some abuse in the use of testing. When we use testing to label children and set up the kind of self-fulfilling prophecy that says to a child, "You look stupid to me," then we give him preposterous school tasks to do and when he fails we say, "See there, you couldn't even do that." And then to confirm that, we test and say, "That proves it." That's test abuse.

We hear the term *culture-free test.* Even if we could devise such a test I would question how useful it could be. We don't live in a culture-free society. How useful would it be for me to take a test on how to survive in the Kalahari Desert when I'm living in Oakland? We need to give tests that give us some notion of how well children are doing those things that society prizes, rewards with better jobs, and with full participation in a highly technical society. At this time in our history, the middle class tends to prize the ability to speak well, to present oneself publicly in a certain way, to be able to listen attentively. Because those skills are held by the middle class as important, doesn't diminish their importance. If the goal of the school is to teach every child those fundamental skills and habits and attitudes that will enable him to reach his highest self-fulfillment and at the same time be able to participate effectively in the society of which he is a part, then speaking prestige English is part of it, reading is part of it, counting is part of it, and we're going to have to know how well our children speak, read, write, and count. So we will be

doing testing. There are certain tests because of the populations on which they have been standardized are unfair to certain type children—we'll have to admit that and change our tests. But it's not the test that's wrong, it's the abuse that's made of test results.

In order to deal with some of the abuses that are made of test results, I propose that we establish a superintendent's committee on testing and include on that committee some of the teachers who raised this question initially, so that we can ferret out what the concerns are, so that our teachers can become skilled diagnosticians in dealing with learning difficulties and can use tests effectively. We hope to have that committee established shortly after the opening of school. One last word on testing. Someone raised the objection and said that teachers used the tests to label. Teachers who do that will find some other way to label children if you take the test away, and I don't want to rob good teachers of that tool. Someone else complained to me that teachers will teach the test or teach in order to test, and I respond that a teacher who would do that, if he teaches the test, probably taught more than he would have taught under any other circumstances.

Another thing we want to do in Oakland is to send out a different signal about the reward system. As you know, in most bureaucracies, whether we're talking about a school bureaucracy or an industrial bureaucracy, the reward system usually works for those who can keep their departments cool and keep things running smoothly. The system has worked for those who could get along with their immediate superior and be nice and smile. But don't let anything exciting happen, don't mark the papers negatively, hold tight and you'll get your reward. *Well the system here in Oakland is changed.* The reward system will work for those who dare to take risks, those who dare to do something that's different—to take a chance. If one dares, it means there may be failure but if everything we do meets success, we may not be reaching far enough beyond our grasp. Sometimes we may have to fall down. The system will work for those who dare to establish meaningful relationships with community, even though at some times that may seem to create a little turmoil in the school. In some of the institutions that are insipid, perhaps a little turmoil would help. You see, we know that in our institutional life the cooling-off process results in a kind of caricature of humanity

and an organizational paralysis. Churchill described this with caustic eloquence in describing the British Empire in the thirties: "We decided only to be undecided, resolved only to be irresolute, adamant for drift, solid for fluidity, all-powerful to be impotent." You see our reward system is just the opposite of that. Dare to be fluid, dare to be potent, dare to be powerful in bringing about the needed change.

I've alluded to the importance of community involvement a number of times, and here I'm talking not about community involvement for window dressing, but involvement because the school as an airtight clinic never was a worthwhile notion. You know that I've already taken steps to give the community a meaningful role in the selection process for the principals at Castlemont High, King Elementary, and Woodrow Wilson Junior High schools. It's the process that's important. Parents can feel free (when they've had a part in the selection process) to say to principals, "Friend, we've brought you here because we believe in you and we want to continue to believe in you." I'm talking about empowering people. And the only way people have power is if they've had meaningful roles in making decisions that affect them. A community that has helped to place a principal in his job is committed by that very act to helping that principal succeed. I used to say to some of my principal friends back East that they didn't have to worry so much about establishing a union to protect principals' working conditions and protect themselves against brutal personnel problems. The best kind of job insurance any principal can have is a faculty, students, and a community at his back saying, "You're doing the job, brother, keep on." That's the kind of job insurance we want.

It's in this belief that we're prepared to develop a kind of multiple option approach. This is based on the notion that there is a different level of readiness on the part of communities across any city to participate in this process. Some are ready to move right in and to continue to perform as parent-teacher associations, as Dad's Clubs, to continue the kind of informal participation that often pays off. I've seen some schools since I've been here that operate their community involvement model on an informal arrangement, and it works. They've established summer programs at one school. This year they're looking forward with great anticipation to beginning a nongraded program at another school. So informal participation can be effective if you want to identify it as an option. Some others may rather operate under a more formal arrangement, a kind of advisory board arrangement, where community people sit down and hear what the principal has to say and offer advice and suggestions. And then there are still other communities where the people may be ready to say, "Let us have a part in the decision-making process, a meaningful role in having the final say." Notice I keep talking about community participation in the decision-making process. I'm not talking about community control, because there's no such thing as community control. Schools are state institutions, and we're bound by state statutes, most of which we can't abdicate and give away to people. But we can *share*, in increasingly effective ways, our decision-making prerogatives with the community. I think that's where we are going to have to move, and we hope to help you work that out. Whatever your level of participation is, be it informal, fairly structured, or highly structured, I feel that the central office must have the resources to help you implement the model that seems most appropriate for your school. We're committed to the notion that the school site is the primary vehicle for parent and community involvement; that it's out there in the field, at the local school site, we're going to get the payoff. The battle will be won or lost in individual classrooms in the field, but at the same time this notion of community involvement will have stretched beyond the school site and encompassed the entire city.

We are committed to establishing the Master Plan Citizens Committee. I will shortly propose to the board of education a plan to bring about such a committee. A public hearing will be held with organizations from throughout Oakland. They will be invited to testify as to the most appropriate means for selecting members, the size of the committee, the mandate, its duration, etc. I believe the most urgent issue before this group will be the development of short- and long-range plans for delivering uniformly excellent school facilities for our students and our staff. It is of course true that many of our buildings do not meet earthquake standards, that our physical arrangements sometimes do not facilitate the reduction of racial isolation, that we may in some cases be operating uneconomically small units. But more than anything else it is a source of anguish to me that so many of our buildings are simply a disgrace. Those buildings are saying something to our children. They're saying that this is good enough for you.

I was at one school site that was in an advanced stage of dilapidation and parents were sitting down talking with me and saying rather timidly, "Dr. Foster, could you get us some paint to paint the buildings," and I was trying to figure out a way to get a bulldozer and knock the whole thing down and clear it out. And when I got back and looked at some of the test results in that school, they were good; they had brought about an increment of growth. Then I really began to despair; because given those adverse conditions, those teachers were able to produce results. What would they have done if they had optimum conditions under which to work? They were talking about dealing with children two grades behind and they were able to improve 1.5 in their special projects, which was excellent; but it still didn't catch them up. And as I looked at that dilapidated school I could think of another school I visited just a week before: beautiful brick structure, grass manicured as though someone was on his knees clipping it with a scissors. I don't want that school to have less. I want that school to have more; but I want to bring other schools up to those standards. Imagine the feeling, especially in these athletic contests, when you leave a dilapidated building to go to some fine school and then play your game and come back to your little hovel. That says to you that you're not quite worthy of fine facilities. That's debilitating, it's debasing, it's denigrating. I don't want to be a part of that, and one of the heavy charges we'll lay on this citizens committee will be to take a look and try to bring to a uniform standard of excellence all of our facilities in Oakland.

Some of you know that before arriving I asked the board of education to authorize a study by a blue ribbon management analysis firm—Price-Waterhouse—to assist me in assessing and making plans for the improvement of management effectiveness in Oakland public schools. You know the board approved that study. The Price-Waterhouse team has labored long and hard, subjecting our operations to arduous scrutiny and gathering opinions and data from a wide variety of sources; and I want to share with you now some of their basic viewpoints and findings. I've lifted these right from the preliminary document.

I. More Effective Resource Allocation and Management—Goals, Priorities, and Objectives

In order to make significant improvements in the use of resources, it is absolutely essential that a clear statement of goals and objectives be developed along with a statement of the priorities among them.

II. Recasting the 1970-71 Budget

In order that the board and superintendent can see how the resources of the system are now being allocated to programs, we propose to develop a plan by which the present budget can be recast into a programmatic format.

Let me explain that just a bit. In one school system where I found myself working, the stated priorities were (1) reading and (2) early childhood education. And we took a line-by-line budget and recast it programmatically to find out where the money was going. And it turned out that reading was fourth. Most of the money in that system was going into physical education, art, and music. I have nothing against those programs. They are beautiful activities as witnessed by music in the lives of the students who have performed for us today; they've lifted us all spiritually. But if we say our priority is reading, then we have somehow to allocate our resources so that allocation matches priority. This is another way of saying, "Put your money where your priorities are." And that's what we intend to do.

Returning now to the Price-Waterhouse study.

III. We believe that the following principles must underly the management reorganization plan

1. The management reorganization should be accomplished within present levels of expenditure for supporting functions.

2. Resources committed to the support of basic skills and other high priority programs should be increased.

3. Some of the management responsibilities now with the central office should be allocated to regional organizations, each headed by an associate superintendent.

4. Within each region, the school should be the basic unit for decentralized management and for community participation.

5. Parents and other members of the community are a resource which should be more effectively utilized.

6. School staff should participate in the development of school objectives.

7. The allocation of authority and responsibility for decision-making must be clarified.

8. Additional management resources should be allocated to the planning function.

9. The management reorganization should result in unifying separate central organizational units with like functions.

10. Adequate resources on a continuing basis should be committed to management training and development.
ment training and development.

These highly generalized statements were lifted out of context from an interim report. They will be elaborated and documented further, but they may give you a sense of the direction in which we will be moving.

We're talking about change in Oakland. Change to catch that gathering wind; not after two years of study or a year of introspection. Change now! Let's begin the process today, right now. First some steps to which I am committing myself and the central administration, and then some challenges for all of us. I propose in the next few minutes to state boldly some of the objectives that central administration will be accepting; objectives for which *we* can be held accountable, because I'm not asking teachers to do what I don't dare to do. It's easy to hold somebody else accountable while you sit in judgment, but it's a little more difficult when you step out into the same arena and subject yourself to the same accountability. And this is what I propose to do in the next few minutes, to let you know what we are saying that we want to do in a given time frame to help reach the goals and objectives of this system.

1. I will submit to the board, by its meeting on October 13, a draft statement of the overall goals of the Oakland Unified School District. Prior to their adoption as policy, I anticipate that the board will want to hold full and complete hearings to receive the maximum number of additions, deletions, and amendments.

What we're saying here is that for a system to formulate objectives we have to have goals that are districtwide and widely accepted by all so that the individual site units will be able to establish objectives that will relate to these goals. The goals that we propose to submit to the board as a point of departure will be goals that have been developed out of my experience with urban education, out of the experience of senior staff members, out of the conversations I've had around the city with a variety of groups, with the study that we've made, with the documents that show what this system is doing performance-wise for children. So we won't just pick these goals out of the air. And then in public hearings, the public can make its input. And the public certainly includes school teachers who want to come and testify. All the organizations and interest groups can look at those goals, and we are promising to have the draft before the board by October 13.

2. Pending board confirmation, we will take immediate steps to appoint three regional associate superintendents, each serving approximately 22,000 children. These executives will be, in effect, my alter ego in the field, providing full administrative and instructional leadership. After their selection, steps will be taken to determine three appropriate regions, free up or establish facilities for them in the regions they will serve, and begin the reallocation of certain central educational resource personnel to each region. We expect to have much of this accomplished by January 1, and the process complete in every respect by the end of the school year.

This is part of the concept of decentralization, a moving of resources closer to people who have to use those resources. Bureaucracies, because they're so ponderous, don't respond quickly enough to the needs of local areas. By having the resources out where they can be utilized, we can have a much more effective delivery system of our educational talent. It's tied in with the notion of accountability. You can't hold a man accountable for 68,000 children in a city, but you can hold him responsible for 22,000 scattered in two high schools, a few junior high schools, some elementaries. As you break your area down, then you can intensify the unit in which you can assess accountability. And we propose to move on with that concept pending board approval.

3. In order to be able to tell how much we're spending in math, reading, physical education, or English, and to learn how better to put our money where our priorities are, I am proposing that we make every effort to recast our budget in program terms by February 1. This will largely be a manual procedure which will not be supported

by complete accounting and reporting systems in the school year 1970-71. We will, however, implement the necessary budget, data processing, payroll, personnel, and accounting support systems so that the Board, staff, and community will be able to make more informed and effective decisions about the limited resources available to achieve progress.

This is just a way of looking at where our money is going. I was studying some figures on vandalism for the schools around the city. When you take the vandalism and add it to the theft and fire damage, it comes to a considerable amount for some schools. I looked up the campus patrols that you have, where citizens are paid to come in and keep order and to keep children from hurting each other, and we spend considerable money on that. When we look at it programmatically and see the need in the reading area, I'm prepared to say to schools that if you can eliminate your vandalism, if you can cut down on the theft, prevent the fires, get volunteer help, and eliminate the need for paying people to keep children from hurting each other, put in a program that makes children enjoy being together; if you can do that, then take that money you save and apply it to reading or one of your other priorities. You can't get that kind of handle on a system until you begin to look at what's happening programmatically to your money. So we propose to have that in place by February 1.

4. We will develop several alternative models for parent and community involvement in local schools, and these multiple options should go out to the schools no later than November 1.

What I'm saying here is that central office will take the responsibility, working along with others, to prepare a series of guidelines for a number of options for bringing parents and community into the operation of the school, and schools should have that by November 1 to begin to look at which option seems to be most feasible. I want to hasten to say that we're not talking in two different ways at the same time. We're talking decentralization and yet I'm saying that the central office is going to send out a *proposal for options.* What I'm stressing here is that you need something to begin with; schools shouldn't have to rediscover the wheel each time. I spent a year in Philadelphia devising, with others on a sixty-eight-member team, a system for decentralization and community control. Now to put sixty-eight people through the agony we went through for a whole year would be wasteful of your time and mine; so we'll draw on some of that experience, along with the experience of other people, and place before you an array of options. You might take A and B and put them together and come up with a kind of C, so that you won't have to follow slavishly the options as presented, but they become a point of departure.

5. Now at the same time, on that November 1 date, we expect to have in operation the full-fledged Master Plan Committee.

6. The district must now move to professionalize and regularize its total pattern of procedures and agreements as they relate to the negotiating council and with various staff components. I will shortly propose to the board of education the creation of an office of staff relations reporting directly to the superintendent and serving an integral part of the superintendent's discharging of his duties.

Here we are saying that the relationship between management and staff is such a critical relationship that it shouldn't be left to a part-time person, as skillful as a part-time person may be. It requires and justifies the utilization of a person who's looking at those relationships continuously and working with the staff to help to develop the kinds of concerns that will resolve some of the learning problems, some of the things that grow into confrontation, that tend to deal with sources of friction so that we can have the highest esprit de corps throughout our system. I don't want to imply that that in any way downgrades the negotiations. It upgrades them to a kind of operation that demands the best talent of the best qualified person full-time. We propose to get that under way shortly.

7. The Bay Area is uniquely rich in resources which can and must be tapped for the strengthening of our schools. Universities, industries, and business firms need to be systematically given opportunities to deepen their roles in the school community. By November 15 we hope to create an office of resource development to coordinate this effort.

It's a shame that we're not making the maximum use of all the rich facilities in this region. I was talking to someone from U.C., Berkeley, and the only thing that person could see—it was almost as with myopic eyes and blinders—was tutorial programs. But at a great university such as U.C., Berkeley, why shouldn't the department that deals with landscape architecture go over to that little school, that almost broke my heart the day that I was there, and sit down and plan with that community how to beautify the place. I'm talking about using the full resources of a university and not limiting it just to a tutorial project here or an intern program there.

We're getting ready to move into a kind of PPBS (Planning, Programming, Budgeting System) arrangement where we're talking about management by objectives and all the rest. It means getting principals and teachers and community geared and tooled up so they can know how to look at resources, then look at their objectives and array those objectives in some kind of priority order and say, "This is where we want to put the most money." That takes training. Why shouldn't the business school of one of these great universities share with us their expertise in the staff development effort to get people ready to deal with this kind of management system? I'm talking about expanding the involvement far beyond the piddling approach that has been used. I'm talking about the kind of relationship with industry and with the commercial establishments that really adds a dimension of reality and relevance to the instruction of children so that they, instead of studying an abstract subject such as biology away from the real world, get a chance to go into some of the hospitals and work along in the laboratories as partners in research. I'm talking about the occupational level courses.

I remember running a large high school and we had some occupational level courses—sign painting, upholstering, drapery, and slipcover making, power sewing, and a couple of others. I made a study one day of how many of our graduates ever got jobs in the areas in which they had been trained. And I went to one of the brothers and I said, "Friend, you've been operating an occupational level course that purports to get people ready to enter the sign painting industry, and I perceive that in the last two years no child has gotten a job painting a sign. Now you came from industry and you have contacts out in the field. I'm going to give you two periods off a week to go and reestablish those contacts, open the door so some children can get jobs, otherwise, we're going to miss you next year." You see that's accountability. The brother went out, had me come down to a little place called the Rickshaw Inn in New Jersey, and I spoke to the Delaware Valley Sign Association about this whole business. I talked to them about my concept that children ought to have "hands-on" experience. We went on and played out the whole thing, "We're not coming asking you to help us; we're really here to help you, to give you a chance to participate in the development of a reservoir of well-trained potential employees." And they got the message. We began to put children out two or three days a week, and they began to learning rigging—something we've never taught at our high schools—how to rig those signs and lift those heavy things up. They learned something about the neon business and how you bend glass; something we've never taught. And every kid who finished the course got a job the next year.

I'm talking about accountability; I'm talking about using resources in the community—not in the usual way, where we go out and visit, although we're going to do some of that, too; we contend that's useful. Not in the usual way, where we bring some chap in and he says, "I made it you can do it, too"; we're going to keep doing that, too, because that's useful; but we're going to do more. We're going to use the community as a living laboratory where children can go out and learn. This addresses itself to the notion that learning of a high quality can take place in a number of settings. Too long we've had the notion that learning had to take place with some chairs, a blackboard, and a teacher standing in the front of the room. So we're hoping, then, by November 15 to have an office charged with this responsibility.

8. I am completely committed to the belief that whatever the outcome of these efforts, the battle will be won or lost out in the field, in your school, in your classroom. The central office must function more as a service center and a foundation and less as a military headquarters. To give meaning to this idea and to assist in freeing up those ideas in the field that will speed us toward our objective, I will establish by October 15 a New Notions for Excellence Fund of $100,000. We will commit funds to those proposals which turn schools more sharply to meet their priorities, which develop, on a one-grant basis, a new instructional capability which has measurable objectives and replicability elsewhere in the system. Tentative plans call for $60,000 of this fund to be for proposals involving a total school, $30,000 for individual teacher's grant for projects up to $500, and $10,000 for activities designed, organized, and carried out by students. Decisions will be made by a fund committee consisting of principals, teachers, and students, with perhaps some central office input.

I want you to get the concept here. What we're saying is that we realized a long time ago that one person sitting behind the desk trying to decide what's best for a city full of children is doomed to mediocre success or abject failure. That the collective wisdom of the group—everybody putting his mind to work on how the job can get done—will give us a better chance of meeting the needs of children. We're not only saying that your ideas are important; we're setting up a fund to pay for the ideas so that it will help you to implement them and to carry them out on a day-to-day basis. It may sound strange that students can have ideas, but we want to give $10,000 so that students can make their proposals and talk about what they can do to improve reading in their schools, that "each one teach one," or "by youth itself," approach. As those programs and proposals hit our desk and this committee searches them through, we'll be funding them. I happened to operate a school one time where I used to say to teachers that the only limitation on what we can do with and for our children is your commitment, your willingness to give of yourself, your own creativity, your own imagination. Those are the only limitations we have because it's wide open. It wasn't surprising to me that when we'd have an innovative teacher grant program, we won more, half again as many, innovative teacher grants than any other school in the city. And they were able, those teachers, to win those grants because they had really begun to realize that their ideas were important, that someone would help get them started. And that's what we want to do here, generate ideas from the field and let the "white house" fund them and get them started.

I've given about eight things that the administration is holding itself responsible for; and we're saying that you can hold us accountable if we don't do it by a certain date. And it's going to be in writing. We have two distinguished columnists here, journalists that I know personally, who are taking all this down—Mrs. Mitchell and Mrs. Stinnett. They'll have it all down and you'll read it. We stand accountable. If we don't make it, you have the right to say, "Well Marc, you said you were going to do this and that. What happened?" And I have to stand before you and let you know. If we're willing to lay that kind of responsibility on ourselves, I don't think it's too much to ask you to join us in taking certain responsibilities, and I'd like to suggest now some of the things that I would want *you* to commit yourself to. And not just you, I'm in it with you. Although I made these commitments, I'm making the same pledge to help you do the things that I'm going to challenge you now to accomplish.

1. I'm calling upon each teacher to take on the heavy personal and professional responsibility of setting your own instructional objectives for this year.

I want to just clarify two terms: the goals are the overarching things that we are trying to do for the system; the objectives are what you are saying you are going to do with and for your children in that year. Whatever the program is, whether it's in the shop area, physical education area, English, basic skills area—wherever your area of responsibility happens to be—I'm asking each teacher to begin now the process of establishing objectives for this year, and setting them in measurable terms. You know the way objectives used to be stated in broad terms: "our objective is to bring about meaningful growth on the part of children so that they will be happy, functioning individuals in a complex society"—and that's a way to say nothing. I'm talking about a teacher who would dare to say, "I'm committed to producing one month's growth for each month of instruction in the basic skills." I want a teacher in areas were children are two and three grades behind—some brave souls—to dare to say, "I'm going to produce 1.5 growth per month for each month." And some real brave sisters and brothers to say, "I'm going to dare you to say I'll give you 2 for 1 in the basic skills." That's the kind of objective I'm talking about, the kind you can measure. If you have a class that children are cutting in the high schools, and you should have forty-five (well I hope not that many), thirty-five children in your room, and only ten are coming on the late shift, then your objective ought to be to change the cutting pattern in your room. That's measurable, and you ought to state that something like, "In three months I'm going to reduce cutting in my room to zero"—a measurable objective. And it means getting on the phone at night and saying, "Johnny, where were you? How dare you cut me, man? You're ruining my whole objective here." Somehow we're going to have to find ways of making our big, anonymous institution more personal—a place where people feel they're a part of something and somebody cares. So, if that's where you have to start, getting the children to come to you, then start there; but state it in measurable terms. If you look at your watch and see that by the time you get down to teaching you've blown fifteen minutes of the period, your first objective ought to be to get a better system, so you don't waste time like that. And if you don't know how to do it you ought to call for some help. I'm talking about using educational resources, but I want everyone to begin to explore—not in any grand-sounding terms—what his and her objectives should be. I want you to lay out your objectives in a very practical way based on the most important needs that your children manifest. I realize that the first effort at this may not be as perfect as you want it to be, but we have to start somewhere. You may come up with a few objectives and decide well, this really wasn't what I should be doing. Then you can change it, but I'm laying upon you, each teacher and everyone else in our schools, a charge to begin that process immediately.

2. Each school shall state its objectives, in similar terms, for the year, with a target date for a brief working statement of November 15.

As each classroom teacher begins to talk about what it is he's trying to do for his children and with them, those objectives collectively become the objectives of the school, because we're talking about schoolwide objectives.

If you have a school, and I could name one in this town, that has a dropout rate in excess of 60 percent, it's obvious you're going to have to do something about it. One of your primary objectives may be to reduce the dropout rate by 50 percent. Set an impossible task, give yourself something to reach for, but the objectives really should be within your grasp. You don't begin talking about "I'm going to raise reading by so many degrees and so many grade levels," if half your children are in the street. If your attendance pattern is running where your ADA is, somewhere down in the 60 percent group, then obviously with 40 percent of your children out in the street you can't claim to have a viable educational program; so *that* becomes one of your early objectives—not by the end of the year but in three months—to raise the average daily attendance 15 percentage points. I'm talking about how you set measurable objectives, so if you don't get there, you have a way of getting handles on it. Why didn't we make it? Accountability and management by objectives is not a technique for getting rid of people. To say, "Aha! I caught you, you didn't do what you said you were going to do—get out." It's not that at all. Management by objectives is a way of getting people to say what they want to do, to look at their resources, to try to match what they say they're going to do with their resources, and then to say at the end of the period—end of the time frame—we either made it or we didn't. And if we didn't make it, let's sit down and talk about it. It's a way of going back, looking at performance, and finding out what the difficulties were. A fellow went around selling one of these performance contracts and found out he was losing money because he hadn't written in a feature that every child in the program must have attended 80 percent of the time. He had signed a performance contract and the children were coming and going, and although they were there and he had the same number of children, he didn't have them over a period of time long enough for the training to take effect. So what I'm saying to you is that if you have objectives you can begin to look at why you made your objectives or why you didn't, and then begin to gear your program to reach those objectives.

I'm asking that each school site have at least a preliminary statement of what their objectives are for the year by November 15. I don't think that's an impossible mission, I think it's an essential one.

3. I have said that we will produce "multiple options" for parent and community participation by November 1.

Discussions as to the ways of strengthening your activities in this area can get under way immediately—some schools might be ready to go with a renewed plan tomorrow, some in two months; but it is my hope that all will come to at least a tentative agreement for submission by February 15. I know that the principals who are in the audience realize that for all intents and purposes February 15 is really tomorrow, but we must capitalize on the forward movement.

If they don't do some of these things in year one in a new administration, they won't be done. So we're going to have to move forward immediately. I'm asking you to lay the responsibility upon yourself, to look at the options for community involvement, ways of deepening and strengthening meaningful contact, and by February 15 to evolve something to which your school is committed, so that we can have the kind of communication with parents that will make a difference in the learning of their children.

4. With your efforts in setting objectives getting under way immediately and the New Notions for Excellence Fund being set up by

October 15, we anticipate that the fund committee can begin receiving and reviewing proposals early in November.

What I'm saying to you here is that if we make $100,000 available for new notions and no new notions are generated, the endeavor becomes futile. I'm depending upon you to submit your proposals, get them ready, related to the objectives of your school and your personal objectives, able to be tested out in measurable terms, get them in, and by early November we should be sending out the checks to get your programs under way.

Well, this is where we are and where we are going. I've taken a long time to lay out the elements, and I'm grateful for your patience. Perhaps I've made it sound unnecessarily complicated, but it's quite simple. Our children are going to perform at grade level or better or we're going to know the reason why. That's what it all boils down to.

I was somewhat shocked once when Mario Fantini said to me, "You know Marc, (and it's in his little book, *Making Urban Schools Work*) the only measure for quality education that makes any sense to parents, especially poor parents (but I submit it makes sense to all parents), the only criteria that makes sense is that quality education can be defined as 'at or above grade level performance in the basic skills as assessed by tests that have national norms.' " That was Fantini's notion. And at the time I was thinking about all the other things—like can they learn to get along together, and some of the other things that happen to children in schools. But poor people, when you ask them "What is the main thing you want to have happen to your children?" They say "We want him to read and write and count." Ask rich people. "We want him to read and write and count so he can go to Harvard or Stanford or somewhere." Whoever you're talking with, they're talking about achievement and that's what we're about. And all the foregoing comes down to that we're going to have our children performing at acceptable standards or we're going to know the reason why.

The time has come to be up and doing. I mean what I say about our time, our moment in the sweep of events in America. I want you to come with me. I earnestly seek your help, your ideas, your zeal, in building a vision of what urban education can be. We will be writing an unprecedented chapter in educational history. We can make Oakland not a place of tumult and turmoil, but a place where they drew on each other, where they built on the best, where they put it *all* together, and showed the nation the way in urban education.

I hope I can count on you!

# C

# Education Research: A Profession in Search of a Constituency

First, let us consider schools, the apparent constituency of education researchers. One of their major characteristics is an extraordinary resistance to change. A sophisticated audience does not require extended argument on this point—but there is one piece of evidence we must consider: there are no incentives in our present education system for administrators to increase the efficiency of instruction. I doubt that any school district has an effective system for measuring and attributing significant improvements in student conduct, learning, or instruction. Thus it is impossible for such improvements to be recognized or rewarded. Some administrators or teachers may on occasion be recognized for apparently promoting better learning. The operative word is *apparently*. They are being rewarded for what appears to be improvement—but while serious researchers emphasize the necessity for recognizing genuinely improved learning, identifying the cause of such improvement strains our current methodologies. At this moment, effective accountability systems have hardly been designed; to the extent that they have been designed, schools do not use them. Therefore, so-called successful educators being recognized today are just as often demonstrating skill in public relations rather than skill in educational improvement.

In this context, the reasonable school administrator must ask: How can research have relevance for me? Essentially, research aims at producing information to assist innovation. Yet a rational administrator—with a wife and children to support, a mortgage to pay, and

---

Edward Wynne. Reprinted from *Phi Delta Kappan* 52, no. 4 (December 1970): 245-247.

colleagues whom he has to work with—might well contend: "Why should I try this innovation? My system will not give me credit for 'simply' improving learning; the improvement must also have sex appeal." In addition, any material innovation will make obsolete some existing practices. Our rational administrator might conclude that the effective innovation could win him enemies or diminish his chances for advancement, as other administrators find their competencies made obsolete or their roles threatened. Finally, some innovations may well disturb parts of the public; at present, there is little incentive for an administrator to attempt to overcome such hostility, or collect allies for change, since there is little likelihood that he will receive credit if an innovation "only" improves learning. In sum, unless the schools are peopled with extremely irrational administrators, we should expect, as Anthony G. Oettinger says, that "innovation will understandably fade before self-preservation."

What are the implications for educational research? Simply that schools—our apparent constituency—at best regard our product as inconsequential, and at worst as a threat to their operations. Who knows? Some crazy parent, judge, board member, or legislator might try to compel a school to carry out the implications of our work. Imagine all the trouble that might cause. Consider Ocean Hill-Brownsville, Title I evaluation, or school desegregation. Schools really don't want our product. But in twentieth-century America they cannot publicly be against research. Under such circumstances, what would a rational man do? He would give the enterprise lip service, do all he can to keep it underfinanced, ignore or belittle the findings of research as long as possible, discourage honest experimentation, and keep accurate data out of the hands of researchers.

Isn't this just what is happening? We all know that school districts spend almost no money on actual research or evaluation. Nearly all research money comes from the federal government. Even then, education research received only .31 percent of the $54 billion spent for education in 1968. For some reason, other less "intellectual" enterprises than education treat research more seriously: 10 percent of the defense budget goes to research, and business spends 3 percent of its national expenditures on research. The figure for health is 5 percent. Knowledgeable observers contend that school representatives have played no role in lobbying to enlarge the federal investment in education research.

Concurrently, schools have frustrated important rcscarch attempts. About 45 percent of of the big-city districts queried in the Coleman study refused to assist with that important survey. The American Association of School Administrators opposed Ralph Tyler's national assessment program—until a former president of the AASA was made president of the guiding board. This was called making the assessment "more representative." Many of us have a pretty good idea of the machinations that surround Title I evaluations within school districts.

But why all this pulling and hauling? Schoolmen are not a terribly forceful lot. Researchers are not innately aggressive. Are the threats posed by research that serious?

Yes! Because they touch on a vital aspect of human nature—so illicit that neither schoolmen nor researchers dare to mention it, so ominous that study after study on the status of research looks at the trees and avoids confronting the forest. The issue revolved about P O W E R!

Research can produce knowledge. This knowledge can givc thc public tools to make new demands on schools. The tools can change the power relationship between schoolmen and their communities. Because researchers can make these tools, we are important threats to schoolmen. We must be tamed, controlled, restricted, and sedated. We are.

While the only important product of research is information, information is the major source of change in any society in which people are not killing each other on a large scale. As Karl Deutsch observed, timely well-focused information may indeed be likened to the power triggering a gun. Only a light tug at the right place is needed to fire the cartridge, and if the cartridge is fired, great force is released. The information can be simple—like the news of the apparent success of the Tet offensive conducted by the North Vietnamese, which soured many Americans on the Vietnam War. It can be subtle—like rises in the cost-of-living index, which promote political stress. But whatever its character nothing important happens differently in a democracy unless some members of the society are told something they didn't realize before. Note that I did not say that the communication of "new" information automatically produces change, but that such communication is a precondition to change. The question of what information will work in what contexts is a complex one, but we should not undervalue the long-range value of scientific data and information. The studies of economist John Maynard Keynes and his followers eventually brought radical revisions in our tax and financial policy, leaving us with the fortunate problem of living in a comparatively affluent society. Gunnar Myrdal's *American Dilemma*—which was a major effort in social science team research—played an important role in demolishing the intellectual and ideological underpinnings of segregation. I needn't touch on the public reaction to us resulting from the research on insecticides, population, ecology, air pollution, and so forth. It's true that the examples do not demonstrate "instant change"—but, frankly, I'm not appalled by a little more debate and thought about some of these issues. In a sense, researchers are playing with dynamite—as Arthur Jensen was told when he wrote about genetic differences in intelligence between races—and unconsciously schoolmen know it. Apparently, not many researchers do.

What are the implications of playing with dynamite? First, that schoolmen, as a class, are not a healthy constituency for promoting dynamic research at this stage in history. They don't want to be blown up! This is not to say there aren't some in-school allies—deviants who are achievement and client-oriented, at the risk of their jobs or the regard of their colleagues. But such enmity needn't be eternal—structures can change and new incentives for improvement can be generated. Indeed, this must be a major focus of our efforts. But for the short run, courting the affection of most schoolmen will simply mean continuing our current ineffectuality.

But we researchers can't go it alone. It's a big world. Where will the dollars and support come from to permit us to conduct our studies? Who will try the experiments we want to attempt? Where will our data come from? Where are our appropriate constituencies?

Our natural constituency consists of persons who may acquire more power as a result of the information we develop: parents, legislators, school board members, taxpayers, academic disciplines that find our information useful. In short, almost everyone without a vested interest in the way schools are now run. Really, we have a plethora of potential allies. The problem is more how to communicate with them, show them how we can help each other, and cultivate their rapport. If we conduct a successful cultivation, our research will be funded; it is even likely that our results will be tried by schools if they make sense to spokesmen for these classes. Public pressures will also get us access to the data we need.

In sum, our new constituency can help us attain the status desired by most substantial persons: a chance to fulfill one's talents and be of service to one's fellows. Other research fields have achieved this effect. Why can't we? Don't people care as much about their children as they do about their own health? If cancer research data about cigarette smoking excites them, why not educational research data some day?

Of course we cannot, at this time, offer anything as dramatic as the cigarette research data. But this doesn't mean that important things don't lie ahead. There has been a tremendous underinvestment in education research; more money may produce important increases in the quality of our product. Our efforts have also been handicapped by the resistance of schools: Suppose cigarette research depended on the wholehearted cooperation of cigarette companies? But despite the comparative ignorance of our profession, we may still underestimate our potency.

The one thing our work does tell us is that the way schools are now run—the teacher-training process, the seniority systems, the salary scales, most of the classroom practices followed, the types of buildings used, the staffing patterns, the tests administered, the promotion criteria for staff, the hiring practices, and almost everything else you can think of—is largely an established wisdom. As Peter Drucker observed:

> We still know very little about learning and teaching. But we do know that what "everybody" knows about learning and teaching is largely wrong. And this may well be a greater and more important advance than any of the new science and new technology of which we are so conscious today.

Let me offer some examples of what this means. Suppose we compared the learning rate of children who went to school only on alternate days with the rate of children following the traditional schedule. Assume the alternate day curriculum was specially revised. Anyone want to make predictions about the results? I doubt that we would dare predict with much certainty.

Or suppose we compared the effectiveness of traditionally trained teachers with groups trained via other radically different modes, or simply against randomly selected college graduates? Or suppose we restructured schools so that most teaching of children was done by other children with teachers simply acting as trainers of teaching students (as Ralph Melaragno and Gerald Newmark are doing near Los Angeles). Would anyone say with certainty that some forms of incentive compensation or output accountability for administrators—coupled with more delegation and other structural changes—couldn't have constructive effects? How do we know that it isn't best to try to recruit our best college graduates into teaching, waive all education course requirements, and assume that they will stay only for a few years? In effect, make teaching a transient career for the cream of society.

Or, considering higher education, suppose we devised modes that spread undergraduate and graduate education more evenly throughout life instead of making it a medicine to be taken all in one dose? Of course this might complicate college record-keeping, but perhaps that's not the most important problem affecting youth maturation.

None of these proposals would necessarily cost more money than we now spend. With some developmental work, they may be as effective as, or better than, our current systems.

All of them would be of interest to important classes of laymen. I don't say all laymen would like all of them; some might require important changes in lay attitudes, as well as in school modes; proponents of such experiments might have to develop allies and court potential opponents. Still, proposals such as I have outlined are just as consonant with existing research as are current school practices—and advancing them might win researchers many friends among the public, as well as enemies among educators.

What are the operational implications of this approach? How can we use such educational alternatives to win lay support? There are a series of steps: (1) decide this is something researchers should strive to do; (2) identify fellow researchers of like mind and communicate with them to develop strategies; (3) enlarge the planning to bring in laymen who share our concerns; (4) try to get money for communications; (5) design and put into operation a communication network to get our perspectives out among laymen—perhaps a periodical, a clearinghouse, lists of researchers who are willing to work with lay groups on school issues; and (6) continuously collect feed-back about our efforts and reconsider our initial priorities.

# Bibliography

This bibliography lists the more important writings relied on in this book. It is divided into four topical areas, which attempt to follow the major divisions of the work. No reference is cited below in more than one of the areas.

## General

Deutsch, Karl W. *The Nerves of Government.* New York: Free Press, 1963.

Drucker, Peter F. *The Age of Discontinuity.* New York: Harper & Row, 1969.

Duncan, Otis Dudley. "Social Forecasting: The State-of-the-Art." *The Public Interest,* no. 17 (Fall 1969): 88-118.

Easton, David. "An Approach to the Analysis of Political Systems." *World Politics* 9 (April 1957): 383-400.

Kahn, Herman & Weiner, Anthony J. *The Year 2000.* New York: Macmillan Co., 1967.

Rivlin, Alice. *Systematic Thinking and Social Action.* In preparation.

Schon, Donald A. *Technology and Change.* New York: Delacorte Press, 1967.

Wilensky, Harold L. *Organizational Intelligence.* New York: Basic Books, 1967.

## School Output Measures

Cohen, David K. "Politics and Research: Evaluation of Social Action Programs in Education." *Review of Educational Research* 40, no. 2 (April 1970): 213-238.

Cohen, Wilbur J. "Education and Learning." *Annals* 373 (September 1967): 79-101.

Coleman, James S. et al. *Equality of Educational Opportunity.* Washington, D.C.: Government Printing Office, 1966.

Cronbach, Lee J. & Suppes, Patrick, eds. *Research for Tomorrow's Schools.* New York: Macmillan Co., 1969.

Division of Planning, Research and Evaluation. *Oakland Public Schools, Achievement Test Results, 1970-71.* Oakland, Calif.: Oakland Public Schools, 1971.

Educational Testing Service. *State Educational Assessment Programs.* Princeton, N.J.: Educational Testing Service,1971.

Guthrie, James W. et al., *Schools and Inequality.* Cambridge, Mass.: MIT Press, 1969.

*Improving Educational Assessment and An Inventory of Measures of Affective Behavior.* Washington, D.C.: Association for Supervision and Curriculum Development, National Educational Association, 1969.

Lennon, Roger. "Accountability and Performance Contracting." Invited address, American Education Research Association, New York, 6 February 1971.

Merriman, Howard O. *The Columbus School Profile: 1970.* Columbus, Ohio: Columbus School District, 1970.

National Assessment of Educational Progress. *Writing–National Results, 1970, Report 3; Science–National Results, 1970, Report 1; Citizenship–National Results, 1970, Report 2.* Washington, D.C. Government Printing Office, 1970.

Silberman, Charles E. *Crisis in the Classroom.* New York: Random House, Vintage Books, 1970.

Stephens, J. M. *The Process of Schooling.* New York: Holt, Rinehart & Winston, 1967.

"Symposium on Evaluating Educational Programs." *Urban Review* 3 (February 1969).

Tyler, Ralph W., ed. *Education Evaluation: New Roles, New Means.* Sixty-eighth Yearbook of the National Society for the Study of Education, Part II. Chicago: University of Chicago Press, 1969.

U.S. Department of Health, Education and Welfare. *Do Teachers Make A Difference?* Washington, D.C.: Government Printing Office, 1970.

U.S. Commission on Civil Rights. *Racial Isolation in the Public Schools.* Washington, D.C.: Government Printing Office, 1967.

Wynne, Edward. "School Output Measures as Tools for Change." *Education and Urban Society* 2, no. 1 (November 1969): 3-21.

## Sociological Aspects of Educational Administration

Bricknell, Henry M. *Organizing New York State for Educational Change.* Albany: University of the State of New York, 1962.

Bushnell, David S. & Rappaport, Donald, eds. *Planned Change in Education.* New York: Harcourt, Brace, Jovanovich, 1971.

Callahan, Raymond E. *Education and the Cult of Efficiency.* Chicago: University of Chicago Press, 1962.

Center for the Study of Public Policy. *Financing Education by Grants to Parents.* Cambridge, Mass.: March 1970.

Coleman, James S. "The Concept of Equality of Educational Opportunity," *Harvard Educational Review,* 38, no. 1 (Winter, 1968), pp. 7-22

Crozier, Michael. *The Bureaucratic Phenomena.* Chicago: University of Chicago Press, 1964.

Lurie, Ellen. *How to Change Schools.* New York: Random House, 1970.

Marsh, Paul E. & Gortner, Ross A. *Federal Aid to Science Education: Two Programs.* Syracuse, N.Y.: Syracuse University Press, 1963.

Marris, Peter & Rein, Martin. *Dilemmas of Social Reform.* New York: Atherton Press, 1967.

"The Public Interest Vis-a-Vis Educational R & D." *Journal of Research and Development in Education* 2, no. 4 (Summer 1969).

Waller, Willard. *The Sociology of Teaching.* New York: Russell & Russell, 1961.

Williams, W. & Evans, J. "The Politics of Evaluation: The Case of Headstart." *Annals* 385 (1969): 118-32.

## Other Themes Affecting Output Developments

Abelson, Robert P. et al. *Theories of Cognitive Consistency: A Sourcebook.* Chicago: Rand McNally, 1968.

Baier, Kurt & Rescher, Nicholas, eds. *Values and the Future.* New York: Free Press, 1969.

Bauer, Raymond A., ed. *Social Indicators.* Cambridge, Mass.: MIT Press, 1966.

Bennis, Warren G. & Slater, Philip E. *The Temporary Society.* New York: Harper & Row, Colophon Books, 1968.

Berelson, Bernard & Steiner, Gary A. *Human Behavior.* New York: Harcourt Brace, 1964.

Brown, Roger. *Social Psychology.* New York: Free Press, 1965.

Chambers, Raymond. *Accounting, Evaluation and Economic Behavior.* Englewood Cliffs, N.J.: Prentice-Hall, 1966.

Cremin, Lawrence A. *The Transformation of the School.* New York: Vintage Books, 1961.

Hoffer, Eric. *The Ordeal of Change.* New York: Harper & Row, 1952.

Hofstadter, Richard. *The Paranoid Style in American Politics.* New York: Alfred A. Knopf, 1966.

Innis, Harold. *Empire and Communication.* Oxford: Clarendon Press, 1950.

Keniston, Kenneth. *The Uncommitted.* New York: Harcourt, Brace & World, 1960.

Levien, Roger E. *National Institute for Education. Preliminary Plan for the Proposed Institute,* R-657-HEW. Santa Monica, Calif.: RAND, 1971.

Mondale, Walter F. "The Institutionalized Presidency." *Law and Contemporary Problems* (Summer 1970).

National Goals Research Staff. *Towards Balanced Growth: Quantity with Quality.* Washington, D.C.: Government Printing Office, 1970.

Rainwater, Lee & Yancey, William L. *The Moynihan Report and the Politics of Controversy.* Cambridge, Mass.: MIT Press, 1967.

Tharp, L. H. *Until Victory.* Boston: Little, Brown & Co., 1953.

Tyack, David B. *Turning Points in American Educational History.* Waltham, Mass.: Blaisdell Publishing Co., 1967.

U.S., Congress, Senate, Committee on Government Operations. *Full Opportunity and Social Accounting Act, Hearings. Before the Subcommittee on Government Research, on S.843.* 90th Cong., 1st sess., 1967.

U.S., Congress, Senate, Committee on Labor and Public Welfare. *Full Opportunity Act, Hearings. Before the Special Subcommittee on Evaluation and Planning of Social Programs, on S.5.* 91st Cong., 1st & 2d sess., 1969, 1970.